CONTENTS

Appraisal Essentials

Advanced Residential Applications and Case Studies

Mark A. Munizzo

Lisa Virruso Musial

CENGAGE
Learning™

Australia • Brazil • Japan • Korea • Mexico • Singapore • Spain • United Kingdom • United States

**Advanced Residential
Applications and Case Studies**

Mark A. Munizzo, Lisa Virruso Musial

Vice President/Editorial Director:
Dave Shaut

Acquisitions Editor: Sara Glassmeyer

Editorial Assistant: Michelle Melfi

Senior Marketing/Sales Manager:
Mark Linton

Production Manager: Jennifer Ziegler

Text Permissions Acquisitions Manager:
Mardell Glinkski Schultz

Senior Manufacturing Coordinator:
Charlene Taylor

Senior Art Director: Pamela Galbreath

Content Project Manager:
Karunakaran Gunasekaran

Production House/Compositor: PrePressPMG

Cover Image: © Mhryciw, Dreamstime.com

For product information and technology assistance, contact us at
Cengage Learning Customer & Sales Support, 1-800-354-9706

For permission to use material from this text or product,
submit all requests online at **cengage.com/permissions**
Further permissions questions can be emailed to
permissionrequest@cengage.com

Library of Congress Control Number: 2010924432

ISBN-13: 978-0-8400-4924-7

ISBN-10: 0-8400-4924-2

Cengage Learning
5191 Natorp Blvd
Mason, OH 45040
USA

Cengage Learning is a leading provider of customized learning solutions with office locations around the globe, including Singapore, the United Kingdom, Australia, Mexico, Brazil, and Japan. Locate your local office at: **international.cengage.com/region**

Cengage Learning products are represented in Canada by Nelson Education, Ltd.

For your course and learning solutions, visit **academic.cengage.com**

Purchase any of our products at your local college store or at our preferred online store **www.cengagebrain.com**

Printed in the United States of America
1 2 3 4 5 14 13 12 11 10

ABOUT THE AUTHORS

Mark A. Munizzo, IFAS, CAE, is a Certified General Real Estate Appraiser in Illinois and the president of The Equity Network, a real estate appraisal and consulting firm. He has served on the education and advisory councils for The Appraisal Foundation Sponsors and is a member of the Examinations Committee for Uniform Standards of Professional Appraisal Practice. Mark has a Certified Assessment Evaluator (CAE) designation with the International Association of Assessing Officers (IAAO). He is also a certified Uniform Standards of Professional Appraisal Practice instructor with The Appraisal Foundation and a national instructor with the National Association of Independent Fee Appraisers (NAIFA), having received NAIFA's Instructor of the Year Award in 2002. In addition to holding a Bachelor of Business Administration degree from St. Norbert College, Mark is currently completing his graduate studies in real estate appraising at the University of St. Thomas in Minneapolis, MN. Mark is coauthor of 13 appraisal books from Cengage Learning including *Basic Appraisal Principles, Basic Appraisal Procedures, Residential Market Analysis and Highest and Best Use, Residential Site Valuation and Cost Approach, Residential Sales Comparison and Income Approaches, Residential Report Writing and Case Studies, Statistics, Modeling, and Finance, Advanced Residential Applications and Case Studies, General Market Analysis and Highest and Best Use, General Report Writing and Case Studies, General Sales Comparison Approach, General Site Valuation and Cost Approach, and General Income Approach.*

Lisa Virruso Musial, IFAS, president of Musial Appraisal Company in Riverside, IL, received her Bachelor of Science degree in Quantitative Methods from the University of Illinois at Chicago. She is a Certified General Real Estate Appraiser in Illinois and a practicing commercial real estate appraiser in the Chicago market. Lisa is a national instructor with the National Association of Independent Fee Appraisers (NAIFA) and received

NAIFA's Instructor of the Year Award in 2004. She also is a certified Uniform Standards of Professional Appraisal Practice instructor with The Appraisal Foundation. Lisa is coauthor of 13 appraisal books from Cengage Learning including *Basic Appraisal Principles, Basic Appraisal Procedures, Residential Market Analysis and Highest and Best Use, Residential Site Valuation and Cost Approach, Residential Sales. Comparison and Income Approaches, Report Writing and Case Studies, Statistics, Modeling, and Finance, Advanced Residential Applications and Case Studies, General Market Analysis and Highest and Best Use, General Report Writing and Case Studies, General Sales Comparison Approach, General Site Valuation and Cost Approach, and General Income Approach.*

INTRODUCTION

Congratulations! You are about to raise your professional knowledge and understanding to a higher and more detailed level of awareness. This course is designed to apply the specialized knowledge that you have cultivated to this point. Even if you are an experienced appraiser, some of this information will likely direct your thoughts toward what your appraisal practice should consist of and how it will apply in the future. In our minds, the subject matter in the following pages should be considered to be part of the heart and soul of a real estate valuation practice.

From this day forward, virtually everything around you will begin to take on a new meaning as you continue to commit yourself to your professional development. We say this with certainty as we ourselves are practicing appraisers, national instructors, and authors of educational materials for appraisers. The profession itself encompasses many disciplines of valuation beyond real estate and transcends such disciplines as economics, the construction trades, business, finance, law, governmental administration, statistics, mathematics, geography, geology, mapping, the information sciences, and, to some degree, psychology, to name a few.

Most of the concepts, methods, processes, and techniques that appraisers use today are directly the result of studies performed within the academic community and are most often from some other related field of study rather than from valuation. Only until recently, as the profession has begun to formally define certain issues, is there a refinement of terms that can be cited as unique to the appraisal profession. We see this as a new beginning for the appraisal profession, and we call for a need for a serious working relationship with formal academicians to further elevate the valuation profession by advancing a more comprehensive and practical education curriculum. We believe our curriculum to be the starting point of such a relationship.

Within these pages you will note that Section 1 is a comprehensive review of the appraisal process, appraisal approaches, appraisal methods, and appraisal techniques. These are concepts and procedures that you should be quite familiar with at this point in your development. The purpose of this section is to provide a comprehensive review of these appraisal concepts as a means of preparing the student for the application of the specialized knowledge required to complete the complex appraisal problem within Section 3. The student should find the complex property assignment in Section 3 to be challenging but not too difficult based on the application of the appraisal concepts and techniques reviewed in Section 1 and applied in Section 2.

Section 2 is largely focused on threading a case study through the appraisal process, sales comparison approach, cost approach and income approach to value with consideration for the appraisal process and the principles as they apply to real estate markets. This text is intended to educate you in the methodology of the cost, sales comparison, and income approaches. Within these pages, there is also coverage of the processes of *scope of work*, *data collection and analysis*, and *highest and best use* to aid you in developing *critical thinking* in all real estate–related analysis. You are responsible for understanding the material in this text and to pursue a greater understanding and application of this information in the future should you choose to incorporate some of these methods and techniques into your appraisal practice. There is no way that a single course in real estate appraisal can qualify you to be proficient in the subject matter discussed. Successful completion of an entire curriculum and application of actual experience is what determines the competency of all professionals.

You will come to find that every action you take as a professional appraiser has the potential to dramatically affect how every appraiser worldwide is perceived. This is an awesome responsibility, and we hope that you are up to the task. With responsibility comes liability, and we are hoping that you act accordingly.

This text is designed to aid in this development. Section 1 is designed with objectives and key terms and is divided into subtopics, each of which concludes with lesson review questions or exercises to reinforce the learning process. It is imperative that you complete all lesson review and section review questions within Section 1 as well as all In Practice problems and note any questions, comments, or concerns that you might have for the instructor to clarify. Section 2 is designed to apply most of the concepts reviewed in Section 1 and walks the student through the process of an appraisal assignment. Section 3 is designed to test the student's ability to perform competently in a complex assignment.

We hope that you enjoy this process, and we wish you success in your professional development.

LEARNING OBJECTIVES

Section 1: The Appraisal Process, Approaches, Methods, and Techniques

By the end of this section, participants will be able to

- distinguish between developing and reporting in an assignment;
- identify the steps in the critical thought process;
- recognize the reporting standards of *USPAP*;
- understand the basis of the scientific method;
- define relevant information in the critical thought process;
- understand relevant characteristics in an assignment;
- identify the four steps involved with scope of work;
- understand the five functions of managing the assignment;
- discern between specific data, general data, primary data, and secondary data;
- define reconciliation;
- understand the difference between data and facts;
- identify the steps involved with the cost approach;
- perform all calculations within the cost approach;
- understand the process of the cost approach;
- comprehend the strengths and limitations of the cost approach;
- understand reconciliation within the cost approach;
- recognize the various methods of costing;
- distinguish between depreciation and obsolescence;
- understand curable and incurable items;
- understand the principles related to the cost approach;
- understand the process of the sales comparison approach to value;

- perform all necessary calculations within the sales comparison approach to value;

- comprehend the strengths and limitations of the sales comparison approach;

- understand reconciliation within the sales comparison approach;

- define a unit of comparison;

- define an element of comparison;

- recognize the difference between quantitative and qualitative adjustments;

- understand the sequence of adjustments;

- distinguish between percentage adjustments and lump-sum dollar adjustments;

- understand the process of the income approach to value;

- comprehend the strengths and limitations of the income approach;

- perform all direct capitalization using IRV;

- understand the operating income statement;

- define potential gross income;

- calculate vacancy and collection loss;

- define and calculate effective gross income;

- define and calculate net operation income;

- calculate the various income multipliers using VIM;

- calculate income and expense ratios with the income approach to value;

- define yield capitalization;

- understand reconciliation within the income approach;

- identify the six land or site valuation techniques;

- value land or site using all six valuation techniques;

- understand correlation;

- understand regression analysis;

- calculate the slope and intercept;

- estimate values using simple linear regression; and

- determine the most reliable unit of comparison.

Appendix A: Appraisal Math and Statistics

By the end of this section, participants will be able to

- explain the order of operations;
- add, subtract, multiply, and divide negative numbers;
- calculate percentages and how to convert them into decimals;
- understand reciprocals;
- round numbers;
- understand exponents;
- understand problem-solving techniques;
- comprehend basic algebra concepts;
- understand interpolation and extrapolation;
- understand units of comparison;
- calculate area and volume;
- convert various units of measure;
- understand the difference between population and sample;
- understand measures of central tendency;
- calculate the mean, median, and mode of an array of numbers;
- understand measures of variability;
- calculate range, variance, and standard deviation;
- calculate weighted averages;
- define *statistics*;
- identify the different sampling techniques;
- understand outliers and how to deal with them;
- calculate the coefficient of variance (COV);
- be familiar with bar charts, scatter plots, and histograms;
- plot *x*- and *y*-coordinates;
- understand frequency distributions;
- understand skewness of distribution;
- understand the properties of a normal curve;
- understand normal distribution;
- define the empirical rule and when it can be used;
- define *correlation*;

- understand the financial principle of time value of money;

- distinguish between simple interest and compound interest;

- understand each of the six functions of a dollar;

- use the various methods to compute each of the six functions of a dollar; and

- calculate a mortgage payment.

Appendix B: Forms of Ownership

By the end of this section, participants will be able to

- be familiar with the various forms of ownership;

- distinguish the difference between the various forms of ownership including joint tenancy, tenancy in common, community property, and tenancy by the entirety;

- understand the concept of right of survivorship;

- describe the difference between condominium ownership and cooperative ownership;

- understand the difference between a living trust and a testamentary trust;

- describe the benefits of land trusts;

- understand the concept of time-sharing;

- identify and define the four unities of ownership;

- identify the benefits of cooperative ownership; and

- distinguish between time-share estate and time-share use.

SUGGESTED READING

Basic Appraisal Principles, Mark A. Munizzo and Lisa Virruso Musial, Cengage Learning (2007)

Basic Appraisal Procedures, Mark A. Munizzo and Lisa Virruso Musial, Cengage Learning (2007)

Residential Site Valuation and Cost Approach, Mark A. Munizzo and Lisa Virruso Musial, Cengage Learning (2007)

Residential Sales and Income Approaches, Mark A. Munizzo and Lisa Virruso Musial, Cengage Learning (2007)

Statistics, Modeling, and Finance, Mark A. Munizzo and Lisa Virruso Musial, Cengage Learning (2007)

THE APPRAISAL PROCESS, APPROACHES, METHODS, AND TECHNIQUES

section one

LEARNING OBJECTIVES

By the end of this section, participants will be able to

- distinguish between developing and reporting in an assignment;
- identify the steps in the critical thought process;
- recognize the reporting standards of *USPAP*;
- understand the basis of the scientific method;
- define relevant information in the critical thought process;
- understand relevant characteristics in an assignment;
- identify the four steps involved with scope of work;
- understand the five functions of managing the assignment;
- discern between specific data, general data, primary data, and secondary data;
- define reconciliation;
- understand the difference between data and facts;

- identify the steps involved with the cost approach;

- perform all calculations within the cost approach;

- understand the process of the cost approach;

- comprehend the strengths and limitations of the cost approach;

- understand reconciliation within the cost approach;

- recognize the various methods of costing;

- distinguish between depreciation and obsolescence;

- understand curable and incurable items;

- understand the principles related to the cost approach;

- understand the process of the sales comparison approach to value;

- perform all necessary calculations within the sales comparison approach to value;

- comprehend the strengths and limitations of the sales comparison approach;

- understand reconciliation within the sales comparison approach;

- define a unit of comparison;

- define an element of comparison;

- recognize the difference between quantitative and qualitative adjustments;

- understand the sequence of adjustments;

- distinguish between percentage adjustments and lump-sum dollar adjustments;

- understand the process of the income approach to value;

- comprehend the strengths and limitations of the income approach;

- perform all direct capitalization using IRV;

- understand the operating income statement;

- define potential gross income;

- calculate vacancy and collection loss;

- define and calculate effective gross income;

- define and calculate net operation income;

- calculate the various income multipliers using VIM;

- calculate income and expense ratios with the income approach to value;

- define yield capitalization;

- understand reconciliation within the income approach;

- identify the six land or site valuation techniques;

- value land or site using all six valuation techniques;

- understand correlation;

- understand regression analysis;

- calculate the slope and intercept;

- estimate values using simple linear regression; and

- determine the most reliable unit of comparison.

KEY TERMS

absorption rate

abstraction method

accrued depreciation

actual age

allocation method

annual debt service (ADS)

bracketing

breakdown method

capitalization rate (R)

cash equivalency

chronological age

coefficient of variance (COV)

comparables

comparable sale

comparable sales method

contract rent

correlation

cost approach

cost index method

critical thought

curable

curable functional obsolescence

curable physical depreciation

data

dependent variable

demand analysis

depreciation

development

direct capitalization

direct costs

discounting

economic age-life method

effective age (EA)

effective gross income (EGI)

effective gross income multiplier (EGIM)

elements of comparison

engineering breakdown method

entrepreneurial profit

expenditures made after purchase

external obsolescence

extraction method

extrapolation

facts

functional obsolescence

general data

gross adjustment

gross income multiplier (GIM)

gross monthly rent multiplier (GMRM)

gross rent multiplier (GRM)

ground lease

ground rent capitalization method

hypothesis

income capitalization

incurable

incurable functional obsolescence

incurable physical depreciation

independent variable

indirect costs

inefficient market

inference

intercept

interpolation

land residual method

linear regression

long-lived items

long-term lease

market delineation

market method

market rent

market study

market value

modified economic age-life method

multiplier (M)

net adjustment

net income ratio (NIR)

net operating income (NOI)

obsolescence

operating expenses

operating expense ratio (OER)

operating income statement

other income

paired sales analysis

personal interviews

physical age

physical depreciation

potential gross income (PGI)

potential gross income multiplier (PGIM)

primary data

qualitative adjustment

quantitative adjustment

quantity survey method

reconciliation

regression line

relative comparison analysis

relevant characteristics

relevant information

remaining economic life (REL)

replacement cost new (RCN)

replacement reserves

reporting

reporting standards

reproduction cost new

rise

run

sales comparison approach

sales comparison method

scientific method

scope of work

secondary data

short-lived items

simple linear regression

site analysis

slope

specific data

square-foot method

straight-line method

subdivision development method

subject property

superadequacy

supply analysis

total economic life (TEL)

unit of comparison

unit-in-place method

vacancy and collection loss

x-axis

y-axis

yield capitalization

y-intercept

LESSON 1: Review of the Appraisal Process, Critical Thought Process, and Market Analysis

THE APPRAISAL PROCESS

At this point in your educational development you have likely mastered the concept of the appraisal process. You will recall that the appraisal process is a two-part *scientific method* of *developing* and *reporting.* The focus of this course is on the application of the entire process with concentration on methods and techniques associated with an appraisal assignment. You will also remember that the appraisal process, like all scientific methods, begins with *problem identification* and concludes with *communicating the results.* Remember that the last step in the *development* aspect of the appraisal process is to *reconcile* to conclusions and that *communicating the results* is the reporting aspect of the two-step function of the appraisal process. This means that communicating or reporting the results of the assignment is the last step in the overall appraisal process. (See Figure 1.1.) **Development,** therefore, begins with problem identification and ends with reconciliation, while **reporting** is synonymous with communicating the results and is the final step of the process. The developing standards for real property appraisal assignments are covered within Standard 1 of the *Uniform Standards of Professional Appraisal Practice (USPAP),* while the developing standards for the other disciplines of appraisal review, appraisal consulting, mass appraisal, personal property, and business valuation are covered in Standards 3, 4, 6, 7, and 9, respectively.

Reporting carries with it a specific standard of practice and, depending upon the assignment type, a different standard is used to govern the requirements placed on the appraisal professional. As an example, Standard 2 dictates the requirements of reporting under a real property appraisal assignment. Likewise, Standards 3, 5, 6, 8, and 10 all address the reporting requirements for the various disciplines of appraisal review, appraisal consulting, mass appraisal, personal property, and business valuation assignments, respectively. These are known as the **reporting standards** (see the current edition of *USPAP*).

The Scientific Method

In scientific study, the **scientific method** is a process that begins with problem identification and hypothesis development and continues with data collection, verification, and analysis to reach a conclusion. A *hypothesis* has a slightly different meaning under the scientific method than typically understood. In common language, a hypothesis is an idea or proposition used to explain certain facts or to provide the primary assumption of an argument. We will discuss argumentation later in this section. In common language, a hypothesis is the basis of an argument or the main point of the argument, while the term has a more formal connotation in scientific analysis.

In the scientific method, a **hypothesis** is a formal statement that is carefully outlined and is the focus of a scientific inquiry that is to be tested based on the use of facts uncovered during the testing process. In scientific analysis a hypothesis is a carefully crafted statement designed to be tested under the scientific method. As an example, Copernicus once set a hypothesis that the earth revolved around the sun.

In most real estate analysis a hypothesis is not required. In fact, to set a hypothesis before data collection runs the risk of unduly directing the assignment toward either proving or disproving the hypothesis rather than allowing the market data to speak for itself. In such a case, the hypothesis becomes the focus rather than the market forces and factors that dictate answers to the identified problem. A hypothesis works well for investigations in the sciences, but it is the scientific method that is important to the real estate appraisal profession. Nonetheless, the scientific method is used without the use of a formal hypothesis as a means of conducting an appraisal assignment. As stated, the focus of this course is to concentrate on the appraisal process, methods, and techniques associated with the appraisal assignment. While developing and reporting are two distinct aspects of the appraisal process, they are completely interrelated and should be conducted as such.

The purpose of setting an assignment to a standard based on the scientific method should be clear. The performance standards of any profession are strict requirements to ensure proper delivery of credible assignment results. By now it should also be understood that simply because the steps in the process are followed does not mean that the conclusions are foolproof. Critical thought plays an important role in reaching accurate conclusions. The appraisal professional must use his or her experience, specialized knowledge, and critical judgment to reach accurate and credible results during the execution of the assignment so that these results may be accurately communicated in the report. As a means of reinforcing where the focus of this course will be placed, let us briefly review the appraisal process.

The following is a detailed description of each step in the appraisal process.

Problem Identification

The professional appraiser must first identify the primary issues during the engagement process and determine from the start whether he or she has the experience and the knowledge to complete the assignment in a competent manner. This is known as the competency requirement for all real estate appraisers. The appraiser must determine whether the results of the assignment will be credible in light of the clients' intended use of the report. Simply because the appraiser has the education to conduct an assignment or may have completed similar assignments in other regions does not necessarily mean that the appraiser has the competency to perform this particular assignment in this area. The competency provision pertains to property types, geographical area, appropriate application of a recognized method or technique, and virtually any other experience or related issue that the appraiser might face. (See the Competency Rule in *USPAP.*)

The information that is required in the problem identification stage is known as **relevant characteristics.** Under the *Uniform Standards of Professional Appraisal Practice* an appraiser must identify all characteristics of the property that are relevant to the type and value and intended users of the appraisal. (See Standard 1-2(e) of *USPAP.*) In the market analysis process, relevant characteristics are also required within the first step. This is to aid the appraiser/analyst in conducting data collection that is relevant to the assignment and, in particular, relevant to the subject property and use of the analysis.

Within this first step in the appraisal process, the appraiser must identify the following:

- The client and other intended users of the report
- The intended use of the report and the appraiser's opinions and conclusions
- The type and definition of value and the source of the definition
- The effective date of the appraiser's opinion and conclusions
- The description and location of the real estate
- The property rights to be valued
- The characteristics that are relevant to the type of value and the intended use of the appraisal, along with the limiting conditions or limitations of the appraisal (determine the scope of work)

Scope of Work

In addition to determining competency during the problem identification step, scope of work is also determined by the appraiser largely during the engagement process and interview with the client. Like competency, the appraiser must maintain the appropriate scope of work throughout the appraisal process. **Scope of work** determination begins with the engagement process and is confirmed once the property is inspected, data is collected and verified, and, in the case of a real property appraisal assignment, highest and best use is completed and the land value is concluded. Scope of work performance takes place from data collection and verification all the way through to reconciliation. Once all opinions and conclusions are completed, the scope of work is disclosed in the reporting or communicating process of the assignment. Therefore, there are four overlapping steps in the scope of work process that help ensure proper conduct within scope of work and market analysis:

1. **Determine** the proper scope of work, a preliminary determination
2. **Confirm** the scope of work, a confirmed determination
3. **Perform** the scope of work necessary, execute the scope of work
4. **Disclose** the scope of work in the report

The scope of work decision is largely dictated by the clients' needs and intended use of the appraisal, along with the assignment conditions. The assignment conditions are those that may have an effect on how the information is analyzed and reported. Such conditions include situations where the appraiser is forced to make reasonable assumptions that are not absolutely known in order to complete the assignment. Assignment conditions must not affect the credibility of the assignment results.

Scope of work can be affected by circumstances in the appraisal, the property itself, or highest and best use analysis. There may be a change in how the appraiser will value the property if any of these circumstances are found to have shifted during the data collection stages. Scope of work is integrated in the appraisal process, and the process of confirming the scope of work and performing the scope of work are overlapped. (See Figure 1.1.)

Manage the Assignment

While it may seem that "manage the assignment" is separate from scope of work on the outline of the appraisal process, they are in fact concurrent processes. Once the engagement process is complete, the professional appraiser should have a clear understanding of the clients' needs and expectations. To enhance performance, the appraiser must manage the assignment. The five basic functions of management are as follows:

1. **Plan**—To determine what is required, and when
2. **Organize**—To determine how the assignment process will be conducted
3. **Staff**—To determine the personnel required for the assignment and to identify that the competency of every individual associated with the assignment is appropriate
4. **Direct**—To be certain that the relevant characteristics are identified and that the scope of work is appropriate throughout the assignment. It is also important to direct other associates working on the assignment, particularly if they are trainees or underlings.
5. **Control**—To ensure that the appraisal process is completed with accurate and verified information

A good management function also includes a feedback mechanism for oversight and for periodically calibrating the manner in which assignments are completed. *Feedback* is perhaps the most important safeguard against proceeding on an assignment in a perfunctory or robotic manner.

Data Collection and Verification

During the data collection and verification stage, the appraiser determines what information is most relevant to the analysis and how this information is related to the definition of the problem to be solved. Further, the quality and durability of the data uncovered during this stage is the basis for the opinions and conclusions that will be completed during the reconciliation stage. Much of the data uncovered will be applied during the various approaches to value, where a clearer interpretation of the data is more formally considered.

There are different types of **data** uncovered during an appraisal assignment. **Specific data** is data that relates directly to the subject property, and much of this information is collected during the inspection of the subject property itself. Typically, specific data is obtained as **primary data,** or data that is uncovered firsthand by the appraiser. **General data** is data that relates to the neighborhood or region. Such information is typically obtained as **secondary data,** or data that is received from a secondary source such as public records or census information. In truth, specific data and general data can be obtained as either primary or secondary data.

Data collection and verification is often where even the most experienced appraisal professionals fail to correctly employ due diligence. Gathering information is one thing; critically thinking about the relevance and accuracy of the information is quite another. Too often an unacceptable appraisal report contains excessive market-derived information that is not presented to the reader in a relevant manner. In short, data collection without analysis is a major omission and a pitfall for appraisers because such actions are below the standard of practice.

Highest and Best Use

The first natural assumption that an appraiser must make is that the property will be properly managed and be put to its highest and best use. Within this use consideration rests the concern that an owner of a given property will seek out the most reasonably probable, physically possible, legally permissible, financially feasible, and maximally productive use of the property. These criteria are based on the market data uncovered and on the physical structure of the subject property.

The following considerations are made in estimating the highest and best use:

- **Possible Use (Physical)**—What uses are physically possible on the subject given by the physical characteristics revealed by property analysis?

- **Permissible Use (Legal)**—Among legally permitted and physically possible uses for the subject property, which uses are appropriate, given the characteristics revealed in the market activity, neighborhood, and property analysis? Which uses would produce any net return to the owner?

- **Feasible Use (Appropriate Use)**—Among legally permitted and physical possible uses for the subject property, which uses are appropriate, given the characteristics revealed in the market activity, neighborhood, and property analysis? Which uses would produce net return to the owner?

- **Maximum Profitability**—What is the most profitable use of the site "as if vacant" and then "as if improved"?

- **Highest and Best Use**—Among appropriate or feasible uses for the subject property, which will produce the highest present value?

APPROACHES TO VALUE

Appraisers are taught early on that there are three traditional approaches to value in the appraisal process that the appraiser should complete if at all possible: the income approach, the cost approach, and the sales comparison approach. Each approach views problem identification from a different perspective. While each approach requires different data to be collected specifically for that approach to value, some of the data that is uncovered is used within each approach in a different manner. There are times when one approach may be more appropriate to value a property than another, particularly if the approach is more indicative of what is taking place in the market. Conversely, an approach may not be at all appropriate because of a lack of data or because the results may be potentially misleading or inaccurate, whereby the appraisal results lack credibility. Sometimes the approach may not be appropriate because of the property itself. As an example, the cost approach is not applicable in the case of vacant land as there are no improvements to cost. An indicated value conclusion within each approach is reconciled after determining the strengths and weaknesses of the data found and analyzed within each approach to value.

Many appraisers believe that the approaches to value are the most critical aspect of an appraisal assignment, and yet these are only tools of valuation, not necessarily the most thought-provoking part of the process. These tools of the assignment help the appraiser to reach conclusions that are uncovered during the market analysis section of the appraisal process. Once trends are identified during data collection and analysis, and value conclusions are indicated after the approaches to value are completed, overall conclusions can be made based on the information uncovered throughout the process. Such overall opinions and conclusions are reconciled from the approaches to value based on validity and quality of the information within each approach.

Reconciliation

During the reconciliation phase of the appraisal process the opinions and conclusions are sorted out in a comprehensive manner. **Reconciliation** is the process of determining and giving weight to the most relevant information to support the conclusions that are an accurate interpretation of the trends relevant to the definition of the valuation problem in the assignment. Reconciliation is performed at the end of each approach to value whereby the appraiser concludes an indication of value using that specific valuation approach. After the appraiser determines the value under each approach, the appraiser further reconciles to a final value conclusion. This *final reconciliation* is the process of giving the most weight to a particular approach over another based on which is most relevant to the problem in order to conclude a final valuation decision.

Another part of reconciliation that is commonly overlooked is the point that market trends and other such information uncovered within the market analysis are supposed to be included in these conclusions. Including this information helps to support or reject notions, either preconceived or concluded. These omissions are the result of an appraiser's unwillingness to use the critical thought process to support the conclusions, another common omission that falls below the standards of practice. As stated above, reconciliation is the final step in the development aspect of the appraisal process, but communicating (reporting) the results is the final step in the appraisal process.

Communicate the Results

The term *communicate the results* refers to reporting the results of the appraisal process. This last step in the appraisal process is sometimes erroneously referred to as the appraisal because the results are generally written in a physical report with a concluded value known as an appraisal. In truth, the appraisal is a process of developing an opinion of value; or the opinion of value itself. In other words, the physical report does not in and of itself constitute an appraisal. It is the process and the value conclusion that make the report an appraisal. The validity and credibility of the appraisal are measured by the accuracy of data, the appropriateness of methods and techniques applied, and the soundness of claims made and conclusions reached and supported by the evidence uncovered and presented. This holds true for any assignment type, not just for appraisal assignments.

The Final Step in the Appraisal Process

Throughout this curriculum, we have discussed the importance of keeping the processes within the appraisal process interrelated. Perhaps nowhere is there a greater risk of disconnection within the appraisal process than in the final step of reporting the assignment results. Because developing and reporting are two distinct parts of the same process, there is a potential for a gap between the two steps. While reconciliation is considered to be the final step in development, it really is the conduit between development and reporting. Reconciliation is the basis for synthesizing the most relevant points of the analysis to reach opinions and conclusions that will be highlighted within the report. In short, reconciliation contains the relevant information that needs to be effectively communicated within the report. The appraiser dictates what information is relevant information based on the client's needs, scope of work, and assignment conditions.

Effective communication plays a large role in reporting to be sure, but accurately communicating the assignment results is the starting point of proper reporting. Depending on the assignment type, the reporting phase should also reflect what has transpired throughout the appraisal assignment beginning with problem identification and moving through the market analysis steps of subject analysis, market delineation and neighborhood identification, supply and demand analysis, and conclusions. The point is that the communication of results takes place only after the appraisal process has reached conclusions, and that such communications are to be properly executed based on the client's needs and the complexity of the assignment.

Summary

Before we proceed, let's take a moment to break down the appraisal process itself and place this course into perspective. It is critical that we take the time to address this point to give you an understanding of why the course is required in this curriculum in the first place. Recently, several appraisal underwriters and review appraisers were queried and it was determined that the major problem with real estate appraisal reports is that the appraisers stop sounding like appraisers when it comes to the report function. The language, terms, techniques, and concepts of real estate appraisal are sometimes forgotten or not properly applied. This is unforgivable!

To take valuable time and effort at considerable cost to sit through an appraisal curriculum and not implement what is learned is a failure to your status as a professional. For this reason alone, we would like to reiterate the appraisal process and the importance of critical thinking and discuss how the focus of this course fits into your learning experience. As you will see, the critical thought process is the basis for gaining agreement with your report from the reader.

Keep in mind that although the course isolates certain portions of the appraisal process or individual processes in detail, the intent here is to allow you to become knowledgeable and proficient in the function of these processes and not to see them as separate functions. Let us remind you about the importance of thinking critically. This will be discussed later in this lesson.

When a process such as highest and best use, critical thought, or scope of work is isolated, you should reflect on how this information fits into

FIGURE 1.1
The Appraisal Process—Communicating the Results

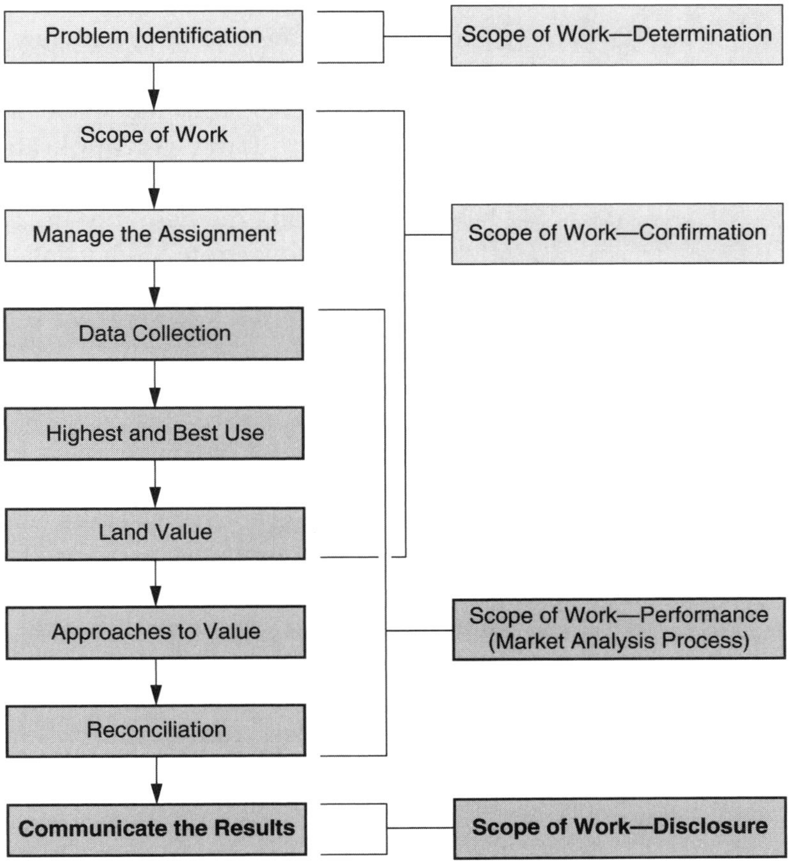

the entire appraisal process. You should also reflect on how these processes overlap or interrelate, and finally, you should reflect on how you will report these overlaps. This course rehearses the connection between appraisal theory and practical application.

We know that as a scientific method, the appraisal process begins with identifying a problem and ends with reaching valid conclusions. What about the proper application and execution of the appraisal process? That is the focus of this course. While we will focus specifically on the application of the appraisal process, methods, and techniques associated with an appraisal assignment, it is extremely important that your focus be directed toward the effects on the entire assignment, even while focusing on the details of these portions. To see the development and reporting portions as separate and unrelated steps within the appraisal process is to risk loss of validity and therefore credibility, which is a violation of *USPAP*.

Our goal has been to elevate the profession by elevating the professional, but we need your help. As a professional you have obligations and responsibilities—as an appraisal student you have the same. Please think about how you will use this information in practice.

The balance of this course is a review and application of the methods and techniques (as outlined in Figure 1.1) with concentration on market analysis, highest and best use, and scope of work, including the critical thought process and concluding with application of case studies for complex properties. As practicing appraisers and real estate appraisal educators, we have tried to bring the field into the classroom and the classroom into the field. As you know, professionalism is a constant achievement that must be attained if public trust is to be preserved.

CRITICAL THOUGHT PROCESS

As part of the cognitive sciences, much has been written about critical thinking. Most of what is written reflects a far more academic approach to the science of the mind with a hefty dose of logic and reasoning. For our purposes, **critical thought** in its simplest form is thinking independently. When the standard of practice calls for an appraiser to remain impartial, independent, and objective, it is implied that critical thought should be part of the process. In fact, it is reasonable for the client to expect that the appraisal professional will use critical thinking to process all information throughout the assignment.

Outside influences have little to do with how the critical thinker processes information. Information is gathered, analyzed, and synthesized, and opinions or conclusions are made. Does this sound familiar? It should, because critical thought is the template for the scientific method of analysis.

For humans, critical thinking develops at an early age when a child begins to form strong tendencies or beliefs and to reject irrational notions presented by others. Critical thinkers are active thinkers who try to figure things out for themselves. Critical thinkers do not passively accept the beliefs of others, nor do they accept unconfirmed information as fact. Critical thinkers thoughtfully form principles of thought and action and they are not unduly influenced by the language of another.

In valuation, critical thought is far less scientific because the appraisal process itself is a scientific method of analysis. The appraisal process, however, does rely on the appraisal professional or market analyst to exercise critical thought. Critical thought is part of the appraisal process and a key component of the performance standard for appraisal professionals. In short, critical thought has a process that also integrates within the appraisal process that all appraisal professionals are required to follow. Critical thought is therefore required as part of any analysis performed within an appraisal practice.

Although in the cognitive sciences critical thinking begins with identifying the problem, this is already done in the appraisal process at the beginning of the appraisal process itself. For the purposes of valuation, therefore, critical thought begins with some kind of data input that is processed into conclusions based on the application of the specialized knowledge and experience of the analyst.

Data

While data collection is a separate step in the appraisal process and the beginning point of market analysis, data in the critical thought process is the input for making valid conclusions. Data can come from many sources and in varied forms.

Facts

Facts are data to be sure, but in valuation, **facts** are data that has been verified in the market by the analyst. This step of data verification is a requirement under the *Uniform Standards of Professional Appraisal Practice.* Without verification the information is just data that may or may not be true or accurate; their reliability is suspect if it has not been verified. If such data is not verifiable, the appraiser/analyst must disclose this fact and determine if the use of such data would render results that are not credible. Unverified data is unreliable and may lead to conclusions that are suspect.

Relevant Information

Relevant information is fact (verified data) that has been selected by the analyst as most important or relevant to the question or problem being investigated. Not all data that is uncovered and verified is relevant to the assignment or the identified problem within the assignment and therefore falls beyond the scope of the assignment. Knowing what is relevant information and knowing what to include or exclude in the system is critical to the outcome of the assignment. Such knowledge is only garnered through education, knowledge, and experience.

Knowledge and Experience

Knowledge and experience go directly to the COMPETENCY provision of the *Uniform Standards of Professional Appraisal Practice.* Competency requires the appraisal professional to know whether he or she is qualified to complete the assignment in a competent manner. Neglecting to perform critical thought is incompetence.

Analysis and Judgment

Proper analysis and judgment come from good data, knowledge, and experience. Analysis is the process of applying critical thought, and judgment is the application of relevant information to the assignment.

Conclusions

Conclusions are supportable decisions or claims that the knowledgeable and experienced analyst determines after collecting and verifying data, selecting relevant information and issues from such data, and applying analysis and judgment to such information. This is all done to answer the key question of problem identification. By now you should recognize this

FIGURE 1.2
The Critical Thought Process

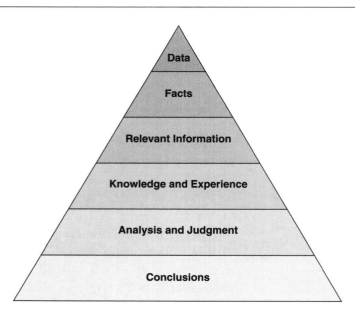

as the scientific method of analysis. Application of analysis and judgment is what this course is designed to exercise.

The pyramid in Figure 1.2 depicts how the critical thought process works from placing data into the system to projecting concluded output from the system.

REVIEW OF MARKET ANALYSIS

Market Analysis   Market analysis is a study process using scientific investigative and problem-solving techniques to gain insight into market conditions (change over time). Further, a market analysis is a study of a real estate market for a particular property type. This type of analysis may lead to a value conclusion, but is not in and of itself an appraisal. An appraisal carries with it the conclusion of an opinion of value. A market study and an appraisal utilize the scientific method as a process to completion. You will recall that the scientific method is a process that begins with problem identification and continues with data collection, verification, and analysis to reach a conclusion. Any scientific method should include the following:

- Identifying a problem or asking a question
- Collecting and verifying data
- Analyzing the data

- Synthesizing or reconciling the data

- Reaching conclusions concerning the data based on the question asked or problem identified

We have already discussed that market analysis is actually a process within the appraisal process. Like all processes, there are several steps that must be completed, although the specifics of each step might be altered slightly to accommodate the particular situation being investigated or the depth of study required, based on the nature of the assignment. The concept of market analysis is not only critical to an appraisal and the appraisal process but can also be seen as a separate study from the appraisal. The information gathered in a market analysis serves to feed the process of highest and best use analysis and the traditional approaches to value. Since this course is specifically focused upon the application of the appraisal process, methods, and techniques, our primary concern will be on how the market analysis feeds this system.

Two important terms in the above-stated definition of market analysis are *study process* and *market conditions*. A study process implies a certain level of research, as in a scientific study, and of course the word process speaks for itself. The term *market conditions* here means "the change that takes place in the market over time." This is not to say that market conditions are a representation of the time that has transpired. *Market conditions* refers to the characteristics of the market such as interest rates, employment levels, vacancy levels, and so forth, at a given point in time. The point here is that a market analysis, or **market study,** as it is sometimes called, is an analysis that includes a scientific process of data study with consideration for the effects of the changes in the market over time. Within the appraisal process the information gathered during data collection and used to support the market study is the basis of the approaches to value and highest and best use analysis. Further, this same data is the relevant information on which conclusions will be based and opinions will be made.

Such information requires critical thinking just to make sense of the data that is uncovered, and yet many appraisers fail to see this all-important consideration. The critical thought process must be employed throughout the appraisal process and play a key role during data collection and throughout the analysis and synthesis portion of the appraisal process, market analysis, highest and best use, and the approaches to value. Further, this data requires analysis under a more scientific approach if it is to be of use to the appraisal professional; otherwise it is just a collection of data. Data analysis, like the four-step process in highest and best use, helps to set up the critical thought process throughout the appraisal process if it is correctly employed. We will speak in more detail about the critical thought process at the end of this lesson, but for now let us focus on how market analysis and critical thought process work within the appraisal process.

Market analysis is extremely important to virtually anyone who is considering the use, value, or ownership of real estate. Real estate market analysis involves demographics, population, migration, and other information that is time specific. Market analysis allows for the application of projecting trends based on market support. In a changing market the data is also changing and, therefore, older information has limited use unless adjusted for changes in conditions. This is why we say that data collected from the market is time specific. This is also why there is a market conditions adjustment within the sales comparison approach and why value within a report is fixed upon a specific date.

THE GENERAL PURPOSE OF MARKET ANALYSIS

Because market analysis is based on the scientific method the process can be redressed to almost any situation. The main differences between assignments are the question at hand, the purpose of the assignment, and the needs of the client—not necessarily the process by which the assignment is completed. While it is true that any process based on the scientific method allows for modifications to support how the assignment might more appropriately be completed, only slight modifications are generally required to address these needs.

In a real estate market analysis the focus is on the demand and supply issues that affect real estate. Real estate market analysis provides guidance for private and public sectors and is used to rank potential uses or change in uses. Real estate market analysis also identifies the risks involved with real estate or its market. Because of the principle of change, real estate market analysis is seen as an ongoing process and, therefore, as time sensitive. Real estate market analysis is also location specific and therefore likely to have limited substitutions for a particular real estate product. All of these issues are addressed within the market analysis portion of the appraisal assignment and much of the data collected is used to support the highest and best use analysis and the approaches to value.

Regardless of the assignment type a real estate market analysis should contain the components listed below, which are known as elements of market analysis and feasibility. These same elements when broken down and placed in specific terms will become the basis of adjustments within the sales comparison approach, and may affect the data used within the cost and income approaches. There are five elements of market analysis and feasibility:

- Site analysis
- Demand analysis (demographics)

■ Supply analysis (competitive market review)

■ Market interviews (verification and perceptions)

■ Conclusions and recommendations

Site Analysis

Site analysis is based on an inspection of the subject property's location and site conditions. The physical, economic, and geographical location of the subject and the immediate surrounding properties are addressed in site analysis. Because the surroundings can a have a profound effect on a property, its use, and its value, site analysis is concerned with both specific data (inside the property lines) and general data (outside of the property lines). Site analysis, at a minimum, should address any of the assignment characteristics and other items such as

■ property address;

■ size and dimension;

■ ownership rights;

■ topography;

■ neighborhood conditions;

■ location;

■ utilities;

■ amenities; and

■ natural resources.

You will notice that when the element of site analysis is placed in specific terms, the results are the basis of adjustment in the sales comparison approach and may lead to issues that affect highest and best use and the cost and income approaches. Depending on the assignment type, site analysis is as vast and varied as the property being considered. Like all analyses the site analysis must address the significant issues within the parameters of the required scope of the assignment. For example, in a residential appraisal the dimensions and location of the lot and size of the house with access to neighborhood amenities are site issues that support the use of the property and the scope of the analysis and incorporate both general and specific data to support this analysis. Likewise the site analysis for an industrial property should focus upon access and egress to and from transportation hubs, utilities, and other issues relevant to industrial properties. To speak to the fact that the dinosaurs roamed the earth several million years ago is outside of the scope of the analysis for this property type and is irrelevant to the issues within the assignment.

Demand Analysis

The general purpose of market analysis is concerned with the identification and study of demand and supply for a product or service. In real estate analysis, the **demand analysis** considers a subject property's market potential and marketability in the current and future market. Demand also focuses upon the buyer's side of the market and is the basis for choosing comparables within the sales comparison and income approaches and identifies the central issues within highest and best use and any potential obsolescence or curable issues within the cost approach. Demand analysis uses a wide variety of data, including but not limited to the following:

- Demographics
- Population
- Households
- Income
- Affordability
- Commuting patterns
- Employment
- Migration patterns

Supply Analysis (Competitive Market Review)

Part of the general purpose of real estate market analysis is concerned with the identification and study of the supply of competing real estate products. Both the existing supply and future supply are considered. In a **supply analysis** (also called a competitive market review) the analyst considers competing properties to the subject and determines the subject property's market potential and marketability in the current and future market. Supply analysis uses data including the following, and more:

- Existing inventory
- Future inventory
- Building permits
- Vacancy rates
- Current projects
- Future projects
- Lease terms
- Absorption rates

Market Interviews

Market interviews have two major benefits to the market analyst:

1. To help verify the information gathered from the marketplace
2. To gather market perceptions concerning almost any question within the marketplace

Provided that the interview process is conducted properly, market interviews can be an effective method of verifying data and helping to identify perceptions of the players in the marketplace. The technical performance of interviewing is critical to the accuracy of the analysis. If incorrectly performed, such qualitative techniques have the potential to steer the analysis in a misleading direction.

Performing an interview to verify data is an effective method, provided that the interviewer understands how to apply proper interviewing techniques. The interviewee must also be qualified to answer the questions accurately and truthfully.

Interviewing methods are regularly used by market analysts as a means of becoming acquainted with the market being studied. This qualitative method of analysis is beneficial for gaining an understanding of how the market perceives itself or how the players within the market perceive the market in which they regularly participate.

Qualitative research is based upon the premise of speaking with a small group of market participants and is largely subjective in nature. This type of information might not have immediate data to support the findings, but perception is the better part of reality and therefore should not be ignored. Qualitative interviewing techniques allow for market perceptions to be probed in depth. Some examples of qualitative research techniques are

- focus groups;
- surveys; and
- one-on-one interviews.

The danger in this type of qualitative analysis is that the information taken from a small number of respondents might not be truly representative of the general market. Such analysis is a double-edged sword. A well-informed professional facilitator is critical to the success and accuracy of qualitative interviewing methods.

While interviewing is generally a good idea and widely considered to be beneficial to methodology, it might also be a weakness if the interviewing process is improperly conducted or if the persons being interviewed are not properly qualified to answer the questions.

There are several areas in which qualitative methods can break down. The persons chosen as interviewees must be properly screened to reflect the target market. Although not statistically significant, the information garnered from such interviewing techniques can be invaluable to the market analyst provided the facilitator understands and employs proper interviewing techniques. The problem stems from giving too much credence to a few interviewees' perceptions or placing too much emphasis on an atypical interviewee's opinions or interpretations of the market.

Conclusions and Recommendations

As in any scientific method, conclusions and recommendations must be supported with verified data relevant to the identified problem. As previously stated, presenting market data without analysis is an unacceptable practice in real estate valuation. Further, to not reach conclusions or recommendations within an assignment likely falls short of the purpose of the assignment. Just as important as the appraisal process and the interrelated processes discussed earlier in this program are the methods of analysis chosen to reach conclusions and make recommendations.

Markets and the Sales Comparison Approach

The concept of a market, although vast, should be relatively ingrained into your knowledge base by this point in your career. At a very basic level we know that a market contains buyers and sellers of a product or service and that a market can be affected by several variables such as those defined within the economic principles. (See *Basic Appraisal Principles,* Cengage Learning.) We also know that supply and demand play critical roles in a market and that supply represents the sellers' side of the equation, while demand represents the buyers' side. Because the information that may be extracted from the market is so broad, it is important to accurately identify the predominant players in a market for a particular product or service.

Also, on a very general scale, markets are ordinarily identified as either efficient or inefficient. An efficient market is a market that has a large and readily identifiable group of buyers and sellers and has goods or services that are easily produced and readily transferable. An **inefficient market** lacks a readily identifiable group of buyers and sellers and consists of goods or services that are not easily produced or readily transferable. Of course real estate tends to operate in an inefficient manner for several reasons. The lack of absolutely verifiable information alone makes real estate an inefficient market, but there are many more reasons.

Real estate has many variables that have an effect on use, supply, demand, and value. We know influences such as social, governmental, economic, and physical/environmental issues all affect real estate. We also know that supply (scarcity), demand (desire), use (utility), and transferability (purchasing power) of real estate are what create value in real estate. The mutations and permutations of these eight issues alone are endless for any given property type in any given market, but combine the economic principles within the equation and almost anything can happen in the real estate marketplace. In an inefficient market, the analysts must exercise great care to accurately perform an analysis that will render credible assignment results. The approaches to value are an attempt to measure with efficiency the issues that are relevant in an inefficient market. As appraisal professionals we should celebrate the fact that real estate is an inefficient market—otherwise there would be no need for our services. But remember, public trust is critical to us all!

THE MARKET ANALYSIS PROCESS

The process of market analysis is a scope-driven process that varies slightly from assignment to assignment to match the complexity of the problem or the assignment conditions identified early on in the appraisal process. If the scope is too narrow, the relevant issues may not be fully addressed and there is a risk of not uncovering accurate information to make critical decisions. If the scope is too wide, relevant issues may become lost in too much minutia or an avalanche of data where there is a danger of misinterpretation. The market analysis process is one area that is truly reflective of the level of experience and quality of an appraisal professional's skill and knowledge.

As previously stated, a real estate market analysis should contain the following elements of real estate market analysis and feasibility:

- Site analysis
- Demand analysis (demographics)
- Supply analysis (competitive market review)
- Market interviews (verification and perceptions)
- Conclusions and recommendations

Each step requires critical thought to accurately make conclusions before moving on to the next step. Such conclusions should speak directly to the relevant issues within the assignment. While it is true that all market analyses should at the very least contain the aforementioned components, there is a formal process of completing a market analysis.

So what are the steps in market analysis, and how can one become more proficient at performing such assignments accurately?

- Step 1: Subject property analysis
- Step 2: Define the market and users (market delineation)
- Step 3: Relevant demand analysis
- Step 4: Relevant supply analysis

- Step 5: Demand and supply relationship analysis
- Step 6: Forecast analysis (subject penetration of the market)
- Step 7: Reconcile to conclusions

Step 1: Subject Property Analysis

Similar to the appraisal process, which begins with a definition of the problem, the market analysis process begins with a definition of the property that specifically speaks to the relevant characteristics of the subject property and the scope of work determination. The location of the subject, economic attributes, access to linkages, competitive advantages or disadvantages, and physical attributes of the subject are all considered in the definition after collecting the following relevant data about the subject:

- Location
- Site dimensions
- Building dimensions
- Condition
- Materials and workmanship
- View
- Setback
- Utilities
- Parking
- Legal issues
- Ownership rights
- Physical boundaries
- Taxes
- Insurance
- Income
- Expenses

Some questions should be asked by the analyst to help direct the relevant characteristics toward the foreground of the assignment. Possible questions include the following:

- Does the subject fill any other potential uses by its physical location or attributes?
- Are there alternate uses for the subject, if modified?
- Is the subject functional and for what uses?

- What is the zoning allowance?

- Is the property included in a governmental comprehensive plan?

This part of the analysis should perhaps do more to provide insight into the property, its highest and best use, and the information required about it than any other section of the analysis. The subject analysis varies with the complexity of the property and the definition of the problem within the assignment. Specific questions should be asked early on that are reflective of the subject and how it fits into the market. The point is that you are beginning to engage in critical thought by asking such questions based on the issues uncovered during data collection and by analyzing your client's needs even though the client might not understand these issues or how they might be relevant.

Remember, our client identification and the intended use of the report would have been completed during the problem identification step of the appraisal process; we are now collecting and verifying data in the market analysis stage of the appraisal process (see Figure 1.1). This information will ultimately be used to support the choice of comparables, the elements of comparison, and the adjustments needed within the sales comparison approach, highest and best use, and data relevant to the cost and income approaches.

The subject and how it fits into the market are the beginning point of the market analysis, and here is where confirmation of scope of work begins. Should there be something found while collecting data in the market that changes scope of work or causes you to not meet your client's expectations, you must notify the client of your findings and re-engage the assignment under a new scope of work or decline the assignment.

Step 2: Define the Market and Users (Market Delineation)

Market delineation is defining the market and the users. The analyst must determine who the potential users of the subject property are and to what use the property would be placed. We know that a user of the real estate represents the demand side of the market, but demand is largely based on the attributes of the subject property. For this reason, step one of market analysis (subject property analysis) flows well into step two in market analysis (market delineation), which in turn flows well into step three (demand analysis).

When an analyst defines the market, it is completed in conjunction with the information gathered from the subject analysis, which is step one of market analysis. The attributes of the subject gathered during the subject analysis and how the market would respond to these attributes is what defining the market is all about. In short, defining the market—or market delineation—is really an analysis of the market segment relevant to the subject property.

Relevant market demographics are important in this stage, but only after identifying who would likely use the subject property. Physical boundaries are also part of this process; so is any submarket that plays a critical role within this market concerning the subject property. Some questions that should be asked include:

- Who is the target market?
- Where do the target markets exist?
- What amenities are demanded?
- What price range is noted?
- What rent or mortgage is affordable?
- What are the absorption rates?
- What property types are wanted?

The appraiser must have a clear understanding of the market in which the subject property competes and the potential for changes in the future. Further, it is critical to identify where the potential players are within a market area so that the all-important influences on value (physical, economic, governmental, and social) relevant to the assignment can be accurately addressed. Here is where an experienced appraiser may fail the due diligence test by not asking the proper questions of the market. Some data to help identify the market area include the following:

- Regional data (to acquire a broad perspective)
- Population size
- Socioeconomic composition
- Employment levels
- Household size
- Travel times to employment centers
- Mass transportation
- Political boundaries
- Growth patterns

The method of data collection is also critical. Sometimes assumptions about the subject, the market, or the data collected can cause analysis errors. Other times not enough due diligence during market delineation can cause an analysis to be inaccurate. Market segmentation should be accurate and relevant to the purpose of the assignment. Some ways that markets can be delineated are by

- property type;

- use;

- submarkets;

- trade area; and

- geographic location.

Step 3: Relevant Demand Analysis

Determine how many potential users there are in the market and, in some assignments, project future growth or shrinkage of potential users. Remember, it says potential users. All potential alternate uses must also be considered.

Once the subject property and the market for the subject have been identified, the relevant demand within the market can be isolated and identified by market research techniques. Gathering data is one thing, but isolating the relevant market segment to make accurate conclusions or render credible opinions is something altogether different. Relevant information is the most important phrase in the text. Relevant data is the basis for adjustments in the sales comparison approach. To supply information that is not relevant to the questions asked about the subject in problem identification falls outside of the scope of the assignment. In data analysis and data collection, it is usually necessary to start with a broader view of the market and then tighten the focus toward a smaller and more relevant view of the data. This technique ensures that nothing relevant is left outside of the view of the data analysis, and that such information is relevant to the scope of work for the assignment. Here are some questions that an analyst must ask during the demand analysis:

- Who can afford this property?

- Who will be attracted by the attributes of the subject property?

- What attributes of the property are relevant to the market players?

- How many potential users are there?

- What is the relationship of current supply to value?

Because there are so many factors that might affect the forces of value, an analyst needs to isolate the relevant factors found in the market that are likely to support the conclusions derived during market analysis. Here is where assumptions are made that might lead the analyst to incorrectly employ analysis techniques that could lead to focusing on the wrong information or gathering irrelevant data. There is no substitute for knowledge and experience, unless of course the experienced analyst has incorrectly assumed something about the data without verification. Major demand factors include the following:

- Household income levels
- Employment
- Age
- Population levels
- Submarket population
- Household composition
- Migration trends
- Migration patterns

Step 4: Relevant Supply Analysis

Determine the competition and the supply of similar properties available in the market. Also determine whether there are substitutions for the subject or alternate uses for other properties that would allow such properties to compete with the subject property. In some assignments, project the future growth or shrinkage of supply. Here is where competition may lead to a different use conclusion. If the market has been properly segmented and submarkets have been properly identified during market delineation (step 2), accurate supply and competition can be identified during this step and forecasts can be made during demand and supply analysis (step 5).

Many well-meaning appraisers will overload a report with local, regional, and national statistics and information without a hint of analysis as an attempt to make the report look substantial. This is what we mean when we say market data without analysis, which does not meet the client's expectations or needs. The slang term is "data dump," and it is not a habit that any appraisal professional should acquire.

The true offense is that often some of this data is good information from which accurate conclusions, projections, or opinions could be drawn and supported if the appraiser would simply take the time to analyze and synthesize the data into meaningful results. The reader of the report is forced to undertake the process of critical thought by completing an analysis of the provided data and trying to make sense of it all.

The best analysts will place in the report the answers to the questions that are asked during the appraisal process for the assignment. As an example, here are some questions that the analyst should ask during the supply analysis:

- How much competition does this market contain?
- How much competition is scheduled to come online?
- What legal issues now and in the near future will affect the supply?
- What other uses does the subject or the supply have?

■ What other property types can have a similar use to the subject?

■ What is the supply in the competing markets?

■ What is the relationship of current supply to value?

There are also factors to consider on the supply side of the equation:

■ Recently completed projects

■ Future projects

■ Recent changes in pricing

■ Substitutability of other properties

■ Vacancy rates

■ Occupancy rates

■ Absorption rates

■ Construction cost changes

■ Changes in financial markets

■ Historical occupancy

■ Comprehensive plan

Step 5: Demand and Supply Relationship Analysis

Compare the trends of both supply and demand analysis and look for interaction between the two. Look for separate trends to emerge. Understand that any preconceived highest and best use conclusion may be dashed here.

An opinion of value is based on the future benefits derived from the ownership of the real estate interest. In particular the market value opinion is for the subject property. It is therefore natural that step 3 (demand analysis) and step 4 (supply analysis) should be folded into step 5 (demand and supply relationship analysis) only after market delineation (step 2) and subject property analysis (step 1) have been completed.

The interaction between demand and supply is what dictates value in the market. There can be no market without demand, and, likewise, there can be no market without supply. The forces behind the principle of supply and demand are what dictate the value of any product in any market. These forces are based not only on the influences presently noted in the market, but also on future expectations within the market.

The market is made up of people, and because wants, needs, and perceptions are a large part of human nature, future activity might be difficult to project. This is where choosing an appropriate method of analysis such as trend analysis or fundamental analysis is critical. Likewise, accurate data for the chosen method of analysis might not be available to the analyst. The analyst has a responsibility to determine if the data and information that can be garnered from the market and within the appraisal process (and, therefore, the market analysis process) will lead to credible results in line with the client's needs and expectations. This decision is solely that of the appraisal professional, and this decision is what competency is all about. Remember you may have the knowledge and experience to complete an assignment and therefore be considered competent, but if you lack the ability to deliver credible results then the assignment should not be performed. This is why accurate and verified data is so critical to credible results. Some examples of sources of data follow:

- Local, county, state, and federal governments

- Census Bureau

- Bureau of Labor

- Trade groups

- Surveys

- Assessor records

- REALTORS®

- Other appraisers

- Trade journals

- Newspaper articles

- GIS databases

- Proprietary databases

Step 6: Forecast Analysis (Subject Penetration of the Market)

Depending on the assignment type, the analyst will forecast projections for the subject property based on supporting data uncovered in the market analysis process, including, in some cases, future projections or absorption of the subject property. This is where the decision of which relevant information will be in the analysis and communicated during the communication of the results (reporting) stage in the assignment. The analyst must determine which details will be communicated to the client and intended users of the report based on the expectations and needs of the client.

Estimate vs. Forecast   An estimate is based on a date from the past and carried into the present, such as Census figures, which are released every ten years. An estimate of these figures can be made based on the growth rate over the prior years. A forecast, on the other hand, is projected into the future using present data.

If the assignment does not call for a forecast, then only a reconciliation of the subject penetration is required here. Since value is based in part on the present value of future interest, some projections are required. The analyst should consider whether the identified market for the subject will still exist in the reasonably near future. Once a forecast is made then reconciliation and conclusions can be drawn, along with any inferences required to reach such conclusions. An **inference** is a qualifier that defines the circumstances under which the conclusions are made, such as a hypothetical condition or an extraordinary assumption. Typically, such inferences are identified in the limiting conditions and scope of work areas of the report.

Step 7: Reconcile to Conclusions

Based on the data uncovered in the market analysis process the basis for highest and best use analysis is presented and supportable conclusions are reconciled. Also, information from the market is applied to the approaches to value and the appraisal process is completed. A properly conducted market analysis should help the appraiser support the comparables chosen and the adjustments made within the sales comparison approach. Reconciliation takes place within each approach to value and then an overall reconciliation for the assignment is used to reach supportable conclusions. Reconciliation should reflect what the market analyst found during the analysis.

This section completes the final step in the market analysis process and the development aspect of the appraisal process, but critical thought that is used throughout these processes must be reiterated within the reporting process as a means of allowing the reader to understand what has taken place in the assignment, and how the opinions and conclusions were reached.

TYPES OF MARKET ANALYSIS

In addition to the different levels of analysis, there are several related types of analysis within the discipline of market analysis. These related but varied types of analysis have more differences in scope than in their processes. A difference in scope means a different assignment type. Of course, a different assignment type also means a difference in what is likely to be relevant information.

Market analysis can be an assignment type or an analytical method. Likewise, different assignments require different methods of analysis. Such methods are dictated by the scope of work, complexity of the property or question, data available, and cost of the analysis.

If the cost of the analysis method in an assignment is ever an issue, the appraiser must weigh the budget against the analysis technique required with the needs of the client and the client's expectations. If the analysis method needed to complete the assignment proves to be too costly, then the assignment should be refused during the engagement process. An appraiser must be able to complete the assignment in a timely manner with credible results. The cost issue might be a particular concern when costly statistical analysis is used or extensive labor-intensive research is required. Here are examples of some assignment types:

- Economic base analysis
- Feasibility analysis
- Market studies
- Marketability study
- Investment analysis

Economic Base Analysis

An economic base analysis is a survey of business, industry, and employment base for an area. The economic base of an area is the economic activity that allows local businesses to generate income from outside the immediate area, as well as within the community. This analysis is concerned with the rate of population growth and the level of income associated with these growth patterns. An economic base analysis is used to forecast future economic activity and to predict future population growth patterns, income levels, and other similar variables that have an effect on real estate values or the use of land.

Feasibility Analysis

A feasibility analysis is sometimes called an economic feasibility analysis and is a cost-benefit analysis to determine whether a project will meet the objectives of an investor. Feasibility as spoken about in highest and best use analysis and in curable/incurable items under the depreciation section of the cost approach to value is very similar to the thought process in a feasibility analysis. Simply put, "Is it worth pursuing?" Feasibility analysis focuses on the profitability of a specific project.

Market Study

A market study is a study that is more macroeconomic in scope than specific to an individual property. A market study focuses on the general market conditions of supply and demand, pricing, and demographics for a specific area or property type. Market analysis sometimes includes construction or absorption trends (rate of market acceptance and consumption of a given item).

Marketability Study

A marketability study is more microeconomic in scope and it focuses on the specific property or class of property and relates the property to demand in a given market. A marketability study is a valuable tool for determining a specific highest and best use, projecting market mix, or projecting tenant mix for a particular property, provided that the appraiser-analyst understands that historic data alone does not predict the future with certainty.

Investment Analysis

Simply put, an investment analysis is an analysis of the cost-benefit relationship for a particular real estate investment's acquisition price versus the anticipated future return of the project. Investment analysis focuses on the expected rate of return, and the risks associated with the project.

Types of Market Analysis: Methods

We know that market analysis covers a broad range of assignments, methods, and techniques. Market analysis techniques with market data are also vast, particularly when statistics, computer software, and graphic analysis are involved. Two market analysis techniques are *qualitative analysis* and *quantitative analysis*. **Quantitative analysis** uses actual quantities such as "430 feet" or "$25,000." **Qualitative analysis** is the study of relative values such as good, average, fair, or poor.

For the most part the cost, income, and sales comparison approaches each use quantitative and qualitative techniques. The actual numbers used in each technique are quantitative, while the reconciliation of the data is qualitative.

SWOT Analysis

Other examples of market analysis as a method can be found in a marketability study where the **S**trengths, **W**eaknesses, **O**pportunities, and **T**hreats are analyzed. Like the first two steps in the market analysis process, the strengths and weaknesses of the subject, along with the opportunities and threats in the marketplace (such as competition), are identified and analyzed. Although the SWOT method of market analysis is typically completed for marketability studies, the technique has merit for other applications where there is ample information to support such an analysis. Some analysts will list the "T" in SWOT as "Trends," but trending really is a separate analysis activity and is typically performed with statistical data. Perhaps the most widely used trending analysis using statistics in real estate valuation is to perform a graph analysis using a linear regression (trending) technique.

Remember, a marketability study is performed for a specific product or service in a specific market at a particular point in time. A SWOT analysis answers the issues of marketability based on evidence found within the market.

In its simplest form, a SWOT analysis begins with listing all relevant information about the current situation. Then the product is identified, and the strengths, weaknesses, opportunities, and threats are outlined, supply and demand are highlighted, and conclusions are made based on the product's ability to "fit" in the market.

When considering a product's ability to "fit" in the market, the relevant information determination is largely affected by the use, demand, and relative desirability of the property. The market analyst using the SWOT method must carefully weigh not only what information is relevant to the general market but also those issues relevant to a specific client and related to the specific property if "fit" is to be properly addressed. This should lead to a more detailed analysis in the conclusion section of the SWOT analysis.

The scope of a SWOT can be from several views and is typically directed based on the property type, market data available, and relevant information uncovered. For the most part, a SWOT analysis has a scope that follows the typical market analysis from a more macro to a more micro view of the market. For example, most market analysts find it in good form to begin with a wide scope such as international, national, regional, then local to district or neighborhood, then specific property type.

While the scope begins with a more broad perspective, the perspective must be relevant. As an example, in the housing or manufacturing market, general market trends and availability of money are two important issues to focus on from a national perspective, but as the scope moves towards a more local perspective, the issues might change dramatically. If the real estate is somehow affected by a national or regional factor, such as manufacturing or larger industrial warehousing, then the SWOT might not move towards a local perspective. Conversely, a residential market is typically so specialized and local that a large discussion about national trends is likely to be barely relevant at best. If the market is not really relevant to the scope then a detailed discussion about that market will likely be eliminated from the analysis. Because the purpose of the assignment and therefore the scope can be specifically requested to focus on a particular scenario, the analyst must clearly identify the situation where the focus is purposely isolated.

Current situation (sometimes called *present state*)   To begin a simple SWOT analysis, the *current situation* is identified. This is usually written in paragraphs with bullet points when appropriate. A listing of the strengths, weaknesses, opportunities, and threats for the current situation should be avoided in this section, as it tends to force a premature analysis of the information, and runs the risk of causing decisions concerning the data to be made before the relevance of the data can be ascertained. The strengths, weaknesses, opportunities, and threats of the current situation are usually discussed as part of the conclusion. Most often the SWOT of the current situation is where support for opinions, arguments, and conclusions are typically garnered.

Product   The product is listed as a focal point of what is to be discussed in the conclusion section to be sure. But sometimes it is essential to speak to how the product "fits" in each market segment (international, national, regional, or local), and how each situation affects the product. Remember, the point of a marketability study is to determine demand for a class of property in a particular market. Identifying the product is just as important as identifying the market and both are therefore essential to this process. Sometimes a marketability study will address the question of finding a market that matches the product. Either way, the product and market must be analyzed.

In a SWOT analysis, the current economic, social, governmental, and sometimes physical trends that affect each category of strengths, weaknesses, opportunities, and threats within each market segment (international, national, regional, etc.) are considered.

Strengths   In a SWOT analysis the strengths are listed first as a means of identifying the positive attributes of the case, or the competitive advantages that the area might have. Other strengths could be based on "potential" changes to the market, but that might be confused with opportunities. Typically strengths are discussed as stemming from past or present perspective and focus on the existing situation. Opportunities typically stem from some "potential" in the future based on a related issue (usually a strength).

Weaknesses   In the SWOT analysis the weaknesses are the readily identifiable relevant issues that are less than desirable. Like strengths, the weaknesses should concentrate on the past or present issues on a general basis and focus on the relevance to the case in the opinions and conclusions section. The potential for pitfalls in the case should also be identified, but these are typically isolated as threats.

Opportunities   As stated under Strengths, opportunities are items that typically stem from some market potential or are the result of some expected change in the market. This is not to say that opportunities are all just future-based; they aren't. Opportunities are issues that make the case more attractive to the needs of those launching the investigation.

Threats   In the SWOT analysis, threats are items that could have disastrous consequences or could negatively affect the case. Similar to weaknesses, threats are issues that are less than desirable, but threats have more potential, or even are expected, to impact some aspect of the case.

Sometimes the distinction between strengths and opportunities, and weaknesses and threats, isn't clearly defined. Depending on how the information is presented and interpreted, some items can fall into multiple categories. It is even possible that, depending on the needs of the client, some issues might be strengths and weaknesses, or opportunities and threats all at the same time. It is all a matter of interpretation.

Supply and demand analysis   The SWOT may call for a brief supply and demand analysis recapturing the significant issues uncovered for the international, national, regional, local, district, neighborhood, or property-specific perspective. This helps keep the focus on the relevant issues that have been uncovered on several levels, and allows for opinions and conclusions to be formulated at the end of the analysis.

Opinions and conclusions   Like all market analysis tools, the SWOT analysis must reach conclusions with opinions and evidence to support them. Remember, data without analysis is a clear violation of the standard of practice in any market analysis project, and a failure to meet the expectations of the client. Further, opinions and conclusions help put the information into perspective, and should reflect the experience of the analyst in a given situation. There is no room for waffling here. If you have an opinion based on experience, it is acceptable practice to render it here. This is why the client is paying you. If you are a competent, knowledgeable, experienced professional, then such consultation assignments should be well within your ability to perform.

LESSON 1 REVIEW QUESTIONS

1. _____ is a study process using scientific investigative and problem-solving techniques to gain insight into market conditions.

2. The act of delineating a market area is called _____.

3. A real estate market analysis is concerned with the identification and study of _____ and _____ for a particular real estate product.

4. Market analysis provides input into _____ and the appraisal valuation approaches.

5. A(n) _____ market is one that has a large and readily identifiable group of buyers and sellers and has goods or services that are easily produced and readily transferable.

LESSON 1 REVIEW ANSWERS

1. Market analysis

2. market segmentation

3. demand; supply

4. highest and best use

5. efficient

LESSON 2: The Cost Approach

The **cost approach** is a methodized process to derive at a value indication whereby the *replacement cost*, or *reproduction cost*, of a building is first estimated including the *entrepreneurial profit*, then *accrued depreciation* is subtracted, and finally the value of the land or site as though vacant is added to conclude a value indication.

Related Principles

There are several appraisal principles related to the cost approach that are worth mentioning. These principles explain how markets work and they describe the interaction of the forces within markets. Therefore it is certainly worth noting how these principles reflect the actual figures involved with the market's decision-making processes.

For example, the *principle of substitution* has applicability within all of the approaches to value, and therefore a slightly different interpretation can be expected within its application relative to each approach. The principle of substitution is the principle that is primary to the cost approach. The principle of substitution is clearly demonstrated in a market comparison (sales comparison) situation whereby the principle states that all things being equal between two items of similar utility and demand, the lower-priced one will sell first. This is the classic margarine versus butter problem. If the price of butter becomes too high, eventually people will substitute a similar product of like utility, in this case margarine. Likewise if two properties of similar utility and demand are on the market, the lower-priced property will likely sell first. Of course this assumes a knowledgeable buyer acting in his or her own best interests and so on. The principle of substitution as it applies to the cost approach has a slightly different interpretation and therefore a slightly different application.

The principle of substitution as it applies to the cost approach states that "no person is justified in paying more for a property than they can build new." This of course assumes that there is no burden of undue delay. In other words, that the person building the property is not in need of the property before the time its construction will be complete. To put it in simpler terms, the principle of substitution under the cost approach asks: "If I can wait for the time it takes to build the property and assemble all of the agents of production, why should I pay more for an existing property of similar utility?" The answer is, "I shouldn't." Therefore, you see there is a slightly different interpretation of the principle of substitution as it relates to the cost approach than the sales comparison (market) approach.

Implied in these principles and forces are other principles such as *supply and demand* and *the four agents of production* (land, labor, capital, and management), and because supply and demand are noted, then so too must the principles of *balance* and *competition*. A student might do well here to review the principles of real estate.

Supply and demand have a correlated effect upon most markets and the interrelationship of these two forces can have a predictable effect on value. However, within a market there are also additional complex forces at work that might make such predictions difficult or impossible to project without further data. These additional complexities are what make a market an imperfect entity—and most markets, in particular real estate, are imperfect markets. While all of these appraisal principles are a solid foundation for explaining or interpreting a market, they are not the forces themselves. Such forces can only be isolated with market analysis and solid market data that is applied and interpreted under the approaches to value.

As an example, the principle of externality is an exact interpretation of the concept of *external obsolescence*, and the basis of a portion of accrued depreciation in the cost approach. You will remember that under the principle of externality, it is recognized that the influences outside of the property lines might have an effect on the property.

The principle of *contribution* applies to the cost approach by supporting the idea that each component of the cost approach has a contribution to the overall value. The principle of *surplus productivity* states that all addition to value after the agents of production have been satisfied will be applied to the land. Therefore the principle of surplus productivity speaks to the land value portion of the cost approach. In addition, of course, one could not complete a highest and best use analysis without the cost approach to isolate financial feasibility, or the value of the land as if vacant.

METHODIZED PROCESS OF THE COST APPROACH

Replacement or reproduction cost new (RCN)

– Accrued depreciation

= Depreciated cost of the improvements

+ Land (site) value as though vacant

= Indicated value using the cost approach

FIGURE 1.3
Replacement Cost

RCN (Replacement Cost New/ Reproduction Cost New)

Replacement cost is the cost of constructing new the existing building at today's construction standards using today's materials. This is also known as **replacement cost new** and is the beginning point of a cost analysis using replacement cost figures for an existing building. *Reproduction cost* is the cost of reproducing an exact duplicate of the existing building using the exact materials and the construction standards as the original construction. This is also known as **reproduction cost new** and is the beginning point of a cost analysis using reproduction cost figures for an existing building.

The main difference between replacement and reproduction is that replacement cost estimates eliminate superadequacy or other functional obsolescence associated with the existing improvement. Reproduction cost might include obsolescence because it is an exact duplicate of the original. A *special-use* property, such as a historic building, church, school, library, or other such unique property, is the typical application for the reproduction cost new.

The construction cost—whether replacement or reproduction—will be for a new structure as of the effective date (the date at which the analysis and opinions apply).

The home at the bottom of Figure 1.3 is a typical use for the replacement cost new. Replacement cost new is used because it would not be economically feasible to reproduce a home of this age with the same quality, materials, and artisanship of the past.

Applicability

The applicability of the cost approach is founded in the principle of substitution as mentioned previously under "related principles." Remember that the principle of substitution related to the cost approach stated that "no person is justified paying more for a property than they could build new without undue delay." This principle applied to the cost approach is virtually an *axiomatic theorem* concerning most knowledgeable buyers and sellers within a market—axiomatic meaning a "self-evident truth" and a theorem in that it is a "statement susceptible of logical proof when certain facts are accepted as true." In short, the principle of substitution as it applies to the cost approach is as close to being written in stone as anything within the market and the appraisal profession can get. The implication of the related principle of substitution is that market value and the cost of the property are closely related with newer properties. This leads to the concept that the cost approach is likely to be most applicable in newly constructed or relatively new properties. In theory, the market is likely to be knowledgeable about the forces that affect and create value, and therefore the property would not be built if the cost to build were not feasible. Likewise, if the cost approach is accurately performed, then depreciation, land value, and costs new are also accurately isolated. This means that the cost approach, in this case, would accurately reflect what a knowledgeable market acting in its own best interest would transfer a property, based on the aforementioned axiom. It is easily accepted that "given that the land value is well-supported and that the costs associated with the construction of the property are similar to the current cost new with little or no accrued depreciation, the cost approach has substantial validity as an indicator of value." But most texts fail to establish that if the weaknesses of the cost approach are overcome in that depreciation and land value are accurately identified, then the cost approach is a strong indicator of market value in that no person is justified paying more than they can build new.

The cost approach is also useful for determining market value in situations where the sales comparison and income approaches lack validity or applicability. For example, in single-family valuation the income approach may not have validity in a market where the income stream associated with the ownership of property does not drive ownership of the property, and the market might lack recent or comparable sales that would support a value conclusion under the sales comparison approach. Likewise, if the property has a low effective age, and therefore little physical depreciation with identifiable or little obsolescence, then the cost approach is likely to be representative of the market value of the property.

Another situation where the cost approach is helpful is when a property is to be considered with proposed renovations or additions. The cost approach will point to overimprovements or superadequacies. Finally, the cost approach has use when the assignment calls for feasibility consideration. If the cost of completing proposed changes is less than the value return associated with the changes, then the project is considered *financially feasible*. The cost approach is therefore instrumental in feasibility analysis as the very definition of feasibility is based on the question of the value return associated with the cost of a proposed change.

Limitations of the Cost Approach

So it goes that the cost approach, like the other approaches, has limitations in applicability or validity. Often, the limitations are found in the data extracted from the market. As previously stated, the obvious limitations are the lack of accurate land value as if vacant or excessive depreciation leaving the accuracy of the cost approach to be questionable. Other limitations are found in the property itself. If the property under analysis is found to be a special use, nonconforming use, or a building that is not to its highest and best use, the cost approach is not likely to be truly representative of the market value of the property. The simple reason is that in these property types the cost is not likely to match the market response of such properties because of their unique niche in the market.

METHODS OF COST ANALYSIS

There are four methods for estimating the construction costs, whether replacement or reproduction: the *cost index method*, the *square-foot method*, the *unit-in-place method*, and the *quantity survey method*. This lesson explains each of these methods.

COST INDEX METHOD

The **cost index method** estimates construction cost by multiplying the known original cost of a building by a factor. Cost index or cost reporting services keep records of all building costs over time. The factor represents the percentage increase in construction costs up to the effective date of value. This factor is then applied to the original cost of the subject building. The formula used is:

$$\frac{\text{Present index}}{\text{Index at time of construction}} \times \text{Original cost} = \text{Present cost}$$

For example, a house was built for $100,000 in 1986. At that time, the construction cost index was 120. Currently (as of the effective date of the appraisal) the cost index is reported at 300. Calculate the present cost as follows:

$$\frac{300}{120} \times \$100{,}000 = \$250{,}000$$

■ **In Practice**

The original construction cost of a building was $130,000, with a cost index of 175. What are the current estimated construction costs for the building if the cost index is now 290?

Solution:

Using the cost index formula:

    Present index = 290
    Index at time of construction = 175
    Original cost = $130,000

$$\frac{290}{175} \times \$130{,}000 = \$215{,}429$$

This method is the least reliable when used alone, but can be used to support or verify cost figures derived from the other methods. Although original construction costs may be available, it is difficult to determine if these costs represent what would be "typical" costs at that time.

FIGURE 1.4
Sample Page from a Residential Construction Cost Manual

Economy 2 Story

Living Area - 2000 S.F.
Perimeter - 135 L.F.

			Labor Hours	Cost Per Square Foot Of Living Area		
				Mat.	Labor	Total
1	Site Work	Site preparation for slab; 4' deep trench excavation for foundation wall.	0.034		0.59	0.59
2	Foundation	Continuous reinforced concrete footing, 8" deep x 18" wide; dampproofed and insulated 8" thick reinforced concrete block foundation wall, 4' deep; 4" concrete slab on 4" crushed stone base and polyethylene vapor barrier, trowel finish.	0.069	2.27	3.04	5.31
3	Framing	Exterior walls - 2" x 4" wood studs, 16" O.C.; 1/2" insulation board sheathing; wood truss roof frame, 24" O.C. with 1/2" plywood sheathing, 4 in 12 pitch; 2" x 8" floor joists 16" O.C. with bridging and 5/8" plywood subfloor.	0.112	4.70	5.63	10.33
4	Exterior Walls	Beveled wood siding and #15 felt building paper on insulated wood frame walls; 6" attic insulation; double hung windows; 2 flush solid core wood exterior doors with storms.	0.107	7.50	4.26	11.76
5	Roofing	20 year asphalt shingles; #15 felt building paper; aluminum gutters, downspouts, drip edge and flashings.	0.024	0.47	0.91	1.38
6	Interiors	Walls and ceilings, 1/2" taped and finished drywall, primed and painted with 2 coats; painted baseboard and trim; rubber backed carpeting 80%, asphalt tile 20%; hollow core wood interior doors.	0.219	7.73	10.17	17.90
7	Specialties	Economy grade kitchen cabinets - 6 L.F. wall and base with plastic laminate counter top and kitchen sink; 30 gallon electric water heater.	0.017	0.83	0.43	1.26
8	Mechanical	1 lavatory, white, wall hung; 1 water closet, white; 1 bathtub, enameled steel, white; gas fired warm air heat.	0.061	2.12	2.17	4.29
9	Electrical	100 Amp. service; romex wiring; incandescent lighting fixtures; switches, receptacles.	0.030	0.58	0.96	1.54
10	Overhead	Contractor's overhead and profit		3.95	4.24	8.19
		Total		30.15	32.40	62.55

Source: Means Residential Cost Data 2005. Copyright Reed Construction Data, Kingston, MA 781-585-7880. All rights reserved.

SQUARE-FOOT METHOD

The **square-foot method** breaks the structure down into a square-foot unit of comparison. The appraiser can either collect cost data of a comparable new structure in the area or refer to published cost manuals. Because construction costs may vary in direct proportion to the size of the building (economies of scale), it is important that the appraiser chooses a comparable sale that is similar in size to the subject. Cost manuals indicate typical constructions, which are usually updated quarterly or monthly. The quality of the construction and material is first rated with similar construction costs, and then the cost per square foot is adjusted for differences in upgrades or options. Sometimes a local factor is required for regional differences as a result of labor, shipping, or access costs due to difficult terrain. Figure 1.4 shows a page from a typical residential cost manual. The total cost for this house is estimated at $62.55 per square foot. This figure can then be adjusted for regional differences. The square-foot method is the most used method for calculating building costs.

■ **In Practice**

You are appraising a single-family home with a total area of 3,100 square feet. The cost to build a local comparable 3,300-square-foot residence is $415,000.

Using construction costs from the comparable single-family home, estimate the construction costs of the subject residence.

Solution:

Cost per square foot of comparable residence:

$415,000 ÷ 3,300 = $125.76 per sq. ft.

Cost estimate of subject:

3,100 × $125.76 = $389,856

UNIT-IN-PLACE METHOD

The **unit-in-place method**, also known as *component costing* or the *segregated cost method*, calculates the improvement costs by analyzing the costs for major components of a structure. Detailed costs are provided from cost manuals or costing services, as well as from local builders and suppliers. These costs include the following building components:

- Appliances
- Ceiling
- Countertops
- Cabinets
- Electrical
- Electrical fixtures
- Exterior walls
- Fireplace(s)
- Floor coverings
- Floor structure
- Foundation
- Heating and cooling system
- Interior construction
- Plumbing
- Plumbing fixtures
- Roof dormers
- Roof structure and covering
- Stairway(s)

Adding together the major components concludes a total cost new of the improvements. Figure 1.5 is an example of costs for an industrial building obtained from a cost manual.

■ **In Practice**

Using the following information about a rectangular warehouse, calculate the cost to construct using the unit-in-place method.

Building dimensions: 100' × 275', building area = 27,500 sq. ft.

Foundation: concrete walls and footing at $41.20 per linear foot

Floor: reinforced concrete at $3.75 per sq. ft.

Roof: built-up tar and gravel at $2.75 per sq. ft.;

roof sheathing at $0.75 per sq. ft.;

fiberboard insulation at $0.65 per sq. ft.

FIGURE 1.5
Cost Data

Component	Cost per Measured Unit
Foundation 12" concrete wall and footings	$30.70 per linear foot
Floor Construction 8" reinforced concrete	$3.60 per sq. ft. of floor area
Framing 14' steel columns, beams, and purlins	$4.50 per sq. ft. of support area
Roof Construction sheathing, 2" polystyrene insulation, 4-ply asphalt and gravel covering	$3.70 per sq. ft.
Exterior Walls 12" concrete block backup	$10.20 per sq. ft.
Windows industrial sash, steel, 50% vented	$14.20 per sq. ft.
Doors hollow metal, 3' × 7' rolling steel, chainhoist operated, 12' × 12'	$355 per door $1,425 per door
Interior Painting	$0.35 per sq. ft.
Electrical Wiring and Fixtures	$3.10 per sq. ft. of building area
Heating and A/C	$5.30 per sq. ft. of building area
Plumbing including Fixtures	$2.25 per sq. ft. of building area
Parking Area 3" asphalt on 3" stone base	$7.20 per sq. yd.

Interior construction: partition walls, interior painting: total cost $5,100

Front exterior wall: common brick on concrete block, 100' × 15' high at $10.25 per sq. ft.;

two windows each 6' × 12' at $16.10 per sq. ft.;

one 10' × 12' overhead door at a cost of $1,400; one 3' × 7' hollow core metal door at $375

Side exterior walls: concrete block 275' long × 15' high at $8.50 per sq. ft.;

windows covering 20% of wall area at $15.25 per sq. ft.

Rear exterior wall: concrete block 100' × 15' at $8.50 per sq. ft.;

one 10' × 12' overhead door at a cost of $1,400

Steel framing: area supported by frame: 75' × 250' with 14" eave height, at $5.10 per sq. ft.

Electrical: $3.75 per sq. ft. of floor area

Heating: $2.80 per sq. ft. of floor area

Plumbing: $2.00 per sq. ft. of floor area

Solution:

Unit-in-place costs:

Foundation:

Perimeter = (2 × 100) + (2 × 275) = 750 ft.

750 feet @ $41.20 $30,900

Floor:

27,500 sq. ft. @ $3.75 $103,125

Roof:

27,500 sq. ft. @ $4.15 ($2.75 + $0.75 + $0.65) $114,125

Interior construction:

Partition walls, interior painting: $5,100

Front exterior wall:

100' × 15' = 1,500 sq. ft.

Windows: 144 sq. ft. (72 sq. ft. × 2)

Overhead door: 120 sq. ft.

Door: 21 sq. ft.

1,215 sq. ft. @ $10.25 $12,454

Windows: 144 sq. ft. @ $16.10 $2,318

Overhead door: $1,400 $1,400

Door: $375 $375

Total $16,547

Side exterior walls:

$2 \times (275' \times 15') = 8{,}250$ sq. ft. $-$ 1,650 sq. ft. (20% for windows)

= 6,600 sq. ft. @$8.50	$56,100
1,650 sq. ft. @ $15.25	25,163
Total	$81,263

Rear exterior wall:

$100' \times 15' = 1{,}500$ sq. ft.

Overhead door: 120 sq. ft. $(1{,}500 - 120 = 1{,}380)$

1,380 sq. ft. @ $8.50	$11,730
Overhead door: $1,400	1,400
Total	$13,130

Steel framing:

75' $\times$ 250' = 18,750 sq. ft. @ $5.10	$95,625

Electrical:

27,500 sq. ft. @ $3.75	$103,125

Heating:

27,500 sq. ft. @ $2.80	$77,000

Plumbing:

27,500 sq. ft. @ $2.00	$55,000
Total replacement/reproduction cost	**$694,940**

Total cost per sq. ft. = **$25.27** ($694,940 ÷ 27,500)

QUANTITY SURVEY METHOD

The **quantity survey method,** sometimes called the *builder's breakdown method,* is the most comprehensive method of costing. It is similar to the unit-in-place method; however, the costs are estimated by accounting for every item in a project, including the cost of individual units of materials, labor, fees, and so on. The appraiser itemizes these costs separately and places them into categories. With the quantity survey method, *direct costs*, *indirect costs,* and *entrepreneurial profit* are computed more precisely than in any other method. **Direct costs,** also referred to as *hard costs*, include expenditures for labor and materials used in the construction of an improvement including the contractor's overhead and profit. **Indirect costs**, also referred to as *soft costs*, include financing costs, construction loan interest, insurance and real estate taxes during construction, building permits, administrative costs, professional fees (appraisal, engineering, and architectural fees), and lease-up and marketing costs involved with stabilizing occupancy.

Entrepreneurial profit, also known as developers' profit, is the difference between the price paid for a new property and the total cost to deliver the property. This includes the direct and indirect costs plus land value. Entrepreneurial profit is only realized when the improved property sells; therefore it is an estimate of anticipated profit to the entrepreneur. Published cost manuals do *not* include entrepreneurial profit.

Often expressed as a percentage of direct costs, direct and indirect costs, direct and indirect costs plus the land value, or the value of the completed project, entrepreneurial profit is market sensitive and varies with changes in economic conditions.

The use of the quantity survey method requires an extensive knowledge of building construction. See Figure 1.6.

DEPRECIATION

Depreciation is a loss in value. While often the term *depreciation* describes all loss of value, the correct term for the loss of value from all causes is **accrued depreciation**. The loss-in-value terms are specific categories of value loss that describe these causes. The definitions are specific, and professional appraisers should take care to use these loss-of-value terms accurately.

PHYSICAL DEPRECIATION

Physical depreciation is the loss in value as a result of general wear and tear. **Short-lived items** are those that will wear out before the useful life of the property has passed. *Useful life* is the amount of time that the existing improvements can be reasonably expected to contribute utility under which the property was designed. *Physical life* is the amount of time that the improvements will still be habitable. The *economic life* is the amount of

FIGURE 1.6
Itemized Costs

Direct Costs	
Clearing the land	$ 723
Rough and fine grading	16,753
Footings	8,760
Slabs	8,341
Entrance and stoops	4,200
Balconies	12,350
Interior stairs	575
Dampproofing	938
Rough and finished carpentry	127,390
Furring	3,480
Doors	3,560
Rough and finished hardware	11,722
Kitchen cabinets	14,250
Flooring	18,764
Refrigerators	11,920
Disposals	2,330
Gas ranges	7,386
Venetian blinds	4,800
Bathroom tile	7,297
Painting	13,750
Insulation	1,070
Glazing	2,483
Structural steel and lintels	4,747
Ornamental iron	8,190
Masonry	79,423
Drywall	35,961
Heating and air-conditioning	39,467
Plumbing	44,200
Electrical wiring	21,870
Water mains	4,102
Water and sewer connections	790
Roofing and sheet metal	6,200
Incidentals	9,340
Cleaning, general and contract	5,900
Landscaping	7,450
Fence	1,800
Temporary utilities	4,728
Temporary roads and structures	2,857
Streets, parking area, sidewalks, curbs, and gutters	33,689
Sanitary and storm sewers	15,042
Supervision and time keeping	21,785

Indirect Costs	
Permit	$ 35
Survey	1,980
Layout	465
Payroll taxes and insurance	8,570
Builder's overhead and profit	64,000

time that the improvements will contribute to the value over the salvage value. Most often the physical life extends beyond the economic life of a property. As an example, the carpeting will likely need replacing several times throughout the useful life of a building.

Long-lived items are items that are not likely to be replaced over the useful life of the property. Framing or floor joists are examples; these are usually too costly to replace. When the cost of repairing or replacing an item exceeds the value return realized by replacing the item, it is said to be **incurable,** hence the term **incurable physical depreciation.**

Conversely, if the value return exceeds the cost of repairing or replacing the worn-out item, then it is said to be **curable,** hence the term **curable physical depreciation.** Curable physical depreciation is also referred to as *deferred maintenance.* The term *cost-to-cure* is reflective of the costs associated with repairing or replacing a defective item.

OBSOLESCENCE

Another form of value loss is *obsolescence.* **Obsolescence** is the negative market response to an item. There are two types of obsolescence, *functional obsolescence* and *external obsolescence* (also called *economic obsolescence*). **Functional obsolescence** is a value loss as a result of the market's negative response to some functionality of the property. This type of obsolescence is a loss in value due to something that exists within the property itself—for example, a poor floor plan or a peculiar carpet color. Suppose that the building is recently constructed. There is no physical depreciation, as both of these items are new, but there is a value loss as the market is not willing to pay the typical price for the building because of the poor floor plan. Likewise the market is also not willing to pay the typical price for carpeting deemed "peculiar." Because replacing the floor plan would not likely be easy without an excessive *cost-to-cure*, the property suffers from **incurable functional obsolescence.** Suppose that replacing the property's carpet with a more desired floor covering is $2,500 and that the property would receive a value return equaling or exceeding $2,500. Then the property has **curable functional obsolescence** of $2,500.

Suppose that the market supports a loss of value of $15,000 from the incurable floor plan. The functional obsolescence calculation is therefore $17,500 ($15,000 + $2,500). Had there been a loss of value as a result of physical depreciation, adding this figure to the obsolescence figures calculates the accrued depreciation. Because there is no physical depreciation, the accrued depreciation remains as $17,500.

Sometimes there may a loss in value as a result of an *overimprovement*. This is a functional obsolescence that results in a **superadequacy.** In such cases the market will not pay the additional costs associated with the item. For example, high-quality gold plumbing fixtures in a tract home would be extravagant items for which the market would not likely pay additional funds.

External obsolescence is a value loss realized as a result of the market's negative response to something that is outside of the property lines. External obsolescence is never curable, as the ability to rectify the issue is beyond the control of the property owner.

METHODS OF DEPRECIATION

Economic Age-Life Method

Perhaps the single most recognized and used method of estimating depreciation in the appraisal field is the *economic age-life method.* The **economic age-life method** of depreciation (also simply referred to as the *age-life method*) is a method of calculating a percent of depreciation by dividing the *effective age* by the *total economic life:*

$$\frac{\text{Effective age}}{\text{Total economic life}} = \% \text{ of depreciation}$$

Effective age (EA) is the age that the property appears to be as of the date of inspection. **Total economic life (TEL)** is the *effective age* plus the *remaining economic life*. The **remaining economic life (REL)** is the time that the existing improvements are likely *to contribute economically* to the value of the property.

For example, if the effective age of a structure is 20 years and the remaining economic life is 30 years, the total economic life estimate is 50 years as illustrated below.

Total Economic Life				
10	20	30	40	50
Effective Age		Remaining Economic Life		

Therefore, the formula for estimating accrued depreciation by the economic age-life method may also be expressed as:

$$\frac{\text{Effective age}}{(\text{Effective age} + \text{Remaining economic life})} \times \text{Cost new} = \text{Accrued depreciation}$$

Five steps summarize the economic age-life method of estimating accrued depreciation:

1. Estimate the total reproduction or replacement cost new of improvements

2. Estimate the effective age (EA) of the property

3. Estimate the total economic life (TEL) of the property

4. Estimate the rate of depreciation (depreciation percentage) by dividing effective age by total economic life (EA ÷ TEL = % of depreciation)

5. Multiply the rate of depreciation by the total cost new of the improvements to arrive at the estimated accrued depreciated amount

The *depreciated cost of the improvements* can now be computed by subtracting the estimated accrued depreciation amount from the estimated cost new.

For example, suppose a property was constructed 35 years ago. That property has a *chronological age* or *actual age* of 35 years. **Chronological age** (also called **actual age** or **physical age**) is the age that the property has actually been in existence from the time of its original construction. Suppose also that because of proper maintenance and property management the property looks to be effectively 15 years old, and that the estimated time that the existing building improvements will continue to contribute under the current use is another 45 years. Then the effective age (EA) is 15 years, the remaining economic life (REL) is 45 years, and the total economic life (TEL) is estimated at 60 years (15 + 45 = 60). Therefore, the estimate of the percent of depreciation under the age-life method is 25 percent (15 ÷ 60 = 0.25). If it were estimated that the subject would have a replacement cost new of $100,000 then the depreciation using the economic age-life method would be calculated as $25,000 ($100,000 × 0.25 = $25,000).

Subtracting the estimated accrued depreciation amount from the estimated cost new now computes the depreciated cost of the improvements.

Estimated cost	$100,000
minus depreciation	− 25,000
Depreciated cost of the improvements	$75,000

The benefit of this method is that it is widely accepted, reasonably accurate, and fairly simple to execute. Some of the drawbacks are that it is somewhat subjective, does not isolate a breakdown of the depreciation, and assumes that the building will depreciate at a projected straight-line rate into the future (depreciate the same amount per year).

■ **In Practice**

The estimated reproduction cost of a commercial building is $600,000. This type of building typically has a total economic life of 55 years. The actual age and the effective age are eight years. Using the economic age-life method, calculate the depreciation percentage, the depreciation amount, and the depreciated cost of the improvement.

Solution:

Use the five steps previously mentioned to answer the following:

1. Estimate the cost new of improvements: $600,000

2. Estimate the effective age (EA) of the property: 8 years

3. Estimate the total economic life (TEL) of the property: 55 years

4. Estimate the rate of depreciation (depreciation percentage) by dividing effective age by total economic life (EA ÷ TEL = % of depreciation):

8 ÷ 55 = 0.15 or 15%

5. Multiply the rate of depreciation by the total cost new of the improvements to arrive at the estimated accrued depreciated amount:

$600,000 × 0.15 = $90,000

The depreciated cost of the improvements:

$600,000 − $90,000 = $510,000

Modified Economic Age-Life Method

The **modified economic age-life method** of depreciation is similar to the economic age-life method except that the curable items such as curable physical depreciation and curable functional obsolescence are removed before the ratio of effective age to total economic life is applied. Any changes in the effective age are considered a result from curing the physical and functional defects. The result is a more accurate representation of how the market will respond to a property with known curable items that can be isolated and quantified.

For example, suppose that a property has a curable cost-to-cure from both physical depreciation and functional obsolescence of $30,000, and a total estimated cost (RCN) of $400,000. The actual and effective age of the property is 20 years, but because the repairs will lower the effective age to 10 years and the remaining economic life estimate is 45 years, the depreciation percent is 18% (EA divided by TEL [10 ÷ 55], where TEL equals EA added to REL [10 + 45 = 55]).

The following is the flowchart of calculations:

Total cost	$400,000
Cost-to-cure	− 30,000
Remaining cost	$370,000
Remaining cost × depreciation percent	− 66,600
Depreciated cost new modified age-life	$303,400

Adding the depreciated cost new of $303,400 to the land value yields an indicated value by the cost approach using the modified economic age-life method of depreciation.

Breakdown Method

The **breakdown method**, also known as the *observed condition method* or the **engineering breakdown method**, is the most detailed and comprehensive method of calculating depreciation. This method estimates each of the five forms of depreciation:

1. Curable physical depreciation, also known as deferred maintenance
2. Incurable physical depreciation
3. Curable functional obsolescence
4. Incurable functional obsolescence
5. External obsolescence

All are individually calculated and then summed to determine the accrued depreciation. This method is predominately used in commercial real estate appraisals.

For example, suppose that the replacement cost new of a 20-year-old, one-story retail building is estimated to be $800,000. This type of structure has an estimated total economic life of 65 years. Upon inspection, you estimate the effective age to be the same as the actual age; however, some of the components have different observed depreciation percentages. There is no functional obsolescence; however, you discovered via the sales comparison approach that the subject suffers from some external obsolescence of $10,000 for being located too close to the railroad line. The reproduction costs as well as the observed depreciation for each component are detailed below.

Component	Reproduction Cost (RCN)	Observed Depreciation	Amount of Depreciation
Heating system	$15,000	40%	$6,000
Plumbing	$20,000	40%	$8,000
Roof	$25,000	50%	$12,500
Total	$60,000		$26,500

Total cost (RCN)	$800,000
Cost-to-cure	– $60,000
Remaining cost adjusted for cost to cure	$740,000
less incurable depreciation ($740,000 × 0.31*)	– $229,400
less depreciation of itemized components	– $26,500
less external obsolescence	– $10,000
Depreciated cost new observed method	**$474,100**

20 ÷ 65 = 0.31, rounded

Straight-Line Method

The **straight-line method** of depreciation is the simplest method and is calculated by dividing the cost new (or 100 percent) by the useful life to find an equal annual percentage of depreciation over the life of the asset. As an example, if the estimated cost of a building is $100,000 and the expected useful life is 40 years, then the estimated annual depreciation is $2,500 ($100,000 ÷ 40) or 2.5 percent per year ($2,500 ÷ $100,000). Straight-line depreciation is not recommended, as most assets do not depreciate in equal amounts year by year. Typically, structures depreciate slowly at first and then more rapidly at the end of the physical life.

■ **In Practice**

If the RCN for a building is $450,000 and the useful life is expected to be 55 years:

a. Calculate the annual dollar amount of depreciation using straight-line depreciation.

b. Calculate the annual depreciation percentage.

Solution:

a.   **$450,000 ÷ 55 = $8,181.81 per year**

b.   **$8,181.81 ÷ $450,000 = 0.018 or 1.8% per year**

Market Method

The **market method,** or *market extraction method,* of determining accrued depreciation finds similar properties and measures their depreciation. Once depreciation as a percent is isolated, this percentage is applied to the subject cost figures to conclude a depreciated cost new of the subject. The main drawback of this method is that the chosen properties from the market must be very similar in quality and condition to the subject. The following steps extract accrued depreciation from the market:

1. Locate a minimum of two improved comparable sales from the market. These sales should appear to suffer from the same amount of depreciation as the subject.

2. Deduct the estimated site value from the sales prices of the comparable sales. The result is the contributory value of the improvements only.

3. Estimate the replacement or reproduction cost new (as of the date of sale) for each comparable sale.

4. Deduct the estimated contributory value of the improvements from step 2 from the estimated RCN in step 3. This results in a lump-sum dollar amount of depreciation.

5. Convert the dollar amount arrived at in step 4 into a percentage. Do this by dividing the lump-sum dollar amount of depreciation by the RCN arrived at in step 3.

6. Estimate the effective age of the comparable property.

7. Convert the lump-sum percentage of depreciation into an annual rate of accrued depreciation. Do this by dividing the lump-sum percentage calculated in step 5 by the effective age in step 6.

8. Calculate the mean of the annual rate of accrued depreciation. Apply this average annual rate of accrued depreciation by multiplying by the effective age of the subject property. This results in an indicated percentage of accrued depreciation.

9. Multiply the indicated percentage of accrued deprecation by the RCN of the subject property. This results in a total accrued depreciation dollar amount.

For an example, use one comparable sale obtained by the market that sold for $320,000 and has an estimated site value of $95,000. The estimated effective age of this comparable sale is ten years and the estimated RCN is $260,000. Take the following steps to arrive at an annual rate of accrued deprecation:

Step 1	Sales price of comparable		$320,000
Step 2	minus the estimated site value		− 95,000
	Contributory value of the improvements		$225,000
Step 3	Estimated RCN		$260,000
	minus contributory value of the improvements		− 225,000
	Lump-sum dollar amount of accrued depreciation		$35,000
Step 4	Lump-sum dollar amount of accrued depreciation		$35,000
	divided by RCN		÷ $260,000
	Lump-sum accrued depreciation %		0.1346
Step 5	Lump-sum accrued depreciation %		0.1346
	divided by the effective age in years		÷ 10
Step 6	Average annual rate of accrued depreciation		**0.0135**
			or **1.35% per year**

LAND OR SITE VALUATION TECHNIQUES

The last step before reconciling to an indicated value conclusion under the cost approach is to add the value of the land to the depreciated cost new of the property. Raw land is distinctly different from a site in that a site has improvements that allow for a certain use. In the cost approach one may either add the cost of land plus the cost of the site improvements or simply add the cost of the site. Either way is acceptable provided that the reader clearly understands which method was performed and that all of the costs are accounted for without double counting the site improvements.

There are six methods of determining site value:

1. *Sales comparison method*—Obtain sales of similar vacant sites from the market. Arrive at a final estimate of value for the subject site as though vacant after making any necessary adjustments for differences.

2. *Allocation method*—When a property is improved, apply the ratio of land to building value of similar properties in the market to the subject improved property to arrive at the land value of the subject.

3. *Extraction method* or *abstraction method*—When the sales price and improvement costs of a property are known, subtract the costs from the sales price to arrive at a land value.

4. *Subdivision development method*—Subtract the costs of developing and subdividing a parcel of land from the expected sales prices of the sub-divided sites. Make adjustments for time needed to sell all subdivided sites in order to derive the value of the undivided raw land.

5. *Ground rent capitulation method*—A *ground lease* refers to the agreement between a landowner and a tenant agreeing to erect a building on the site. To derive a land value, capitalize the net income associated with the ground lease. For example, if a ground lease generates an annual income of $50,000 and the market reflects a capitalization rate of 9 percent, the value using the IRV formula is:

$$\text{Value (V)} = \text{Income (I)} \div \text{Capitalization rate (R)}$$

$$= \$50,000 \div 0.09$$

$$= \$555,555$$

6. *Land residual method*—With this method, the income from the building is deducted from the total net income derived from the entire property (land and building). The balance is then income derived from just the land, which is then capitalized using the IRV formula.

INDICATED VALUE UNDER THE COST APPROACH

Once the land or site value has been added to the depreciated cost new of the improvements, the final step in the cost approach is to conclude an indicated value. The basis for this value indication may or may not be in reality of market driven forces that are present at the time of the assignment. As investigated earlier, there are strengths and weaknesses of the cost approach, and sometimes the concluded value from the approach may not be what the property is truly worth in the market. For this reason the often quoted maxim "Cost does not necessarily equal value" is stated.

One strength of the cost approach is that it is relatively easy to produce an accurate cost using resources such as cost manuals or proprietary software. Also, as stated earlier, in the case of a new property it is likely that the cost is closely indicative of the value in the market. Nevertheless, this is not always true. For this reason, appraisers use more than one approach to value, and apply the theory behind economic principles known as *the appraisal principles.*

Some of the weaknesses of the cost approach are that there may be too much depreciation to accurately measure, or that the land value may be extremely difficult to determine, thereby causing the approach to lose validity.

LESSON 2 REVIEW QUESTIONS

1. The cost approach is a methodized process to derive at a value indication whereby the _____, or the _____, of a building is first estimated.

2. No person is justified in paying more for a property than they can build _____.

3. _____ cost is the cost of constructing an exact duplicate of the existing building using the exact materials and the construction standards of the original building.

4. Replacement cost is the cost of constructing new the existing building at _____ construction standards using _____ materials.

5. The cost approach has applicability and _____ depending on the situation and data available.

6. The principle of _____ is the primary principle of the cost approach.

7. A special-use property is a typical use of the _____ cost.

8. Another situation where the cost approach is helpful is when a property is to be considered with proposed _____ or additions.

9. If the property has a low effective age, it is likely to have little _____ depreciation.

10. If the cost of completing proposed changes is less than the value return associated with the changes, then the project is considered _____.

11. The _____ method estimates construction cost by multiplying the known original cost of a building by a factor.

12. The use of the _____ method requires an extensive knowledge of building construction.

13. Indirect costs are also referred to as _____ costs.

14. The _____ method of calculating the cost of improvements is also known as component costing or the segregated cost method.

15. Entrepreneurial profit is also known as _____ profit.

16. With the square-foot method, the structure is broken down into a square foot _____.

17. The _____ method is the most comprehensive method of costing.

18. _____ costs are also referred to as hard costs.

19. _____ costing is also known as the segregated cost method.

20. With the _____ method, direct costs, indirect costs, and entrepreneurial profit are computed more precisely than in any other method.

21. The modified age-life method of depreciation is similar to the economic age-life method except that the _____ items are removed before the ratio of effective age to total economic life is applied.

22. _____ is the negative market response to an item.

23. Most often the _____ life extends beyond the _____ life of a property.

24. The _____ depreciation method is the simplest method.

25. _____ age is also referred to as actual age.

26. With the _____ method, the income from the building is deducted from the total net income derived from the entire property.

27. Physical depreciation is the loss in value as a result of general _____.

28. _____ is defined as the age that the property appears to be as of the date of inspection.

29. _____ is the effective age plus the remaining economic life.

30. The last step before reconciling to an indicated value conclusion under the cost approach is to add the value of the _____ to the depreciated cost new of the property.

LESSON 2 REVIEW ANSWERS

1. replacement cost; reproduction cost
2. new
3. Reproduction
4. today's; today's
5. limitations
6. substitution
7. reproduction
8. renovations
9. physical
10. financially feasible
11. cost index
12. quantity survey
13. soft
14. unit-in-place
15. developers'
16. unit of comparison
17. quantity survey
18. Direct
19. Component
20. quantity survey
21. curable
22. Obsolescence

23. physical; economic

24. straight-line

25. Chronological

26. land residual

27. wear and tear

28. Effective age

29. Total economic life

30. land/site

LESSON 3: The Sales Comparison Approach

The **sales comparison approach**, also referred to as the *market approach* or the *market data approach*, is a methodized process of directly comparing the property being valued or analyzed in the assignment known as the **subject property** to other properties that have recently sold, known as **comparable sales** or **comparables.** The main benefit of this approach is that it is perhaps the most indicative of what the "market value" of the subject is likely to be as the comparables are a direct reflection of the willingness of buyers and sellers to transact. The sales comparison approach is most useful when there is an ample number of similar sales to the subject property (an active market) that have recently sold as *arm's-length transactions.*

The process in the sales comparison approach is to itemize the subject and comparable sales into *elements of comparison* whereby *adjustments* are made to the sales price of the comparable based on the differences between the elements.

The adjustment is first extracted from the market's perceived response to a particular element, and then the adjustment is applied to the comparable in order to conclude an indication of value for the subject.

Elements of comparison are categorized characteristics of properties that explain the variances in property values.

When appraising *improved properties*, elements of comparison that would be considered include:

1. Property rights conveyed
2. Financing
3. Conditions of sale
4. Market conditions (time)
5. Location
6. Physical characteristics
7. Economic characteristics

When appraising a *vacant parcel of land or a site,* elements of comparison that would be considered include:

1. Property rights conveyed

2. Financing

3. Conditions of sale

4. Market conditions (time)

5. Location

6. Physical characteristics

7. Economic characteristics

8. Zoning and land-use restrictions

9. Availability, capacity, and proximity of utilities (amount of site development)

UNIT OF COMPARISON

A **unit of comparison** is a physical or economic component that reflects the relationship between the sales price and various elements of comparison. (See Figure 1.7.) A unit of comparison creates a more standardized method of comparison. Choosing the proper unit of comparison as a basis for comparison is essential and depends on the type of property.

For a detailed discussion on gross living area and gross building area, see Appendix A.

The following are examples of units of comparison on a *physical unit* basis:

- Price per square foot of gross living area (residential)

- Price per square foot of gross building area (residential building with 1–4 units)

- Price per square unit (residential building with 1–4 units)

- Price per bedroom (residential building with 1–4 units)

- Price per front foot (vacant land)

- Price per acre (vacant land)

- Price per room (residential condominium, commercial condominium, residential building with 1–4 units, commercial building, etc.)

FIGURE 1.7
Unit of Comparison Formula

Unit of comparison = Sales price ÷ Element of comparison

The following are examples of units of comparison on an economic (income ratios) basis for income-producing properties:

- Gross income multiplier (GIM)
- Gross rent multiplier (GRM)
  - Potential gross income multiplier (PGIM)
  - Effective gross income multiplier (EGIM)
- Gross monthly rent multiplier (GMRM)

Adjustments can be either *quantitative or qualitative* adjustments. A **quantitative adjustment** is one that is numeric in nature and has a direct measurable market response to the element of comparison. As an example, the market reflects that people are willing to pay $5,500 more for a house with a fireplace. The adjustment is quantified and a positive or negative adjustment of $5,500 is applied to a comparable sale under the sales comparison approach. If the subject does not have a fireplace and a comparable has a fireplace, then a negative adjustment of $5,500 is applied to the sales price of the comparable with the fireplace amenity. This is done because if all other things are equal between the subject and the comparable sale, the subject is likely to sell for $5,500 less than the comparable that has the desired amenity of a fireplace.

A **qualitative adjustment** is without a numeric conclusion, and is based on a relative rating of an element of comparison. The adjustment works the same way under the sales comparison approach, with the exception of the numeric adjustment. An example of a qualitative adjustment is more along a rating system such as a superior or inferior rating. As an example, if the comparable sold for $200,000 and had several elements of comparison that reflect an inferior rating when compared with the subject, then the appraiser may reasonably reconcile that the subject is likely to be worth more than $200,000. An appraiser must be prepared to support market extracted adjustments whether they are quantitative or qualitative in nature.

Methodized Process of the Sales Comparison Approach

The methodized process under the sales comparison (market) approach is as follows:

1. Research the relevant sales data collected from the market
2. Verify the data and validity of the arm's-length transaction
3. Choose the units of comparison that are relevant
4. Adjust for differences in elements of comparison
5. Reconcile a to value indication under the sales comparison approach

Research Relevant Sales Data What determines relevance of data is the applicability of the information when compared with the market and the subject property. As stated previously, the property that is the subject of the appraisal assignment is called the *subject property*. The *subject*, as it is sometimes called, has features and characteristics that are likely to have value in the marketplace.

Verification To determine the value, take similar properties that have transacted at a known sales price from the market and compare them to the subject. The sale has to be at arm's length and verified as a market transaction if market value is to be sought.

Choosing Relevant Units of Comparison Within a specified market, the appraiser must analyze information gathered during the general data collection process and determine which unit or units of comparison accurately depict the expectations of the market participants.

Adjustments Next, adjust these comparable properties for their differences with the subject and render an indicate value from each similar sale (comparable).

The adjustments are derived by performing a **paired sales analysis,** also referred to as *paired data analysis* or *matched pairs analysis*, whereby the differences are isolated between other recently sold properties, and a quantitative or qualitative adjustment is applied to the comparable where there is a difference from the subject.

These differences result in either a positive or a negative adjustment.

Note: The *positive* adjustment and *negative* adjustment are often quite confusing to the novice appraiser. The important point to remember is that the *comparable adjusts to the subject*. Therefore, if the comparable is *superior to the subject*, the adjustment must be *negative* to make the comparable similar to the subject. Likewise, if the comparable is *inferior to the subject*, a *positive* adjustment must be made to the comparable sales price to make the comparable similar to the subject.

Reconciliation Recall that reconciliation is the last step in the development aspect of the appraisal process. There are actually several places in which reconciliation takes place. Reconciliation takes place at the end of each approach to value, and then at the end of the development phase of the appraisal process but before reporting. The reconciliation that takes place at the end of the development aspect of the appraisal process is sometimes called the overall reconciliation, and it is concerned with the conclusion that has the most validity and is the most appropriate to solve the original problem.

It is critical for reconciliation to take place at the end of each approach. This is for the benefit of accurately reaching conclusions within the approach using critical thinking. The indicated value by the approach is then submitted, and the strengths and weaknesses of the approach and conclusions are carefully considered before the final reconciliation and the overall value conclusion.

IDENTIFICATION, DERIVATION, AND MEASUREMENT OF ADJUSTMENTS

Quantitative Analysis—Making Quantitative Adjustments

As mentioned earlier, the sales comparison approach is a methodized process of directly comparing the subject property with the comparables. The process in the sales comparison approach is to itemize the subject and comparable sales into elements of comparison whereby adjustments are made to the sales price of the comparable based on the differences between the elements.

Property Rights Conveyed

Comparable sales must be adjusted for differences in property rights conveyed; for example, if the owner of a comparable sale has a leased fee estate (the property is encumbered by long-term leases) and the owner of the subject has a fee simple estate. These differences can have a significant impact on property value. In addition, there may be nonrealty interest items, such as personal property, that were included in the sale of a comparable property.

Financing

Implicit in the definition of market value is that payments to the seller are made in terms of cash or cash equivalency, and that the property is unaffected by special or creative financing or sales concessions. If a comparable sale involved special sales or financing concessions, adjustments whether positive or negative must be made. Seller financing with terms and conditions different from what is offered in the financing market, special loan types, and usual terms of a loan are all examples of special sales and financing concessions.

Cash equivalency is the adjustment made to the comparable sales price if it was sold with atypical financing. For example, the sales price of a comparable sale that reflects a premium paid for the benefit of receiving seller financing is needed to determine the present value of property. This *cash equivalency adjustment,* which is calculated from the buyer's point of view rather than the lender's point of view, can be made either in the sales comparison approach by paired sales analysis or in the income approach.

Conditions of Sale

Implicit in the definition of **market value** is that buyer and seller are typically motivated and that both parties are well informed and acting in what they consider their best interests. For example, if the appraiser interprets a comparable sale transaction as a sale that occurred under duress, then appropriate adjustments need to be made. In addition, if it is determined that the comparable sale was *not* an arm's-length transaction, adjustments would need to be made. Another example would be when the sales price of a property is affected by **expenditures made after purchase.** Examples of such expenditures include costs needed for deferred maintenance, costs for repairs, costs to demolish and/or remove improvements, costs incurred to receive necessary zoning changes, and costs involved with environmental issues.

A knowledgeable buyer who understands that these costs will be incurred immediately after the purchase of a property uses such information in negotiations with the seller. An adjustment must be made to the sales price to reflect these costs, as they were anticipated at the *time of the sale only.* Whether or not these costs actually increased or decreased over time is of no consequence.

Generally speaking, if the market supplies an abundance of comparable data, then these comparable sales with the various issues mentioned should be omitted.

Market Conditions (Time)

Because the principle of *change* dictates that nothing remains static and that everything changes over time, the date that a sale occurred is extremely important. The greater the difference between the effective date of an appraisal and the sale date of the comparable sale, the greater the potential for significant impacts on value. However, even if a short time has transpired since the comparable sale date and the effective date, a major change on the market economic base can significantly impact values in that market. For example, even a recent comparable sale, two months prior to the effective date, may need to be adjusted for market conditions. An adjustment may be needed because it was just announced that a large manufacturing plant in the immediate area will be closing. Property values can be significantly impacted due to large layoffs and the subsequent market reaction to the forces that affect value.

Likewise, property values can be significantly enhanced if the arrival of a new airport or large business that creates employment opportunities is announced.

Location

Under ideal circumstances, the subject and all comparable sales would be located within the same neighborhood. However, this is not always possible; therefore, any differences in location even within the same neighborhood must be accounted for.

Physical Characteristics

Physical characteristics of an improved property include:

- View
- Design

- Age (effective or physical)

- Condition

- Construction type

- Number of rooms

- Site size

- Building size (gross living area or gross building area)

- Number of bedrooms

- Number of baths

- Appeal

- Amenities

- Floor/ceiling height

The appraiser must consider these elements and compare them to the subject. The appraiser must also consider how these physical characteristics will affect the highest and best use of the property.

Economic Characteristics

Economic characteristics of an improved income-producing property include:

- Potential gross income

- Effective gross income

- Net operating income

- Operating expenses

- Tenant mix

- Rent concessions

- Management

- Lease terms

Zoning and Land-Use Restrictions

Police power is one of the four public restrictions that supersede the rights of an individual owner. Police power allows for zoning ordinances (land-use restrictions), building codes, health codes and regulations, environmental regulations, subdivision development regulations, and historical restrictions. In addition to public restrictions, private restrictions (deed restrictions or restrictive covenants) may also exist that would need to be adjusted for.

Availability, Capacity, and Proximity of Utilities

Land on which no improvements have been made is known as *raw land*, or sometimes called *unimproved land*. Raw land can be land that is simply undeveloped or put to an agricultural use. When land has had some

TABLE 1.1
Sales Grid #1

	Subject	Sale #1	Adjust	Sale #2	Adjust	Sale #3	Adjust	Sale #4	Adjust
Sales Price	N/A	$120,000		$115,000		$116,000		$113,000	
Finance	N/A	Conv.		Conv.		Conv.		Conv.	
Bedroom	3 BR	3 BR		3 BR		2 BR (1 & 3)	+$4,000	3 BR	
Construction Material	Brick	Brick		Frame (1 & 2)	+$5,000	Brick		Frame	+$5,000
Garage	1-car	2-car	−$2,000	2-car (2 & 4)	−$2,000	2-car	−$2,000	1-car	
Net Adjust (%)			−$2,000 (−1.7%)		+$3,000 (2.6%)		+$2,000 (1.7%)		+$5,000 (4.4%)
Gross Adjust (%)			$2,000 (1.7%)		$7,000 (6.1%)		$6,000 (5.2%)		$5,000 (4.4%)
Indicated Value		$118,000		$118,000		$118,000		$118,000	

improvements that would support a specific use, then it is said to be a *site.* The term *site* is specific, and it means there are improvements that would allow for further appurtenances to be developed. As an example, in a single-family subdivision, development site improvements would typically include utility connections, driveways and sidewalks, and appropriate lot size and shape to allow for setback requirements. An industrial site is vacant land that would allow for truck access and loading docks and that possesses the necessary utilities to support an industrial building.

Site improvements such as utilities, curbs, and roads are elements of value and, therefore, contribute to the value of the land. Adjustments for differences between the subject and all comparables then need to be made accordingly.

Making Adjustments

Sales Grid   To accurately extract and track adjustments, the appraiser will place the subject and comparable on a *sales grid* similar to the one found in Table 1.1.

Extracting Adjustments   Necessary calculations within the sales comparison approach include adjustments using paired sales analysis (a methodized process to extract adjustments) and reconciling to a value within this approach.

The following *lump-sum dollar adjustments* were extracted using a paired sales analysis from the four comparables.

Bedroom adjustment—Sale 1 and sale 3 are the same in every element except for the difference in bedroom count. Sale 1 has three bedrooms while sale 3 has two bedrooms. In comparing the difference in sales prices between the two sales, a $4,000 adjustment is extracted ($120,000 – $116,000). Because the subject has three bedrooms, a positive adjustment of $4,000 applies to sale 3 to make it more comparable to the subject. Likewise, if there were any other sales with two bedrooms, then a similar positive adjustment would apply to the two-bedroom comparables.

Construction material—Sale 1 and sale 2 are the same in every element except for the difference in construction material. Sale 1 is brick and sale 2 is frame. In comparing the difference in sales prices between the two sales, a $5,000 adjustment is extracted ($120,000 – $115,000). Because the subject is a brick construction, a positive adjustment of $5,000 applies to sale 2 to make it more comparable to the subject. Likewise because sale 4 is frame construction, sale 4 receives a positive adjustment of $5,000.

Garage adjustment—Sale 2 and sale 4 are the same in every element except for the difference in garage size. Sale 2 is a two-car garage and sale 4 is a one-car garage. In comparing the difference in sales prices between the two sales, a $2,000 adjustment is extracted ($115,000 – $113,000). Because the subject is a one-car garage, a negative adjustment of $2,000 applies to sale 2 to make it more comparable to the subject. Likewise, because sale 1 and sale 3 are also two-car garages, sale 1 and sale 3 are also a negative adjustment of $2,000.

Net adjustment—These lump-sum dollar adjustments within each sale are then "netted out" and the net result is either added or subtracted from the sales price to reach an indicated value for each comparable. A **net adjustment** is then the sum of all positive and negative adjustments. A shortcoming of net adjustments is that a series of net adjustments can potentially zero each other out. Because of this, *gross adjustments* must be considered as well. A **gross adjustment** is the result of adding of the adjustments for a comparable and ignoring the signs. In other words, it is the total dollar amount of adjustments ignoring whether the adjustment is negative or positive. Gross adjustments indicate whether a comparable sale is reliable. The comparable with the least amount of gross adjustments is usually the most reliable indicator of subject value. For example, looking at the sales grid in Table 1.1, while the net adjustments for sale #2 and sale #3 are +$3,000 and +$2,000, the gross adjustments are $7,000 and $6,000, respectively. So, while the net adjustments for sale #2 and sale #3 are similar to the other sales, they are less reliable when comparing the gross adjustments. Both net and gross adjustments can be expressed as a percentage of the sale price of the comparable sale.

■ In Practice

1. Using the following sales grid, calculate the net and gross adjustments for each comparable expressed as a lump-sum dollar amount and as a percentage of the comparable sales price.

	Subject	Sale #1	Adjust	Sale #2	Adjust	Sale #3	Adjust	Sale #4	Adjust
Sales Price	N/A	$630,000		$640,000		$645,000		$655,000	
Property Rights	Fee simple	Fee simple		Fee simple		Fee simple		Fee simple	
Financing	Cash	Cash		Special financing	−2.3% (−$15,000)	Cash		Cash	
Conditions of Sale	Arm's-length	Arm's-length		Arm's-length		Arm's-length		Arm's-length	
Market Conditions (time)	Current	1 year prior	+3.2% (+$20,000)	4 weeks prior		5 weeks prior		1 week prior	
Location	Average	Good	−$10,000	Average		Good	−$10,000	Good	−$10,000
Lot Size	Good	Good		Good		Average	+$15,000	Good	
GLA (sq. ft.)	3,500	3,400		3,400		3,500		3,500	
Bedrooms	3	4	−$8,000	3		4	−$8,000	4	−$8,000
Baths	2.5	2.5		2.5		2.5		2.5	
Age (yrs.)	15	12		13		15		8	−$10,000
Condition	Good	Good		Average	+$5,000	Good		Good	
Parking	3-car garage	2-car garage	+$5,000	2-car garage	+$5,000	3-car garage		2-car garage	+$5,000
Porch/Deck/Patio	Deck	Deck		Deck		None	+$1,000	Deck	
Net Adjust (%)									
Gross Adjust (%)									
Indicated Value									

2. Based on the net and gross adjustments, which comparable is the most reliable indicator of value?

Solution:

	Subject	Sale #1	Adjust	Sale #2	Adjust	Sale #3	Adjust	Sale #4	Adjust
Sales Price	N/A	$630,000		$640,000		$645,000		$655,000	
Property Rights	Fee simple	Fee simple		Fee simple		Fee simple		Fee simple	
Financing	Cash	Cash		Special financing	−2.3% (−$15,000)	Cash		Cash	
Conditions of Sale	Arm's-length	Arm's-length		Arm's-length		Arm's-length		Arm's-length	
Market Conditions (time)	Current	1 year prior	+3.2% (+$20,000)	4 weeks prior		5 weeks prior		1 week prior	
Location	Average	Good	−$10,000	Average		Good	−$10,000	Good	−$10,000
Lot Size	Good	Good		Good		Average	+$15,000	Good	
GLA (sq. ft.)	3,500	3,400		3,400		3,500		3,500	
Bedrooms	3	4	−$8,000	3		4	−$8,000	4	−$8,000
Baths	2.5	2.5		2.5		2.5		2.5	
Age (yrs.)	15	12		13		15		8	−$10,000
Condition	Good	Good		Average	+$5,000	Good		Good	
Parking	3-car garage	2-car garage	+$5,000	2-car garage	+$5,000	3-car garage		2-car garage	+$5,000
Porch/Deck/Patio	Deck	Deck		Deck		None	+$1,000	Deck	
Net Adjust (%)			+$7,000 (+1.1%)		−$5,000 (−2.3%)		−$2,000 (−0.03%)		−$23,000 (−3.5%)
Gross Adjust (%)			$43,000 (+6.8%)		$25,000 (+3.9%)		$34,000 (+5.2%)		$33,000 (5.0%)
Indicated Value			**$637,000**		**$625,000**		**$643,000**		**$632,000**

2. Comparable #2 is the most reliable comparable sale because it has the lowest gross adjustment.

ORDER OF ADJUSTMENTS

In addition to the lump-sum adjustments described above, another type of adjustment, a percentage adjustment, can be used. A *percentage adjustment* is an amount based on a percentage of the sales price of the comparable property.

When applying percentage adjustments, you must make the adjustments in a specific order, creating a new base after each element of comparison adjustment. The order is as follows:

1. Property rights conveyed

2. Financing

3. Conditions of sale

4. Market conditions (time)

5. Location

6. Physical characteristics

7. Income characteristics

> An easy way to remember the order of adjustments: **P**rivate **F**irst **C**lass **M**akes **L**ow **P**ay **I**nitially.

Generally, but not always, adjustments to the first five elements of comparison are adjusted with percentage adjustments. The remaining elements of comparison are adjusted using lump-sum dollar amounts. With lump-sum dollar adjustments, the adjustments within each sale are then "netted out," and the net result is either added or subtracted from the sales price to conclude an indicated value for each comparable.

For example, after careful consideration of pertinent elements of comparison, the appraiser needs to adjust one of the comparable sales downward by 10 percent for favorable financing. This is considered a percentage adjustment; therefore, the order of adjustment is important. If it is also determined that a positive $10,000 adjustment needs to be made for location because several of the comparables have a location that is considered inferior to the subject, then this would be a lump-sum adjustment. (See the sales grid in Table 1.2.)

> The acronyms **CIA** and **CBS** are an easy way to remember whether the adjustment to the comparable is a negative or positive adjustment:
> - Comparable Inferior Add (CIA)
> - Comparable Better Subtract (CBS)

Whether using a lump-sum dollar amount or a percentage adjustment, you adjust the comparable to the subject. If the comparable is superior to the subject, the adjustment must be negative to make the comparable similar to the subject. Likewise, if the comparable is inferior to the subject, a positive adjustment must be made to the comparable to make the comparable similar to the subject.

TABLE 1.2
Sales Grid #2

	Subject	Sale #1	Adjust	Sale #2	Adjust	Sale #3	Adjust	Sale #4	Adjust
Sales Price	N/A	$230,000		$245,000		$235,000		$260,000	
Property Rights	Fee simple	Fee simple		Fee simple		Fee simple		Fee simple	
Financing	None	None		None		None		Special financing	−10% (−$26,000)
Conditions of Sale	None	Equal		Equal		Equal		Equal	
Market Conditions (time)	Current	5 weeks prior		4 weeks prior		5 weeks prior		1 week prior	
Location	Good	Average	+$10,000	Good		Average	+$10,000	Average	+$10,000*
Physical Condition	Good	Good		Good		Good		Good	
Net Adjust (%)			+$10,000 (4.3%)		$0 (0%)		+$10,000 (4.3%)		−$16,000 (−6.2%)
Gross Adjust (%)			$10,000 (4.3%)		$0 (0%)		$10,000 (4.3%)		$36,000 (13.8%)
Indicated Value		$240,000		$245,000		$245,000		$244,000	

*Because the financing percentage adjustment must be calculated first, the $10,000 location adjustment is added to the new base sales price [($260,000 − $26,000) + $10,000] resulting in a concluded value of $244,000. If the minus 10 percent financing adjustment were calculated last, it would be −$27,000 [($260,000 + $10,000) × 10%] instead of −$26,000.

RECONCILIATION WITHIN THE APPROACH

After the indications of value from each comparable are completed, the appraiser must *reconcile* which of the sales are most similar (*comparable*) to the subject. After this weighting process is completed, the appraiser determines a value indication based on the value range before and after the adjustment process. Sales that have more adjustments are less similar to the subject and should be given less weight in the reconciliation process. The sales with the fewest adjustments are likely to be more indicative of what the subject's value is likely to be and should, therefore, be given greater weight in the indicated value conclusion under the sales comparison approach. See Appendix A for a discussion on how to calculate a weighted average within the sales comparison approach.

■ **In Practice**

Based on the sales grid in Table 1.2, which comparable would you give the most weight to and why? What is the indicated value of the subject property?

Solution: Sale 2 deserves the most weight because it has the fewest adjustments. The indicated value of the subject is $245,000.

■ In Practice

Your assignment is to value a residential lot. In your data collection process, you find four comparable sales that are most similar to the subject. Upon completing a paired sales analysis, you extracted the following adjustments:

1. A lot with a frontage of 100 feet sells for $5,000 more than lots with frontages of 60 to 80 feet.

2. A lot with a good location is 5 percent more valuable than a lot with an average location.

3. A rectangular-shaped lot is $6,000 more valuable than an irregular-shaped lot.

4. Favorable financing conditions warrant a 5 percent downward adjustment.

5. Residential lots, no matter what size, that are zoned R-3 are $10,000 more valuable than lots that are zoned R-2.

The following sales grid organizes the information about the subject as well as the four comparable land sales. Based on this information, complete the sales grid provided.

	Subject	Sale 1	Adjust	Sale 2	Adjust	Sale 3	Adjust	Sale 4	Adjust
Sales Price	N/A	$330,000		$340,000		$335,000		$350,000	
Property Rights	Fee simple	Fee simple		Fee simple		Fee simple		Fee simple	
Financing	None	None		Special financing		None		None	
Conditions of Sale	None	Equal		Equal		Equal		Equal	
Market Conditions (time)	Current	2 months prior		1 month prior		3 weeks prior		1 week prior	
Location	Good	Average		Average		Good		Good	
Shape	Rectangular	Rectangular		Irregular		Irregular		Rectangular	
Dimensions	80' × 180'	100' × 175'		80' × 180'		100' × 180'		100' × 180'	
Zoning	R-3	R-3		R-3		R-2		R-3	
Net Adjust (%)									
Gross Adjust (%)									
Indicated Value									

Solution:

	Subject	Sale 1	Adjust	Sale 2	Adjust	Sale 3	Adjust	Sale 4	Adjust
Sales Price	N/A	$330,000		$340,000		$335,000		$350,000	
Property Rights	Fee simple	Fee simple		Fee simple		Fee simple		Fee simple	
Financing	None	None		Special financing	−5% −$17,000	None		None	
Conditions of Sale	None	Equal		Equal		Equal		Equal	
Market Conditions (time)	Current	2 months prior		1 month prior		3 weeks prior		1 week prior	
Location	Good	Average	+5% +$16,500	Average	+5% $16,150*	Good		Good	
Shape	Rectangular	Rectangular		Irregular	+$6,000*	Irregular	+$6,000	Rectangular	
Dimensions	80' × 180'	100' × 175'	−$5,000	80' × 180'		100' × 180'	−$5,000	100' × 180'	−$5,000
Zoning	R-3	R-3		R-3		R-2	+$10,000	R-3	
Net Adjust (%)			$11,500 (+3.4%)		$5,150 (+1.5%)		$11,000 (+3.3%)		−$5,000 (−1.4%)
Gross Adjust (%)			$21,500 (6.5%)		$39,150 (11.51%)		$21,000 (6.3%)		$5,000 (1.4%)
Indicated Value			$341,500		$345,150		$346,000		$345,000

*Because the financing percentage adjustment must be calculated first, the positive 5 percent location adjustment is calculated based on the new base sales price after the financing adjustment is made ($323,000; $340,000 − $17,000). This results in a location adjustment of +$16,150 ($323,000 × 5%).

■ In Practice

Based on the sales grid in the previous In Practice section, which comparable would you give the most weight to, and why? What is the indicated value of the subject property?

Solution: Sale 4 would carry the most weight because it has the fewest adjustments. The indicated value of the subject is $345,000.

■ In Practice

1. Complete the grid using the following information about four comparable sales and perform paired sales analysis using the grid provided.

Note: The differences in age and market conditions are slight and, therefore, do not require adjustments.

	Sale 1	Sale 2	Sale 3	Sale 4
Sales Price	$343,000	$325,000	$338,000	$335,000
Property Rights	Fee simple	Fee simple	Fee simple	Fee simple
Financing Concessions	None	None	None	None
Conditions of Sale	Arm's-length	Arm's-length	Arm's-length	Arm's-length
Market Conditions	4 weeks prior	2 months prior	6 weeks prior	1 month prior
Location	Average	Average	Average	Good
Lot Size	50' × 150'	50' × 150'	50' × 150'	50' × 150'
GLA (sq. ft.)	1,800	1,600	1,800	1,600
Bedrooms	3	3	3	3
Baths	2	2	2	2
Age (yrs.)	35	32	35	35
Condition	Good	Good	Average	Good
Parking	1-car garage	1-car garage	1-car garage	1-car garage
Porch/Deck/Patio	Deck	Deck	Deck	Deck

	Subject	Sale 1	Adjust	Sale 2	Adjust	Sale 3	Adjust	Sale 4	Adjust
Sales Price	N/A								
Property Rights	Fee simple								
Financing Concessions	None								
Conditions of Sale	Arm's-length								
Market Conditions (time)	Current								
Location	Average								
Lot Size	50 × 150								
GLA (sq. ft.)	1,800								
Bedrooms	3								
Baths	2								
Age (yrs.)	34								
Condition	Good								

(continued)

	Subject	Sale 1	Adjust	Sale 2	Adjust	Sale 3	Adjust	Sale 4	Adjust
Parking	1-car garage								
Porch/Deck/ Patio	Deck								
Net Adjust (%)									
Gross Adjust (%)									
Indicated Value									

Comparison	Element Difference	Difference in Sales Price
vs.		
vs.		
vs.		

2. Based on the sales grid, which comparable would you give the most weight to and why? What is the indicated value of the subject property?

Solution:

1.

	Subject	Sale 1	Adjust	Sale 2	Adjust	Sale 3	Adjust	Sale 4	Adjust
Sales Price	N/A	$343,000		$325,000		$338,000		$335,000	
Property Rights	Fee simple	Fee simple		Fee simple		Fee simple		Fee simple	
Financing Concessions	Conventional	Conventional		Conventional		Conventional		Conventional	
Conditions of Sale	Arm's-length	Arm's-length		Arm's-length		Arm's-length		Arm's-length	
Market Conditions (time)	Current	4 weeks prior		2 months prior		6 weeks prior		1 month prior	
Location	Average	Average		Average		Average		Good	−$10,000
Lot Size	50' × 150'	50' × 150'		50' × 150'		50' × 150'		50' × 150'	
GLA (sq. ft.)	1,800	1,800		1,600	+$18,000	1,800		1,600	+$18,000
Bedrooms	3	3		3		3		3	
Baths	2	2		2		2		2	
Age (yrs.)	34	35		32		35		35	
Condition	Good	Good		Good		Average	+$5,000	Good	

(continued)

	Subject	Sale 1	Adjust	Sale 2	Adjust	Sale 3	Adjust	Sale 4	Adjust
Parking	1-car garage	1-car garage		1-car garage		1-car garage		1-car garage	
Porch/Deck/ Patio	Deck	Deck		Deck		Deck		Deck	
Net Adjust (%)			+$0 (0%)		+$18,000 (+5.5%)		+$5,000 (+1.5%)		+$8,000 (+2.4%)
Gross Adjust (%)			$0 (0%)		$18,000 (5.5%)		$5,000 (1.5%)		$28,000 (8.4%)
Indicated Value		$343,000		$343,000		$343,000		$343,000	

Paired Sales Analysis:

Comparison	Element Difference	Difference in Sales Price
1 vs. 3	condition	$5,000
2 vs. 4	location	$10,000
2 vs. 3	size & condition	$18,000 or $90/sq.ft.*

*For this adjustment, the sales price of sale 3 needed to be adjusted for condition (+$5,000) before being compared to sale 2.

Condition adjustment—Sale 1 and sale 3 are the same in every element except for the difference in condition count. Sale #1 is in good condition, while sale 3 is in average condition. In comparing the difference in sales prices between the two sales, a $5,000 adjustment is extracted ($343,000 – $338,000). Because the subject is in good condition, a positive adjustment of $5,000 applies to sale 3 to make it more comparable to the subject. If there were any other sales listed as being in average condition, then a similar positive adjustment would apply to those comparables.

Location—Sale 2 and sale 4 are the same in every element except for the difference in location. Sale 2 has an average location, and sale 4 has a good location. In comparing the difference in sales prices, a $10,000 adjustment is extracted ($335,000 – $325,000). Because the subject has an average location, a negative adjustment of $10,000 (–$10,000) applies to sale 4 to make it more comparable to the subject. In addition, sale 1, sale 2, and sale 3 all have an average location; therefore, they do not need a location adjustment to make them similar to the subject.

Size adjustment—Sale 2 and sale 3 are the same in every element except for the difference in condition and size. Sale 2 has 1,600 square feet of living area, and sale 3 has 1,800 square feet. In order to extract the size adjustment, sale 3 needs to be adjusted for condition first, using the condition adjustment calculated earlier. Since sale 3 has a condition of average, and sale 2 has a condition of good, the sales price of sale 3 needs to be adjusted by $5,000. When comparing the difference in sales prices between the two sales, an $18,000 adjustment is extracted ($343,000 – $325,000). This also translates into a unit of comparison adjustment of $90 per square foot ($18,000 ÷ 200 sq. ft.). Because the subject has 1,800 square feet, a positive adjustment of $18,000 applies to sale 2 to make it comparable to the subject. Also, because sale 4 is only 1,600 square feet, it will have to be adjusted by +$18,000.

2. Based on the sales grid, greatest weight would be given to sale 1 because it has no adjustments and is most similar to the subject. However, the indicated value is the same for all four comparables, and the indicated value for the subject property would therefore be $343,000.

QUALITATIVE ANALYSIS—MAKING QUALITATIVE ADJUSTMENTS

As mentioned earlier, a qualitative adjustment is without a numeric conclusion and is based on a relative rating of an element of comparison. The method of determining the qualitative adjustment is referred to as **relative comparison analysis**. With a relative comparison analysis, the qualitative adjustment is a rating system where the comparable is rated similar, superior, or inferior to the subject. By applying the rating system to the comparables and considering their sales prices, the appraiser can conclude to a value range for the subject. Earlier, we learned that if a comparable sold

TABLE 1.3
Relative Comparison Analysis Grid

	Subject	Sale #1	Sale #2	Sale #3	Sale #4
Sales Price	N/A	$450,000	$460,000	$475,000	$500,000
Property Rights	Fee simple	Similar	Similar	Similar	Similar
Financing	Cash	Similar	Similar	Similar	Similar
Conditions of Sale	Arm's-length	Similar	Similar	Similar	Similar
Market Conditions (time)	Current	2 months prior	2 weeks prior	6 months prior	Current
Location	Good	*Inferior*	*Inferior*	Similar	*Superior*
Lot Size	75 × 100	75 × 100	75 × 100	75 × 100	75 × 100
GLA (sq. ft.)	3,300	3,400	3,300	3,250	3,300
Bedrooms	3 bedrooms	*Inferior*	Similar	*Superior*	Similar
Baths	2.5	2.5	2.5	2.5	2.5
Age (yrs.)	25	22	28	28	25
Condition	Average	Similar	Similar	Similar	*Superior*
Parking	2-car garage	2-car garage	2-car garage	2-car garage	2-car garage
Porch/Deck/Patio	Deck	*Inferior*	Similar	Similar	Similar

for $200,000 and had several elements of comparison that reflect an inferior rating when compared with the subject, the appraiser might reasonably reconcile that the subject would likely to be worth more than $200,000. For example, the relative comparison analysis grid in Table 1.3 shows the relative rating of four comparables sales when compared to the subject.

Superior comparables define the upper limit of value, while inferior comparables define the lower limit of value. Based on the qualitative analysis grid in Table 1.3, it is reasonable to assume that the subject market value is greater than the sales prices of sales 1 and 2 and less than the sales prices of sales 3 and 4—in other words, between $460,000 and $475,000.

It is easy to see that a qualitative analysis enables an appraiser to define a value range for the subject, without defining a precise value dollar amount. Placing the subject within a range of inferior comparables and superior comparables is known as **bracketing.**

■ **In Practice**

Using the grid below, define a value range for the subject property.

	Subject	Sale 1	Sale 2	Sale 3
Sales Price	N/A	$322,000	$348,000	$355,000
Property Rights	Fee simple	Similar	Similar	Similar
Financing	Cash	Similar	Similar	Similar
Conditions of Sale	Arm's-length	Similar	Similar	Similar
Market Conditions (time)	Current	Current	4 weeks prior	1 week prior
Location	Good	Similar	Similar	Similar
Lot Size	50' × 100'	55' × 100'	50' × 100'	55' × 100'
GLA (sq. ft.)	1,800	1,850	1,800	1,900
Bedrooms	2 bedrooms	*Inferior*	*Superior*	*Superior*
Baths	1.5	1.5	1.5	1.5
Age (yrs.)	15	11	12	16
Condition	Average	*Inferior*	Similar	Similar
Parking	2-car garage	*Inferior*	2-car garage	2-car garage
Porch/Deck/Patio	Patio	Similar	Similar	*Superior*

Solution:

It is reasonable to assume that the subject market value is greater than the sales price of comparable sale 1 and less than the sales price of comparable sale 3. Therefore, the subject market value is between $322,000 and $355,000.

The mind-set of market participants is very important information that can be garnered by an appraiser's **personal interviews**. Personal interviews provide secondary data, which can be useful, and the appraiser may come to value conclusions; however, secondary data should not be used exclusively if primary data is available and plentiful. Qualitative analysis is often combined with quantitative analysis, but only after all quantitative adjustments have been made.

LESSON 3 REVIEW QUESTIONS

1. The _____ approach is sometimes called the market approach.

2. A physical or economic measure used to standardize the comparison between properties is known as _____.

3. A(n) _____ adjustment is known as a quantitative adjustment.

4. An adjustment that is not numeric and is based on a relative comparison is known as a(n) _____ adjustment.

5. A categorized characteristic of a property that explains the variance in property values in known as a(n) _____.

6. A positive or negative adjustment is applied to the _____ under the sales comparison approach.

7. Sales that have more adjustments are less _____ to the subject, and should be given less weight in the reconciliation process.

8. The property that is the subject of the appraisal assignment is called the _____.

9. To accurately extract and track adjustments, the appraiser will place the subject and comparable on a(n) _____.

10. Adjustments are derived by an extraction method known as the _____ analysis method.

11. A(n) _____ adjustment is the sum of all positive and negative adjustments.

12. A(n) _____ adjustment is the result of adding all of the adjustments for the comparables and ignoring the signs.

13. _____ adjustments indicate whether a comparable sale is reliable.

14. Using the following information, perform a paired sales analysis to complete the sales grid. Calculate net and gross adjustments.

    Note: The size adjustment can be determined using the price per square foot unit of comparison.

	Sale 1	Sale 2	Sale 3
Sales Price	$205,000	$224,000	$230,000
Property Rights	Fee simple	Fee simple	Fee simple
Financing Concessions	None	None	None
Conditions of Sale	Arm's-length	Arm's-length	Arm's-length
Market Conditions (time)	2 weeks prior	3 months prior	6 weeks prior
Location	Good	Good	Good
Lot Size	25' × 125'	25' × 125'	25' × 125'
GLA (sq. ft.)	1,400	1,500	1,700
Bedrooms	3	3	3
Baths	2	2	2
Age	25	26	25
Condition	Average	Good	Good
Parking	1-car garage	1-car garage	1-car garage
Porch/Deck/Patio	Patio	Deck	Deck

	Subject	Sale #1	Adjust	Sale #2	Adjust	Sale #3	Adjust
Sales Price	N/A						
Property Rights	Fee simple						
Financing Concessions	None						
Conditions of Sale	Arm's-length						
Market Conditions (time)	Current						
Location	Good						
Lot Size	25' × 125'						
GLA (sq. ft.)	1,700						
Bedrooms	3						
Baths	2						
Age (yrs.)	25						
Condition	Good						
Parking	1-car garage						
Porch/Deck/Patio	Deck						
Net Adjust (%)							
Gross Adjust (%)							
Indicated Value							

Paired sales analysis:

Comparison	Element Difference	Difference in Sales Price
vs.		
vs.		
vs.		

15. _____ comparables define the upper limit of value, while _____ comparables define the lower limit of value.

16. Placing the subject within a range of inferior comparables and superior comparables is known as _____.

17. A(n)_____ adjustment is an amount based on the sales price of the comparable property.

18. When using percentage adjustments, _____ is the first element of comparison to be adjusted.

LESSON 3 REVIEW ANSWERS

1. sales comparison

2. unit of comparison

3. numeric

4. qualitative

5. element of comparison

6. comparable sales price

7. comparable or similar

8. subject property

9. sales grid

10. paired sales

11. net

12. gross

13. Gross

14.

	Subject	Sale #1	Adjust	Sale #2	Adjust	Sale #3	Adjust
Sales Price	N/A	$205,000		$224,000		$230,000	
Property Rights	Fee simple	Fee simple		Fee simple		Fee simple	
Financing Concessions	None	None		None		None	
Conditions of Sale	Arm's-length	Arm's-length		Arm's-length		Arm's-length	
Market Conditions (time)	Current	2 weeks prior		3 months prior		6 weeks prior	
Location	Good	Good		Good		Good	
Lot Size	25' × 125'	25' × 125'		25' × 125'		25' × 125'	
GLA (sq. ft.)	1,700	1,400	+$9,000 ($30 × 300 sq. ft.)	1,500	+$6,000 ($30 × 200 sq. ft.)	1,700	
Bedrooms	3	3		3		3	
Baths		2		2		2	
Age (yrs.)	25	25		26		25	
Condition	Good	Average	+$16,000	Good		Good	
Parking	1-car garage	1-car garage		1-car garage		1-car garage	
Porch/Deck/Patio	Deck	Patio		Patio		Patio	
Net Adjust (%)			$25,000 (+12%)		+$6,000 (+2.7%)		
Gross Adjust (%)			$25,000 (+12%)		+$6,000 (+2.7%)		
Indicated Value			$230,000		$230,000		$230,000

Paired sales analysis:

Comparison	Element Difference	Difference in Sales Price
2 vs. 3	GLA	$30/sq. ft. ($6,000/200 sq. ft.)
1 vs. 2	Condition	$16,000

Size adjustment—Sale 2 and sale 3 are the same in every element except for the difference in size. When comparing the difference in sales prices between the two sales, a $6,000 adjustment is extracted ($230,000 − $224,000). This also translates into a unit of comparison adjustment of $30 per square foot ($6,000 ÷ 200 sq. ft.). Because the subject has 1,700 square feet, a positive adjustment of $6,000 applies to sale 2 to make it comparable to the subject. In addition, because sale 1 is also only 1,400 square feet, it must be adjusted by +$9,000.

Condition adjustment—In order to extract the size adjustment, sale 1 needs to be adjusted for size first, using the size adjustment of $30 per square foot calculated earlier. Since sale 1 is 1,400 square feet and the subject is 1,700 square feet, sale 1 needs to be adjusted with a positive

$9,000 (+$9,000). When comparing the difference in sales prices between the two sales, they both need to be adjusted for size first. A +$10,000 adjustment is extracted (sales price of sale 2 after size adjustment vs. sales price of sale 1 after size adjustment). This translates into a condition adjustment of +$16,000 ($230,000 – $214,000). Because the subject is listed as being in good condition, a positive adjustment of $18,000 applies to sale 1 to make it comparable to the subject.

15. Superior; inferior

16. bracketing

17. percentage

18. property rights conveyed

LESSON 4: The Income Approach

The *income approach* to value has within it several methods of determining value based on the property's ability to create and maintain an income stream. The major premise behind the income approach is that the future benefits of the income stream have value in the present time. The income approach is generally used with income-producing properties, such as apartment buildings (5+ units), office/retail buildings, and shopping centers; however, it is also used for small residential income-producing properties (1–4 units), vacant land, and single-family homes. The price that a buyer should be expected to pay for a property should be reflective of the expected *net* income level that the property will produce. The more net income that a property produces, the greater the return on the investment for the buyer. Therefore, the more desirable the property is, the greater the price that the property is likely to command.

Income capitalization is a process to convert income to value. The income, whether gross income or net operating income, can be capitalized using direct capitalization or yield capitalization. Yield capitalization is briefly discussed in this text; however, because the scope of this text is residential properties, greatest emphasis will be on direct capitalization.

DIRECT CAPITALIZATION

Extracting income and value information from the market to determine how the subject property would compare, and converting a single year's projected net income for the subject property directly into value, is known as the **direct capitalization** method. The income approach, or *income capitalization approach*, has a simple formula (known by the acronym IRV) that includes the rate of return known as the **capitalization rate (R)** and the **net operating income (NOI).** The capitalization rate is divided into a single year's future net operating income to estimate present value. (See Figure 1.8.)

Depending on which of the three variables is unknown, the income capitalization approach may be applied in one of the following ways:

Net operating income (I) = Capitalization rate (R) × Value (V)
or
Capitalization rate (R) = Net operating income (I) ÷ Value (V)
or
Value (V) = Net operating income (I) ÷ Capitalization rate (R)

FIGURE 1.8
Direct Capitalization Relationships (IRV)

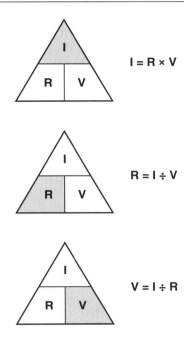

In order to solve for the unknown variable, the remaining two variables must be known. For example, to find the capitalization rate for a comparable property that sold for $200,000 and has a net operating income of $10,000 (income after vacancy and expenses are removed), the following formula would be used:

Capitalization rate (R) = Net operating income (I) ÷ Value (V)

where I = $10,000 and V = $200,000 and the capitalization rate equals 5 percent ($10,000 ÷ $200,000).

■ In Practice

Calculate the income approach to value using direct capitalization if the net operating income of the subject is $45,000 and the market-derived capitalization rate is 8 percent.

Solution:

Since Value (V) = Net operating income (I) ÷ Capitalization rate (R), Then V = **$562,500** ($45,000 ÷ 0.08).

■ **In Practice**

What annual net operating income is needed to support a sales price of $562,500 using an 8 percent capitalization rate?

Solution:

Since Net operating income (I) = Value (V) × Capitalization rate (R), then I = **$45,000** ($562,500 × 0.08).

■ **In Practice**

What can an investor expect as a rate of return for a $562,500 investment and a projected annual net operating income of $45,000?

Solution:

Since Capitalization rate (R) = Net operating income (I) ÷ Value (V), then R = **0.08 or 8%** ($45,000 ÷ $562,500).

CAPITALIZATION RATE (R)

The capitalization rate is derived from the market by using the comparable sales method. The **comparable sales method** calculates a market capitalization rate assuming that all sales and income information from the comparable sales is reliable. (See Table 1.4.)

Before the capitalization rates are derived from the comparables, the sales prices of the comparables may need to be adjusted for elements of comparison such as property rights conveyed, financing concessions, conditions of sale, or market conditions (time). These adjustments, if needed, are made

TABLE 1.4
Comparable Sales Method

Sale Number	Net Operating Income (I)	Value (V)	Cap Rate (R) (Net operating income ÷ Value)
1	$10,000	$200,000	5%
2	$15,000	$300,000	5%
3	$18,000	$360,000	5%
4	$25,000	$500,000	5%

to the comparable sales price before calculating the capitalization rate. Any physical characteristics adjustments are accounted for in the reconciliation process within the approach.

It is worth noting that the values range from $200,000 to $500,000, and yet the capitalization rate for all values is 5 percent. The capitalization rate is reflective of the return that an investor may expect for a similar property type in this market.

NET OPERATING INCOME (NOI)

Net operating income is calculated by first determining a single year's **potential gross income (PGI)** and subtracting vacancy and collection loss, resulting in the effective gross income (EGI), and then subtracting operating expenses. The net operating income is sometimes referred to as *net income*.

Potential gross income (PGI) at full occupancy

+	Other income (nonrental income)
=	Total potential gross income (PGI)
−	Vacancy and collection loss
=	Effective gross income (EGI)
−	Operating expenses (OE)
=	**Net operating income (NOI)**

Potential Gross Income (PGI)

Potential gross income is the annual income that could be potentially generated at full occupancy after estimating and analyzing market rents. It typically includes rent and any other nonrent income (*other income*) before the removal of vacancy and collection loss. The potential gross income estimate is for a specified period of time, usually one year. For properties that are encumbered by a *long-term lease*, the **contract rent**, which is rent under any current leases, of the subject is usually used to calculate potential gross income (PGI). A **long-term lease** is usually considered to be a lease that has a remaining lease term of five yearts or more. Generally, long-term leases are not used with residential properties. For properties that are not encumbered by long-term leases, the appraiser first needs to estimate *market rent* for the subject. Recall that **market rent**, or economic rent, is the rent that is typically expected for a particular property type. Market rent is rent that a typical investor can expect to receive if the property were made available to a new tenant under current market conditions. The appraiser considers

TABLE 1.5
Market Rent Grid

Sale	Square Feet	Annual Rent	Annual Rent per Square Foot
1	1,600	$9,000	$5.63
2	1,670	$9,100	$5.45
3	1,650	$8,900	$5.39
4	1,600	$9,200	$5.75

the *historical rent,* which is the past rent and the contract rent, for the subject as well as the comparables. By analyzing both the historical and the current contract rent of the subject and comparables, the appraiser can identify how the subject is faring under current market conditions. Information sources of comparable sales include discussions with owners, lessees, REALTORS®, and property management firms. Once this data is collected for the comparables from the same or similar neighborhood, it can be compared to the subject property using a grid like the one in Table 1.5.

Before the appraiser can reconcile to the market rent number for the subject, other elements of comparison must be considered. Other elements of comparison of the comparables include location, age of leases (market conditions), construction type of buildings, age/condition, parking availability, expenses that are the responsibility of the tenant, and so on. The monthly or annual rents of the comparables are then adjusted for these differences when compared to the subject.

Other Income

Other income is additional income, other than rent, that is associated with the property but that is usually incidental to the property's use. Examples of other income include coin laundry machines, additional parking fees, and vending machines. The vacancy and collection loss may or may not affect the other income. For example, a guaranteed fee from a vending machine company that wishes to place the machine in the building would not be affected by the occupancy level of the property (vacancy rate); however, coin-operated laundry machines or parking fees would be affected by the occupancy level of the property. Fewer tenants mean less laundry being washed.

Vacancy and Collection Loss

Vacancy and collection loss is an annual allowance for expected future vacancies resulting in a loss of rental income. The vacancy and collection loss is influenced by the subject's rental losses, past and present; the rental levels of the subject as well as competing properties in the market; the projected population and economic trends in the area; and the quality, quantity, and durability of the leases.

FIGURE 1.9
Replacement Reserves Calculation

Replacement reserves = Replacement cost new (RCN) ÷ Remaining economic life (REL)

Effective Gross Income (EGI)

Effective gross income (EGI) is the annual income obtained by subtracting the market-derived vacancy and collection loss from potential gross income that may or may not include income other than rents.

Operating Expenses (OE)

Operating expenses are the expenses necessary to maintain the property. Operating expenses include fixed expenses, variable expenses, and **replacement reserves** as follows:

- *Fixed expenses* are expenses that are unaffected and need to be paid regardless of the occupancy level of an income-producing property. The most common fixed expenses are real estate taxes and hazard insurance.

- *Variable expenses* are expenses that vary depending upon the occupancy level of the building. These expenses include property management fees, building employee wages and benefits, expenses for fuel and utilities, decorating expenses, repair expenses, legal and accounting fees associated with the building, and any other expenses needed to maintain the cash flow and occupancy level of the property. Variable expenses are commonly expressed as a percentage of EGI.

- *Replacement reserves* are funds that should be set aside for the replacement of building and equipment items that wear out before the end of the economic life of the building. The reserves are usually calculated by dividing the replacement cost new of the item by the estimated remaining economic life. The result is a straight line depreciation that assumes that the time will depreciate at the same rate every year. (See Figure 1.9.)

For example, the cost to replace the carpeting in a three-unit building is $1,200 per unit. Upon observation, it is determined that the carpet in all of the units will need to be replaced at the end of the next five years. The annual replacement reserve for carpeting would then be $720 per year:

$$($1,200 \times 3 \text{ units}) \div 5 \text{ years}$$

■ **In Practice**

What is the replacement reserve to replace a 700-square-foot roof that has a remaining economic life of 8 years and an RCN of $12 per square foot?

Solution:

(700 sq. ft. × $12) ÷ 8 years = $1,050 per year

INCOME MULTIPLIER METHOD (VIM)

Another method of direct capitalization is the *income multiplier method*, which extracts the various income *multipliers* from the market. The income multiplier method has a simple formula (known by the acronym VIM), which includes value (sales price) and income. A **multiplier (M)** is the result after dividing the sales price (value) by the income. Income multipliers are extracted from comparable sales in the market (comparable sales method) by dividing the value (sales price) by various types of annual (and sometimes monthly) income of the comparables. The multiplier is then multiplied by the income of the subject resulting in an estimated value for the subject. These formulas can be expressed graphically, as shown in Figure 1.10.

Depending upon which of the three variables is unknown, the income multiplier method may be applied in one of the following ways:

Value (V) = Income (I) × Multiplier (M)
or
Income (I) = Value (V) ÷ Multiplier (M)
or
Multiplier (M) = Value (V) ÷ Income (I)

In order to solve for the unknown variable, the remaining two variables must be known.

FIGURE 1.10
Income Multiplier Method (VIM)

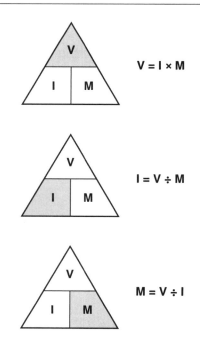

There are several types of multipliers that can be extracted from the market. The type of multiplier that is used depends upon the property type and the type of income.

The various types of income multipliers include:

- Gross income multiplier (GIM)
- Gross rent multiplier (GRM)
  - Potential gross income multiplier (PGIM)
  - Effective gross income multiplier (EGIM)
- Gross monthly rent multiplier (GMRM)

Gross Income Multiplier (GIM)

The **gross income multiplier (GIM)** is the relationship between value (V) or sales price and either the potential gross income (PGI) or the effective gross income (EGI) of a property. If potential gross income is used, the multiplier is known as the **potential gross income multiplier (PGIM)**. For example, if a comparable sale that sold for $432,000 and had a potential gross income of $90,000, the following formula would be used:

$$\text{PGIM (M)} = \text{value (V)} \div \text{potential gross income (I)}$$

Where,

V = $432,000

I = $90,000

PGIM = 4.80; ($432,000 ÷ $90,000)

However, if effective gross income is used, the multiplier is known as the **effective gross income multiplier (EGIM)**. For example, to find the EGIM of a comparable sale that sold for $600,000 and had an annual potential gross income of $120,000, other annual income of $20,000, and a vacancy and collection loss rate of 5 percent, the following formula would be used:

$$\text{EGIM (M)} = \text{Value (V)} \div \text{Effective gross income (I)}$$

Where

V = $600,000

I = $140,000; ($120,000 + $20,000)

EGI = $133,000; [$140,000 − (5% × $140,000)]

EGIM = 4.51; ($600,000 ÷ $133,000)

Gross Rent Multiplier (GRM)

Exclusively used for residential properties, the **gross rent multiplier (GRM)** is similar to the GIM, but the income is potential or effective gross rent only; any other income, such as coin laundry, vending machines, or parking, is not included. The GRM is then the relationship between value (V) or sales price and the potential or effective gross rent of a *residential* property. For example, to find the GRM of a comparable sale that sold for $900,000 and had a gross rent of potential gross income of $200,000, the following formula would be used:

$$\text{GRM (M)} = \text{Value (V)} \div \text{Potential/effective gross rent (I)}$$

Where

$\qquad$ V $\qquad$ = $900,000

$\qquad$ I $\qquad$ = $200,000

$\qquad$ GRM $\;$ = 4.50 ($900,000 ÷ $200,000)

Gross Monthly Rent Multiplier (GMRM)

Exclusively used for residential properties, the **gross monthly rent multiplier (GMRM),** also known as the *gross rent monthly multiplier (GRMM),* is similar to the GRM; however, the income is gross rent on a monthly basis (gross monthly rent). The GMRM is then the relationship between value (V) or sales price and the gross monthly rent of a *residential* property. For example, to find the GMRM of a comparable sale that sold for $870,000 and had a monthly gross rent of $20,000, the following formula would be used:

$$\text{GMRM (M)} = \text{Value (V)} \div \text{Gross monthly gross rent (I)}$$

Where

$\qquad$ V $\qquad$ = $870,000

$\qquad$ I $\qquad$ = $20,000

$\qquad$ GMRM $\;$ = 43.50 ($870,000 ÷ $20,000)

VALUATION USING MULTIPLIERS

To find the estimated value of the subject, the type of income used in the income multiplier method must be applied to the same type income for the subject. For example, the EGIM must be multiplied by the EGI of the subject in order to estimate value, and the PGIM must be multiplied by the PGI of the subject in order to estimate value, and so on.

TABLE 1.6
Gross Rent Multiplier (GRM)

Sale Number	Gross Rent	Value	GRM (Value ÷ Gross Rent)
1	$40,000	$500,000	12.50
2	$38,000	$475,000	12.50
3	$35,000	$450,000	12.85
4	$25,000	$315,000	12.60

For example, if the gross rent of a three-unit residential property was $40,000, other income from laundry was $3,000, and the sales price was $500,000, the gross rent multiplier would be 12.50 ($500,000 ÷ $40,000). Remember, with the GRM, income other than rent is not included. Further, if the market supported similar multipliers, then the multiplier would be applied to the subject's gross rent, as noted in Table 1.6.

Based on the range of multipliers in Table 1.6, the appraiser may reconcile anywhere between 12.50 and 12.85. If for example, the subject, which is most similar to comparable 2, has a projected gross rent of $39,000, using 12.50 as the GRM is reasonably supported. Because the subject's value is being sought, the formula V = Gross rent × GRM is used. The indicated value of the subject is then estimated at $487,500 ($39,000 × 12.50).

■ In Practice

The subject is a residential two-unit building with a projected monthly rent of $975 per unit. Complete the table below. Since all four sales are identical to the subject, estimate the value of the subject using the mode (most frequently occurring number) of the GMRM. *(Note:* Round the calculated multiplier to the nearest 1/10th.)

Sale Number	Value (sales price)	Monthly Rent	GMRM (Value ÷ Monthly rent)
1	$475,000	$1,979	
2	$475,000	$1,945	
3	$485,000	$2,020	
4	$500,000	$2,083	

Solution:

Sale Number	Value (sales price)	Monthly Rent	GMRM (Value ÷ Monthly rent)
1	$475,000	$1,979	240.0
2	$475,000	$1,945	247.2
3	$485,000	$2,020	240.0
4	$500,000	$2,083	240.0

The estimated value of the subject using the GMRM = $468,000 [($975 × 2) × 240].

LIMITATIONS OF THE INCOME MULTIPLIER METHOD (VIM)

Although it's the most straightforward, the income multiplier method using the VIM formula is only reliable when current, accurate, and comparable market data is available. It is important that the subject and the comparables are indeed similar. One way to check this is by comparing the ratio of net operating income to effective gross income. This net income ratio (NIR), which is explained in detail later in this lesson, will be similar for like properties. The reliability of VIM will be compromised when this ratio is dissimilar and is an indication that either the subject or the sales comparables have different vacancy and collection loss rates, different operating expenses, and/or a dissimilar lease structure (gross vs. net lease).

YIELD CAPITALIZATION

Yield capitalization is an income capitalization process that converts projected future benefits into a present value. Yield capitalization considers the expected cash flows (annuities) and the expected resale value (*reversion*). An investor of an income-producing property needs to value the income stream that is expected as well as the capital gain or loss at the end of the investment period following the sale of the property. The projected future benefit is the net operating income that the property produces during a specified period of time. The projected income stream as well as the capital gain or loss at the end of the investment is *discounted* to determine the present value. The use of Ellwood tables or financial calculators simplifies the discounting process. For a discussion on discounting, see "Six Functions of a Dollar" in Appendix A. Yield capitalization and discounting are advanced techniques associated with commercial properties.

THE OPERATING INCOME STATEMENT

The **operating income statement** gives an accounting of the pertinent income and expenses for managing a property. The *income statement,* as it is sometimes called, starts with the potential income and works through to the net operating income. Some of the information is market derived, and some is actual information collected from the property. In fact, the property manager or the accountant for the property often supplies this information to the appraiser. However, many of these expenses given to the appraiser are not relevant, accurate, or truly indicative of the actual situation. The appraiser must then make adjustments to the information acquired based on what is a more realistic interpretation of the actual income and expense figures. The result is a *reconstructed operating income statement.* In addition, the appraiser must remove expenses that are not considered to be operating expenses and, therefore, not to be included in the reconstructed operating income statement. Such expenses include:

- *Capital improvements.* Payments made for capital improvements, such as a new roof, new carpeting, or new appliances, are not considered to be a fixed expense. While these costs may ultimately add to the net operating income of a property, they typically do not recur every year and are accounted for in the replacement reserves.

- *Financing costs.* Owner financing costs, such as mortgage principal and interest payments (**annual debt service,** or **ADS**), are not considered to be an operating expense of the building and, therefore, are not considered in the calculation of the net operating income of the building. Available or probable financing is considered under different income capitalization methods.

- *Book depreciation.* Depreciation charges are an accounting method of recapturing the cost of the investment (property) over a period of time. Since these charges are considered operating expenses, they are not considered in the net operating income of the property. Other capitalization methods consider the recapture of the investment.

- *Personal income tax payments.* Income taxes can affect the investment behavior of an individual investor. Personal income taxes are influenced by an individual's personal income, age, number of dependents, and so on. These expenses do not reflect the property's productivity.

The new reconstructed operating income statement is much more accurate and truly indicative of the subject's financial performance. Table 1.7 is an example of an operating income statement; however, the appraiser has adjusted the operating income statement. Necessary expenses were added, and expenses that were not relevant for the appraisal were removed. The right-hand column reflects these changes.

TABLE 1.7
Operating Income Statement

The Operating Income Statement	Accountant	Appraiser's adj.
Gross Income (Rent)	$80,000	$85,000
Additional income (parking)	$5,000	$5,000
Total PGI affected by V/C	$85,000	$90,000
(Less)		
Vacancy and Collection Loss 5%	----------	($4,500)
Total	$85,000	$85,500
Plus		
Additional income (vending)	$1,000	$1,000
Effective Gross Income	$86,000	$86,500
(Less) **Expenses**		
Variable Expenses		
Management	$12,959	$13,000
Maintenance	$1,202	$1,200
Janitorial	$5,300	$5,300
Common area electric	$300	$300
Pest control	$50	$600
Fixed Expenses		
Taxes	$3,000	$3,000
Insurance	$600	$600
Reserves and replacements		
Roof ($15,000/30 years)	----------	$500
Total Expenses and Reserves	**($23,411)**	**($24,500)**
Net Operating Income	**$62,589**	**$62,000**

Note: In this example, the yearly income from vending machines is guaranteed by the vendor regardless of the building's occupancy level; therefore, it is added *after* vacancy and collection loss was removed from rental income.

◾ In Practice

The following information is about the subject three-unit (each unit has two bedrooms, one bath) income-producing property. After further research, you determine that market rent is $1,200 per unit per month; the market vacancy and collection loss rate (V/C) is 5 percent; the RCN for a roof is $4,800, and the roof has an estimated remaining economic life of 12 years; property taxes are expected to increase by 10 percent; the RCN for 1,600 square feet of carpeting is $2 per square foot, and the remaining economic life is 8 years; and management is 5 percent of EGI. Based on the information supplied by the property owner and data that you uncovered, complete a reconstructed operating income statement. *(Note: Round all figures to the nearest dollar.)*

Property Address: 1439 S. 51st Court

Construction type	Frame
Contract rent	$1,100 per month per unit; all leases have expired
Vacancy and collection losses	$1,200
Real estate taxes	$7,200
Decorating	$250
Pest control	$300
Insurance	$1,300
Janitorial	$1,200
Maintenance	$600
Common electric	$600
Natural gas	$4,800
Water	$720
Management	$0; owner managed
Replacement reserves	$1,000
Coin laundry	$1,400; influenced by the occupancy level
Legal and accounting fees	$400

RECONSTRUCTED OPERATING INCOME STATEMENT

Potential Gross Income (Rent) _____

Other income _____

Total PGI affected by V/C _____

(Less)

Vacancy and Collection Loss 5% (_____)

Effective Gross Income   _____

(Less)

Operating Expenses

Fixed Expenses

_____

_____

_____

_____

Variable Expenses

_____

_____

_____

_____

_____

_____

Replacement Reserves

_____

_____

Total Operating Expenses   (_____)

Net Operating Income   _____

Solution:

RECONSTRUCTED OPERATING INCOME STATEMENT

Potential Gross Income (Rent) ($1,200 × 3 units × 12 months)	$43,200	
Other income (coin laundry)	$1,400	
Total PGI affected by V/C	$44,600	
(Less)		
Vacancy and Collection Loss 5%		($2,230)
Effective Gross Income	**$ 42,370**	
(Less)		

Operating Expenses

Fixed Expenses

Taxes ($7,200 × 1.10)	$7,920
Insurance	$1,300

Variable Expenses

Management 5%	$2,119
Maintenance	$600
Janitorial	$1,200
Common area electric	$600
Natural gas	$4,800
Water	$720
Pest control	$300
Decorating	$250
Legal and accounting fees	$400

Replacement Reserves		
Roof ($4,800 ÷ 12)	$400	
Carpeting (3,200 ÷ 8)	$400	
Total Operating Expenses		**($21,009)**
Net Operating Income	**$ 21,361**	

■ **In Practice**

Using the solution grid in the previous in practice problem, value the subject property by direct capitalization. The market capitalization rate is 8.3 percent.

Solution:

Using the IRV formula, Value (V) = Net operating income (I) ÷ Capitalization rate (R), Value = $257,361 ($21,361 ÷ 0.083).

INCOME AND EXPENSE RATIOS

By analyzing *income and expense ratios* of comparable properties in the marketplace, we can determine how the subject is faring in the market under current market conditions. *Operating statement ratios*, which study the effects that income and expense levels have on property value, include the *operating expense ratio (OER)* and the *net income ratio (NIR)*.

Operating Expense Ratio (OER)

The **operating expense ratio (OER)** is the ratio of total operating expenses (OE) to effective gross income (EGI). (See Figure 1.11.)

For example, using the solution reconstructed operating statement in the previous in practice problem, the operating expense ratio is 0.496 or 49.6 percent ($21,009 ÷ 42,370).

Net Income Ratio (NIR)

The **net income ratio (NIR)** is the ratio of net operating income to effective gross income. (See Figure 1.12.)

FIGURE 1.11
Operating Expense Ratio

Operating expense ratio = Operating expenses ÷ Effective gross income
or
OER = OE ÷ EGI

FIGURE 1.12
Net Income Ratio

Net income ratio = Net operating income ÷ Effective gross income
or
NIR = NOI ÷ EGI

For example, using the solution reconstructed operating statement in the previous in practice problem, the net income ratio is 0.504 or 50.4 percent ($21,361 ÷ 42,370).

It is clear that both operating statement ratios have an inverse relationship to each other. In other words, adding the two ratios together results in a solution of 1 (0.496 + 0.504).

So, we can say that

$$OER = (1 - NIR)$$

and

$$NIR = (1 - OER)$$

Reliability of Income and Expense Ratios

The subject's operating expense ratios should be consistent with those of truly similar comparable properties. Potential problems can be identified if the subject's income and expense ratios fall outside of range when compared to operating expense ratios of similar comparable properties. Significant differences can be an indication that either the subject or the sales comparables have different vacancy and collection loss rates, different operating expenses, and/or a dissimilar lease structure (gross vs. net lease).

Although published studies of operating expenses ratios are available by national associations to assess reasonableness of these ratios for particular property types, the appraiser needs to check these ratios and how they compare to ratios developed from comparable properties.

LESSON 4 REVIEW QUESTIONS

1. Capitalization is a process to convert _____ to value.

2. The major premise behind the _____ is that the future benefits of the income stream have value in the present time.

3. The _____ rate is reflective of the return that an investor may expect for a similar property type in this market.

4. A single future income stream is <u>multiplied/divided</u> by the capitalization rate in order to estimate value.

5. The _____ method extracts a multiplier from comparable sales in the market by dividing the value by the income of the property.

6. If gross income of a property was $60,000 and the sales price was $500,000, the potential gross income multiplier (PGIM) would be _____.

7. If the subject has a gross income of $55,000, what is the indicated value using the multiplier calculated in question 6?

8. What is the value of a property that has a net operating income of $55,000 in a market where the capitalization rate is 13.75 percent?

9. The acronym for the income capitalization formula is _____.

10. The acronym for the income multiplier formula is _____.

11. _____ is the process of discounting a projected income stream as well as the capital gain or loss at the end of the investment to determine the present value.

12. The subject is a residential four-unit building with a projected monthly rent of $850 per unit and an estimated 5 percent vacancy and collection loss rate. Complete the table below. Comparable 3 is the most similar to the subject and has sold most recently. Estimate the value of the subject using the EGIM. *(Note:* Round the calculated EGI to the nearest one and the EGIM to the nearest 1/10th).

Sale Number	Value (sales price)	Gross Rent	Vacancy and Collection Loss	EGI	EGIM
1	$600,000	$38,747	5%		
2	$595,000	$39,000	5%		
3	$590,000	$37,000	5%		
4	$589,000	$38,000	5%		
5	$590,000	$37,500	5%		

13. If the net income multiplier (NIM) is 0.67, what is the operating expense ratio (OER)?

Using the following reconstructed operating income statement, answer questions 14–17.

RECONSTRUCTED OPERATING INCOME STATEMENT

Potential Gross Income (Rent) $40,800

($850 × 4 units × 12 months)

Other income (coin laundry) $3,800

Total PGI affected by V/C $44,600

(Less)

Vacancy and Collection Loss 3%   ($1,338)

Effective Gross Income   **$43,262**

(Less)

Operating Expenses

Fixed Expenses

Taxes $4,500

Insurance $1,100

Variable Expenses

Management 5% $1,126

Maintenance $600

Janitorial $800

Utilities $2,800

Water $650

Pest control $300

Decorating and painting $200

Legal and accounting fees	$200

Replacement Reserves

Roof ($6,000 ÷ 10 yrs)	$600
Carpeting ($2,100 ÷ 5 yrs)	$420
Mechanical ($7,000 ÷ 15 yrs)	$467
Total Operating Expenses	**($13,763)**
Net Operating Income	**$29,499**

14. What is the operating expense ratio?

15. What is the net income ratio?

16. What is the value of the subject if the market capitalization rate for this type of property is 8.3?

17. What is the value of the subject if the GRM from the market is 105.3?

LESSON 4 REVIEW ANSWERS

1. income

2. income approach

3. capitalization

4. divided

5. income multiplier

6. 8.33 ($500,000 ÷ $60,0000)

7. $458,150 ($55,000 × 8.33)

8. $400,000 = $55,000 ÷ 0.1375

9. IRV

10. VIM

11. Yield capitalization

12.

Sale Number	Value (sales price)	Gross Rent	Vacancy and Collection Loss	EGI	EGIM
1	$600,000	$38,747	5%	$36,810	16.3
2	$595,000	$39,000	5%	$37,050	16.1
3	$590,000	$37,000	5%	$35,150	16.8
4	$589,000	$38,000	5%	$36,100	16.3
5	$590,000	$37,500	5%	$35,625	16.6

Estimated EGI of the subject:

PGI ($850 × 4 units × 12 months)	$40,800
minus Vacancy & collection loss (5%)	$2,040
EGI	**$38,760**

The estimated value of the subject using the EGIM = **$634,368** ($37,760 × 16.8)

13. 0.33 (1 − 0.67)

14. 0.68 ($29,499 ÷ $ 43,262)

15. 0.32 ($13,763 ÷ $ 43,262)

16. $355,409 ($29,499 ÷ $0.083)

17. $358,000 ($850 × 4 units × 105.3)

LESSON 5: Land/Site Valuation Techniques

SALES COMPARISON METHOD

The last step before reconciling to an indicated value conclusion under the cost approach is to add the value of the land to the depreciated cost new of the property. Since land does not depreciate, the land is added after depreciation has been removed from the reproduction or replacement cost new of the property. In the cost approach one may either add the cost of land plus the cost of the site improvements or simply add the cost of the site. Either way is acceptable provided that the reader clearly understands which method was performed and that all of the costs are accounted for without double counting the site improvements.

Land or site valuation techniques are used even if the cost approach is not used. In other words, the appraisal assignment may be just to value vacant land or a site.

As in the sales comparison approach discussed earlier in this course, the **sales comparison method** utilizes sales of vacant sites that are obtained from the market and compared to the subject. A final estimate of value for the subject site as though vacant is then arrived at after any necessary adjustments are made for differences. This method is considered to be the most reliable and most preferred method to value land or sites. The sales comparison method of site analysis is most useful when there is an ample number of similar sales to the subject property (an active market) that have recently sold as arm's-length transactions (transactions between two or more unrelated parties acting independently of each other).

The process in the sales comparison method is to itemize the subject and comparable sales into *elements of comparison* whereby adjustments are made to the sales price of the comparable based on the differences between each element.

ELEMENTS OF COMPARISON

Elements of comparison are categorized characteristics of properties that explain the variances in property values. You will note that in the sales comparison method of site analysis there are two additional elements of comparison (zoning/land-use restrictions and availability/capacity/proximity of utilities) that are considered. When appraising a parcel of land or site, the following elements of comparison would be considered:

1. Property rights conveyed

2. Financing

3. Conditions of sale

4. Market conditions (time)

5. Location

6. Physical characteristics

7. Zoning and land-use restrictions

8. Availability, capacity, and proximity of utilities (amount of site development)

Because the first six elements have already been discussed in detail within the sales comparison approach section of this text, only the last two elements, zoning/land-use restrictions and availability/capacity/proximity of utilities are given here in detail. For a full discussion on the previous six elements of comparison, please refer to Lesson 3, which discusses the sales comparison approach.

Zoning and Land-Use Restrictions

Police power is one of the four public restrictions that supersede the rights of an individual owner. Police power allows for zoning ordinances (land-use restrictions), building codes, health codes and regulations, environmental regulations, subdivision development regulations, and historical restrictions. In addition to public restrictions, private restrictions (deed restrictions or restrictive covenants) may also exist and would need to be adjusted for.

Availability, Capacity, and Proximity of Utilities

Land on which no improvements have been made is known as *raw land* or sometimes *unimproved land*. Raw land can be land that is simply undeveloped or put to an agricultural use. When land has had some improvements that would support a specific use, it is said to be a site. The term *site* is specific and it means that there are improvements that would allow for further appurtenances to be developed. As an example, in a single-family subdivision development site improvements would typically include utility connections, driveways and sidewalks, and appropriate lot size and shape to allow for setback requirements. An industrial site is vacant land that would allow for truck access and loading docks and possesses the necessary utilities to support an industrial building.

Site improvements such as utilities, curbs, and roads are elements of value and therefore contribute to the value of the land. Adjustments for differences between the subject and all comparables then need to be made accordingly.

When there is a lack of comparable sales data, other methods are used. These methods, discussed in the remainder of this lesson, can also be used to support a value conclusion by the sales comparison method.

Allocation Method

The **allocation method** is based on the principle of balance. The principle of balance states that there is a proportional relationship between the four agents of production: land, land, labor, capital, and coordination. Because land is one of these agents, there should be a relationship between land value and total property value. When a property is improved, applying the ratio of land to building value of similar properties in the market to the subject improved property will provide the land value of the subject.

For example, if the typical ratio of land to building is one to five (expressed as L:B =1:5), and a parcel improved with a structure has a *total* estimated value of $200,000, then the land is one-sixth (there are six total parts) of that total value, or $33,333. This translates into land percentage of 16.67 percent (1 ÷ 6 or $33,333 ÷ $200,000). Thus part of the total property value is *allocated* to the site and part is allocated to the improvements.

■ In Practice

The typical ratio of land to building ratio is 1:5 and the total estimated *building* value is $250,000. Using this information, answer the following questions:

1. What is the estimated land value?

2. What is the total property value?

3. What is the land percentage?

4. What is the building percentage?

Solution:

Because there are five parts allocated to the building value only, the first step is to determine the value of one part. Remember, there are six parts total.

1. Land value = $50,000 ($250,000 ÷ 5), because the land value is equal to one part and one part is equal to $50,000

2. Total property value = $300,000 ($250,000 + $50,000)

3. Land percentage = 0.167 or 16.7% (1 ÷ 6 or $50,000 ÷ $300,000)

4. Building percentage = 0.833 or 83.3% (5 ÷ 6 or $250,000 ÷ $300,000)

■ **In Practice**

If the typical ratio of land to building ratio is 1:3 and the total estimated land value is $130,000:

1. What is the estimated building value?

2. What is the total property value?

3. What is the land percentage?

4. What is the building percentage?

Solution:

1. Building value = $390,000 ($130,000 × 3), because the building value is equal to 3 parts and 1 part = $130,000

2. Total property value = $520,000 ($130,000 + $390,000)

3. Land percentage = 0.25 or 25% (1 ÷ 4 or $130,000 ÷ $520,000)

4. Building percentage = 0.75 or 75% (3 ÷ 4 or $390,000 ÷ $520,000)

■ **In Practice**

If the typical ratio of land to building ratio is 1:5 and the total estimated total property (land and building) value is $900,000:

1. What is the estimated land value?

2. What is the building value?

3. What is the land percentage?

4. What is the building percentage?

Solution:

1. Land value = $150,000 ($900,000 ÷ 6), because there are a total of 6 parts and land equals 1 part

2. Building value = $750,000, ($150,000 × 5)

3. Land percentage = 0.167 or 16.7%, (1 ÷ 6 or $150,000 ÷ $900,000)

4. Building percentage = 0.833 or 83.3%, (5 ÷ 6 or $750,000 ÷ $900,000)

The allocation method can be used if there is adequate comparable sales data available. When applying the allocation method, it is assumed that there is a typical land to building ratio for similar property types in a similar location.

A shortcoming of this method is that it can be inaccurate because it uses average (typical) ratios for a particular type of property. The actual configuration (building sizes and appeal) of particular property types with similar values can differ substantially. The allocation method does not take these differences into account. Therefore, if used alone, the allocation method is not a reliable indicator of land or site value; however, it can be used to support a land or site value conclusion using other techniques discussed in this section or when it would be impractical to value a mass amount of properties with land and improvements segregated, such as in the case of property tax assessment.

If there are not sales of vacant land in the subject's neighborhood, then the following steps need to be completed in order to perform the allocation method of land or site valuation:

- Find average *improved* property sales and *vacant* land sales with a similar neighborhood as the subject are located.

- The typical vacant land sales price is divided by the sales price of improved properties. This results in a land value to total property value ratio.

- The land value to total property ratio is then multiplied by the sales price of improved comparables sales located in the same neighborhood as the subject. This results in a land value range for the subject.

■ In Practice

The following information was gathered from closed sales of vacant land as well as improved property, located in a *similar* neighborhood as your subject property. The typical sales price of improved comparables located in the same neighborhood as the subject range between $565,000 and $580,000. What is the land value range for the subject?

Vacant land sales:

Sale Number	Sales Price
1	$146,000
2	$141,000
3	$141,500
4	$142,700

Improved property sales:

Sale Number	Sales Price
1 (high)	$585,000
2	$579,000
3 (low)	$568,000
4	$571,500
5	$575,000

Solution: First, determine the typical land sales price by determining the mean of the four sales:

$$\$146,000 + \$141,000 + \$141,500 + \$142,700 = \$571,200$$

$$\$571,200 \div 4$$

$$= \$142,800$$

To determine the land value range, first divide the typical land sales price (the mean) by the highest and lowest improved property sales.

$$\$142,800 \div \$585,000 \text{ (highest)} = 24\%$$

$$\$142,800 \div \$568,000 \text{ (lowest)} = 25\%$$

In this example, the land value range is approximately 24 percent to 25 percent of the total property value.

To determine the land value range for the subject, multiply the land value range percentages by the highest and lowest improved property sales in the subject neighborhood.

$$\$580,000 \times 0.24 = \$139,200$$

$$\$565,000 \times 0.25 = \$141,250$$

Therefore, the land value range for the subject would be from $139,200 to $141,250.

EXTRACTION OR ABSTRACTION METHOD

When the sales price of a comparable property is known, the depreciated improvement costs of the comparable can be subtracted to arrive at a land value. This technique of land or site valuation is known as the **extraction**

method or **abstraction method.** The extraction method utilizes the following methodized process of the cost approach:

	Replacement or reproduction cost new (RCN)
–	Accrued depreciation
=	Depreciated cost of the improvements
+	Land (site) value
=	Indicated value

The indicated value is the result of adding the depreciated cost of the improvements to the land (site) value.

In order to use this technique of land or site valuation, the following steps should be taken:

1. Obtain sales prices of comparable properties located within the subject or similar neighborhood.

2. Calculate an estimate of the comparable's RCN as of the date of the sale.

3. Estimate the accrued depreciation of the comparable sale as of the date of sale.

4. Subtract the estimated accrued depreciation (step 3) from the RCN of the comparable (step 2). This results in the depreciated cost of the improvements.

5. Subtract the depreciated cost of the improvements (step 4) from the total sales price of the comparable (step 1). This results in the indicated land/site value of the comparable.

FIGURE 1.13
Extraction Method

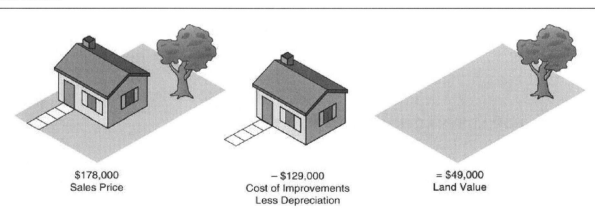

$178,000	– $129,000	= $49,000
Sales Price	Cost of Improvements Less Depreciation	Land Value

6. Compare the indicated land/site value of the comparable (step 5) to the subject site and adjust for any differences.

Steps 1–5 simply rearrange the basic cost approach formula in order to isolate land or site value as follows:

> Replacement or reproduction cost new (RCN)
>
> −   Accrued depreciation
>
> =   Depreciated cost of the improvements
>
>
> Indicated value (sales price)
>
> −   Depreciated cost of the improvements
>
> =   **Land (site) value**

For example, a comparable property sold for $360,000. The replacement cost new (RCN) is estimated at $450,000 and the estimated accrued depreciation is 32 percent as of the date of sale. What is the estimate of land/site value?

Using the rearranged basic cost approach formula:

> $450,000   (RCN)
>
> −   144,000*   (Accrued depreciation)
>
> $306,000   (Depreciated cost of the improvements)
>
>
> $360,000   (Sales price)
>
> −   306,000   (Depreciated cost of the improvements)
>
> =   **$ 54,000   (Land (site) value)**

*$144,000 represents the accrued depreciation calculated by multiplying the accrued depreciation percentage by the RCN ($450,000 × 0.32).

■ **In Practice**

There are no comparable vacant land sales within the subject's neighborhood. However, there are comparable sales of *improved* properties similar to the subject. Accrued depreciation for improved properties similar to the subject in age, size, condition, and appeal is estimated at 35 percent. The following grid shows the estimated cost of improvements for all six comparables using the cost approach. Use the extraction method to estimate *typical* land/site value as well as the *typical* land/ site percentage by using the following table:

Sale	Sales Price	Cost of Improvements (RCN)	Depreciated Cost of Improvements	Land Value	Land Value Percentage
1	$440,000	$550,000			
2	$442,000	$545,000			
3	$430,000	$520,000			
4	$439,000	$525,000			
5	$450,000	$560,000			
6	$455,000	$560,000			

Solution:

Sale	Sales Price	Cost of Improvements (RCN)	Depreciated Cost of Improvements	Land Value	Land Value Percentage
1	$440,000	$550,000	$357,500	$102,500	22.3%
2	$442,000	$545,000	$354,250	$107,750	23.3%
3	$430,000	$520,000	$338,000	$102,000	23.2%
4	$439,000	$525,000	$341,250	$97,750	22.3%
5	$450,000	$560,000	$364,000	$106,000	22.6%
6	$455,000	$560,000	$364,000	$111,000	23.4%
Mean				$104,500	22.8%

*The depreciated cost of the improvements is calculated by deducting the estimated accrued depreciation percentage (35%) from the RCN. Land value is calculated by subtracting depreciated cost of improvements from the sales price.

The typical land/site value is $104,500 and the typical land/site percentage is 22.8 percent.

SUBDIVISION DEVELOPMENT METHOD

With the **subdivision development method,** the costs of developing and subdividing a parcel of land can be subtracted from the expected sales prices of the subdivided sites. Adjustments are made for time needed to sell all subdivided sites in order to derive the value of the undivided raw land.

This method is used primarily to value land that is in transition from one use to another where direct sales of similar uses are not available. The subdivision development method theoretically matches the thinking process in which a developer would engage when considering a higher and better use of the land.

For example, assuming that the highest and best use for 60 acres of raw land is to develop it into a subdivision of 80 residential lots, the total project cost including developer's profit is $5,000,000. The appraiser estimates the lots will sell for $110,000 each for a total of $8,800,000. The raw land is then valued at $3,800,000 ($8,800,000 – $5,000,000) or $47,500 per residential lot. This theoretical value is based on the recapture (recovery) of the costs including the profits. The result is consistent with what a developer should be willing to pay for the land if he could sell all of the lots at once. Because the lots will not sell all at once, it is necessary for this theoretical value to be discounted to a present value.

The principle of anticipation is fundamental to the subdivision development method, because the basis for this method is the present value for a developer to undertake a project. According to Fisher, Martin, and Mueller (*The Language of Real Estate Appraisal*), the process of analysis under this method is as follows: "[T]he number and size of lots that can be economically, legally, and physically created is first analyzed. Then comparable sales of finished lots are used to develop an absorption rate, development period, and total estimated sales price. Next, income and expenses are forecasted. Finally, the net cash flows are discounted to a present value in order to estimate the value of the land."

The **absorption rate** refers to the amount of time over which it is estimated that the individual lots will sell. **Discounting** is the financial concept of converting an estimated future income into a present value using a discount rate. Discounting an expected future cash flow into a present value bases on the concept that the rights associated with receiving the cash flow in the future is less valuable than receiving the income today. Simply stated, it is the present value of a future benefit. For a complete discussion on the time-value of money and present value factors (present value of $1) see Appendix A, Lesson 4.

For example, 80 acres of raw land is to be developed into a subdivision of 100 residential lots. The total project cost including developer's profit is $7,500,000. The appraiser estimates the lots will sell for $125,000 each for a total of $12,500,000. If it is expected that the absorption of the project will take four years (25 lots per year), and that the discount rate is estimated to be 10 percent per year, what is the present value of the raw land?

Because the lots will not sell all at once, it is necessary for the theoretical land value to be discounted. The present value factors for the four years at 10 percent are:

Year 1 = 0.909090*

Year 2 = 0.826446*

Year 3 = 0.751314*

Year 4 = 0.683013*

*The present value factor of $1 is calculated using the following formula:

$$\text{Present Value of } \$1 = \frac{1}{(1 + i)^n}$$

where

i = interest rate

n = number of time periods

Hint: Set calculator to six decimal places

First, calculate the theoretical raw land value:

$5,000,000 ($12,500,000 – $7,500,000) or $50,000 per lot

Next, because it will take four years to sell off at 25 lots per year, this translates into a cash flow of:

$50,000 × 25 = $1,250,000 per year

Year 1 $1,250,000 × 0.909090 = $1,136,363

Year 2 $1,250,000 × 0.826446 = $1,033,058

Year 3 $1,250,000 × 0.751314 = $939,143

Year 4 $1,250,000 × 0.683013 = $853,766

Present value total   **$3,962,330**

$3,962,330 ÷ 80 = $49,529 per acre raw land

Therefore, the developer is justified in paying $49,529 per acre. This is an oversimplified example because the developer's costs and revenues will more than likely fluctuate during each absorption period.

■ In Practice

Assume that the highest and best use of 50 acres of raw land is to be developed into a subdivision of 75 residential lots. You estimate that the lots will sell for $150,000 each for a total of $11,250,000. After a thorough investigation of the market, you conclude that the absorption of the project will take 3 years with 20 lots selling in year 1, 35 lots selling in year 2, and 20 lots selling in year 3. The costs for developing each lot is $10,000 per lot, while other hard and soft costs total, including developer's profit, is 25 percent of the gross lot sales.

The discount rate is estimated to be 9.5 percent per year, what is the present value of the raw land?

Solution:

The total projected sales:

75 lots @ $150,000 per lot	$11,250,000
Development costs	
$10,000 per lot	$750,000
Hard and soft costs @25% of projected sales	$2,812,500
Total development cost	$3,562,500
Theoretical raw land value	$7,687,500
Theoretical raw land per lot ($7,687,500 ÷ 75)	$102,500

Because it will take three years to sell off 75 lots at 20, 35, and 20 lots per year, this translates into a cash flow of:

Year 1: $102,500 × 20 lots = $2,050,000

Present value factor of $1 for one year at 9.5% = 0.913242

0.913242 × $2,050,000 =   **$1,872,146**

Year 2: $102,500 × 35 lots = $3,587,500

Present value factor of $1 for two years at 9.5% = 0.834011

0.834011 × $3,587,500 =   **$2,992,014**

Year 3: $102,500 × 20 lots = $2,050,000

Present value factor of $1 for three years at 9.5% = 0.761654

0.761654 × $2,050,000 =   **$1,561,390**

Present value total   **$6,425,550**

GROUND RENT CAPITALIZATION METHOD

The **ground rent capitalization method** involves a **ground lease,** which refers to the agreement between a landowner and a tenant to erect a building on the site. Ground leases are usually long term (50 years or more). The tenant in a long-term lease wants the lease to run as long as the estimated useful life of the building. Occasionally, the owner of land used for commercial or other purposes decides to retain the fee simple title to the land yet lease the building erected on the site. The income associated with the ground lease is then capitalized using the IRV formula to derive a land value. (See Figure 1.14.)

For example, if the ground lease generates an annual income of $60,000 and the market reflects a capitalization rate of 8 percent, the value using the IRV formula is:

$$\text{Value (V)} = \text{Income (I)} \div \text{Capitalization rate (R)}$$

$$= \$60,000 \div 0.08$$

$$= \$750,000$$

FIGURE 1.14
Direct Capitalization Relationships

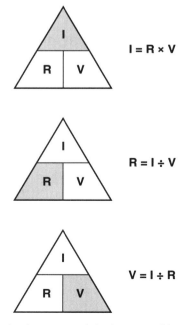

The vertical line represents multiplication and the horizontal line represents division.

■ **In Practice**

If a ground lease generates a monthly income of $35,000 and the market reflects a capitalization rate of 10 percent, what is the value using the IRV formula?

Solution:

Value (V) = Income (I) ÷ Capitalization rate (R)

= ($35,000 × 12 months) ÷ 0.10

= $420,000 ÷ 0.10

= $4,200,000

The appraiser must know the quantity, quality, and durability of the ground lease. This method can be used when there is an active market for ground leases and a direct capitalization rate can be derived from the market. In other words, the appraiser knows the income derived from the ground leases and the sales prices of comparable sales.

LAND RESIDUAL METHOD

With the **land residual method**, deduct the building's net income from the entire property's total net income (land and building). The balance is then the net income derived from just the land, which the appraiser capitalizes using the IRV formula:

Value (V) = Income (I) ÷ Capitalization rate (R)

Use this method to value commercial income-producing property using market-derived capitalization rates for land and building.

There are four components necessary with this valuation technique:

1. The value (depreciated cost) of the building only (V_B)
2. The market capitalization rate for the building (R_B)
3. The market capitalization rate for the land (R_L)
4. The total property (land and building) net income or income overall (I_O)

By applying the IRV formula to the building capitalization rate and the value of the building, the net income attributed to the building only can be determined. The net income attributed to the building can then be subtracted from the total property (land and building) net income, resulting in the net income attributed to the land only. Finally, this net income attributed to the land can then be capitalized using IRV to arrive at the land value.

For example, an office building with a construction cost of $2,000,000 ($V_B$) is being developed on a commercial site. The market capitalization rates for building and land are 9 percent (R_B) and 7 percent (R_L), respectively. When the office building is constructed, the total expected annual net operating income for the improved property is estimated at $340,000 ($I_O$).

First, apply the IRV formula to the building capitalization rate and the value (depreciated cost of the building) to arrive at the building net income.

$$\text{Income } (I_B) = \text{Value } (V_B) \times \text{Capitalization rate } (R_B)$$

$$= \$2,000,000 \times 0.09$$

$$= \$180,000 \ (I_B)$$

Next, subtract the income of the building from the total estimated property income to arrive at the income attributed to the land only:

$$\text{Land income } (I_L) = \text{Total property income } (I_O) - \text{Building income } (I_B)$$

$$\$160,000 = \$340,000 - \$180,000$$

Finally, capitalize the land income (I_L) to arrive at the land value (V_L):

$$\text{Value } (V_L) = \text{Income } (I_L) \div \text{Capitalization rate } (R_L)$$

$$= \$160,000 \div 0.07$$

$$= \$2,285,715 \ (V_L)$$

■ In Practice

A commercial site is to be developed with a 2,000-square-foot retail building. The cost to construct the building is $190 per square foot. The market-derived capitalization rate for land and building is 9 percent and 11 percent, respectively. The annual net operating income attributed to the entire property (land and building) is estimated at $50,000. What is the value of the land using the land residual method?

Solution:

$$\text{Income } (I_B) = \text{Value } (V_B) \times \text{Capitalization rate } (R_B)$$

$$= (\$190 \times 2{,}000) \times 0.11$$

$$= \$380{,}000 \times 0.11$$

$$= \$41{,}800 \ (I_B)$$

$$\text{Land income } (I_L) = \text{Total property income } (I_O) - \text{Building income } (I_B)$$

$$\$8{,}200 = \$50{,}000 - \$41{,}800$$

$$\text{Value } (V_L) = \text{Income } (I_L) \div \text{Capitalization rate } (R_L)$$

$$= \$8{,}200 \div 0.09$$

$$= \$91{,}111 \ (V_L)$$

LESSON 5 REVIEW QUESTIONS

1. Which method of land or site valuation is considered to be the most reliable and preferred method?
   a. Allocation method
   b. Extraction method
   c. Sales comparison method
   d. Land residual method

2. Which formula calculates a unit of comparison?
   a. Sales price ÷ element of comparison
   b. Element of comparison ÷ sales price
   c. Sales price × 50%
   d. None of the above

3. If an element of the comparable is *superior* to the subject then there is a
   a. negative adjustment made to the subject.
   b. positive adjustment made to the subject.
   c. negative adjustment made to the comparable sale.
   d. positive adjustment made to the comparable sale.

4. If an element of the comparable is *inferior* to the subject then there is a
   a. negative adjustment made to the subject.
   b. positive adjustment made to the subject.
   c. negative adjustment made to the comparable sale.
   d. positive adjustment made to the comparable.

5. In which order should the adjustments be made when making percentage adjustments?
   a. Property rights conveyed, location, time, physical characteristics
   b. Property rights conveyed, financing, conditions of sale, market conditions (time)
   c. Lot size, market conditions, topography, soil conditions
   d. Lot size, topography, shape, financing

6. The allocation method
   a. is not a reliable indicator if used alone.
   b. can be used to support a land or site value conclusion using other techniques.
   c. is sometimes used in mass appraisal.
   d. is all of the above.

7. If the typical land to building ratio is 1:4, then land is
   a. ¼ of the total building value.
   b. ⅕ of the total property value.
   c. ¼ of the total property value.
   d. ⅕ of the total building value.

8. If the typical land to building ratio is 1:3 then
   a. the building is ¾ of the property value.
   b. land is ¼ of the total property value.
   c. both a and b are true.
   d. neither a nor b are true.

9. If the typical ratio of land to building is 1:6 and the total estimated total property value (land plus building) is $600,000, what is the estimated land value?
   a. $66,666
   b. $85,714
   c. $50,000
   d. $120,000

10. Using the information in question 9, what is the building value?
    a. $66,666
    b. $85,714
    c. $514,284
    d. Cannot be determined

11. Using the information in question 9, what is the land percentage?
    a. 16.67%
    b. 14.29%
    c. 85.71%
    d. 83.33%

12. Using the information in question 9, what is the building percentage?
    a. 16.67%
    b. 14.29%
    c. 85.71%
    d. 83.33%

13. The typical ratio of land to building is 1:5, and the total estimated total property value (land plus building) is $500,000. What is the estimated land value?

   a. $125,000
   b. $50,000
   c. $100,000
   d. $83,333

14. Using the information in question 13, what is the estimated building value?

   a. $416,665
   b. $50,000
   c. $100,000
   d. $83,333

Please use the following information to answer question 15.

The information was gathered from closed sales of vacant land as well as improved property, located in a neighborhood *similar* to your subject property. The typical sales price of improved comparables located in the same neighborhood as the subject range between $855,000 and $890,000.

Vacant land sales:

Sale Number	Sales Price
1	$225,000
2	$210,000
3	$227,000

Improved property sales:

Sale Number	Sales Price
1 (high)	$885,000
2	$885,000
3 (low)	$860,000
4	$877,500
5	$875,000

15. What is the land value range for the subject?
    a. Between $210,000 and $227,000
    b. Between $222,300 and $222,500
    c. Neither a nor b
    d. Cannot be determined

16. The extraction method is also known as the
    a. allotment method.
    b. allocation method.
    c. abstraction method.
    d. ratio method.

17. The extraction method is used when
    a. the sales price of a comparable property is known.
    b. the depreciated improvement costs of the comparable are estimated.
    c. both a and b are true.
    d. neither a nor b are true.

18. The extraction method of valuing land or site includes
    a. obtaining sales prices of comparable properties located within the subject or similar neighborhood.
    b. calculating an estimate of the comparable's RCN as of the date of the sale.
    c. estimating the accrued depreciation of the comparable sale as of the date of sale.
    d. all of the above.

19. Which statement is true?
    a. Depreciated cost of the improvements = RCN – Accrued deprecation
    b. Land value = Sales price – Depreciated cost of the improvements
    c. Depreciated cost of the improvements + Accrued depreciation = RCN
    d. all of the above.

20. A comparable property sold for $775,000. The replacement cost new (RCN) is estimated at $925,000 and the estimated accrued depreciation is 29 percent as of the date of sale. What is the estimate of land/site value?
    a. $268,250
    b. $656,250
    c. $118,250
    d. $150,000

Answer questions 21–24 using the following information:

A comparable property sold for $425,000. The replacement cost new (RCN) is estimated at $550,000 and the estimated accrued depreciation is 42 percent as of the date of sale.

21. What is the accrued depreciation?

22. What is the depreciated cost of the improvements?

23. What is the estimate of land/site value?

24. What is the land or site value percentage?

25. A comparable new construction property sold for $680,000. The replacement cost new (RCN) is estimated at $475,000 and the estimated accrued depreciation is 0 percent as of the date of sale. What is the estimated site value?
    a. $205,000
    b. $475,000
    c. $680,000
    d. Cannot be determined

26. Which statement is true?
    a. The subdivision development method is used primarily to value land that is in transition from one use to another where direct sales of similar uses are not available.
    b. The principle of anticipation is fundamental to the subdivision development.
    c. Adjustments are made for time needed to sell all subdivided sites in order to derive the value of the undivided raw land.
    d. All of the above

27. Which statement is true?
    a. The absorption rate refers to the amount of time over which it is estimated that the individual lots will sell.
    b. Discounting is the financial concept of converting an estimated future income into a present value using a discount rate.
    c. Discounting is the present value of a future benefit.
    d. All of the above

28. Five acres of raw land are to be developed into a subdivision of ten residential lots. The total project cost including developer's profit is $150,000 per lot. The appraiser estimates the lots will sell for $250,000 each. Without discounting, what is the theoretical value of the raw land?
    a. $1,000,000
    b. $2,500,000
    c. $1,500,000
    d. $4,000,000

29. The present value factor for one year at a 9 percent discount rate is 0.917431. What is the present value of the raw land in question 3, if all ten lots are expected to sell within one year's time?
    a. $2,293,578
    b. $917,431
    c. $1,376,147
    d. None of the above

30. What is the present value of the raw land in question 3, if five lots are expected to sell each year over two years' time? The present value factor for year 2 at a 9 percent discount rate is 0.841680.
    a. $917,431
    b. $841,679
    c. $879,556
    d. Cannot be determined

31. Which statement is true?
    a. The ground rent capitalization method can be used when there is an active market for ground leases and a direct capitalization rate can be derived from the market.
    b. The appraiser must know the quantity, quality, and durability of the ground lease.
    c. Both a and b
    d. Neither a nor b

32. Using the IRV formula, value is calculated by
    a. dividing the income by the capitalization rate [Income (I) ÷ Capitalization rate (R)].
    b. multiplying the income by the capitalization rate [Income (I) × Capitalization rate (R)].
    c. dividing the capitalization rate by the income [Capitalization rate (R) ÷ Income (I)].
    d. using all of the above formulas.

33. If a ground lease generates an annual net income of $25,000 and the market reflects a capitalization rate of 9 percent, the value using the IRV formula is
    a. $277,777.
    b. $3,333,333.
    c. $1,500,000.
    d. $259,000.

34. If a ground lease generates a monthly net income of $6,000 and the market reflects a capitalization rate of 7 percent, the value using the IRV formula is
    a. $85,715.
    b. $80,029.
    c. $72,000.
    d. $1,028,571.

35. If a ground lease generates a quarterly net income of $5,000 and the market reflects a capitalization rate of 8 percent, the value using the IRV formula is
    a. $750,000.
    b. $60,000.
    c. $250,000.
    d. $62,500.

36. Which statement is true about the land residual method of land/site valuation?
    a. The net income from the building is deducted from the total net income derived from the entire property (land and building). The balance is then net income derived from just the land, which is then capitalized using the IRV formula.
    b. By applying the IRV formula to the building capitalization rate and the value of the building, only the net income attributed to the building can be determined.
    c. Both a and b
    d. Neither a nor b

37. In order to value land using the land residual method, what needs to be known about the property?
    a. The value (depreciated cost) of the building (V_B)
    b. The market capitalization rate for the building (R_B) and the land (R_L)
    c. The total property (land and building) net income or income overall (I_O)
    d. All of the above

38. A commercial site is to be developed with a 2,500-square-foot retail building. The cost to construct the building is $170 per square foot. The market-derived capitalization rate for land and building is 7 percent and 10 percent, respectively. The annual net operating income attributed to the entire property (land and building) is an estimated $60,000. What is the value of the land using the land residual method?

    a. $17,500

    b. $250,000

    c. $425,000

    d. $60,000

39. A commercial site is to be developed with a 2,800-square-foot industrial building. The cost to construct the building is $200 per square foot. The market-derived capitalization rate for land and building is 7 percent and 10 percent, respectively. The annual net operating income attributed to the entire property (land and building) is an estimated $80,000. What is the value of the land using the land residual method?

    a. $56,000

    b. $560,000

    c. $24,000

    d. $342,857

40. Using the information in question 39, what is the building income (I_B)?

    a. $56,000

    b. $560,000

    c. $24,000

    d. $342,857

LESSON 5 REVIEW ANSWERS

1. c

2. a

3. c

4. d

5. b

6. d

7. b

8. c

9. b; $600,000 \div 7$

10. c; value of one part × number of building parts = $85,714 × 6

11. b; one part ÷ total number of parts = 1 ÷ 7

12. c; six parts ÷ total number of parts = 6 ÷ 7

13. d; one part ÷ total number of parts = 1 ÷ 6

14. a; value of one part × number of building parts = $83,333 × 5

15. b

First, determine the typical land sales price:

$$\$225,000 + \$210,000 + \$227,000 = \$662,000$$

$$\$662,000 \div 3 = \$220,667 = \$221,000 \text{ rounded}$$

Because the improved properties in a similar neighborhood have generally sold from $860,000 to $885,000, the land value would range from approximately 25 percent to 26 percent of total property value ($221,000 ÷ $885,000 and $221,000 ÷ $860,000).

Because improved properties in the same neighborhood as the subject are selling for between $855,000 and $890,000, the land value range for the subject would range from $222,300 to $222,500 (0.25 × $890,000 and 0.26 × $855,000).

16. c

17. c

18. d

19. d

20. c

$$\begin{array}{r} \$925,000 \\ - \quad 268,250 \\ \hline \$656,750 \end{array}$$

$$\begin{array}{r} \$775,000 \\ - \quad 656,750 \\ \hline = \quad \$118,250 \end{array}$$

21. $231,000 ($550,000 × 0.42)

22. $319,000 ($550,000 − $231,000)

23. $106,000 ($425,000 − $319,000)

24. 24.9% ($106,000 ÷ $425,000)

25. a

    $475,000
    −_____0
    $475,000

    $680,000
    − 475,000
    = $205,000

26. d

27. d

28. a ($250,000 × 10) − ($150,000 × 10)

29. b ($1,000,000 × 0.917431)

30. c

    Year 1: $500,000 × 0.917431 = $458,716

    Year 2: $500,000 × 0.841680 = $420,840

    Total present value $879,556

31. c

32. a

33. a ($25,000 ÷ 0.09)

34. d ($6,000 × 12) ÷ 0.07

35. c ($5,000 × 4) ÷ 0.08

36. c

37. d

38. b

$$\text{Income } (I_B) = \text{Value } (V_B) \times \text{Capitalization rate } (R_B)$$

$$= (\$170 \times 2{,}500) \times 0.10$$

$$= \$425{,}000 \times 0.10$$

$$= \$42{,}500 \ (I_B)$$

$$\text{Land income } (I_L) = \text{Total property income } (I_O) - \text{Building income } (I_B)$$

$$\$17{,}500 = \$60{,}000 - \$42{,}500$$

$$\text{Value } (V_L) = \text{Income } (I_L) \div \text{Capitalization rate } (R_L)$$

$$= \$17{,}500 \div 0.07$$

$$= \$250{,}000 \ (V_L)$$

39. d

$$\text{Income } (I_B) = \text{Value } (V_B) \times \text{Capitalization rate } (R_B)$$

$$= (\$200 \times 2{,}800) \times 0.10$$

$$= \$560{,}000 \times 0.10$$

$$= \$56{,}000 \ (I_B)$$

$$\text{Land income } (I_L) = \text{Total property income } (I_O) - \text{Building income } (I_B)$$

$$\$24{,}000 = \$80{,}000 - \$56{,}000$$

$$\text{Value } (V_L) = \text{Income } (I_L) \div \text{Capitalization rate } (R_L)$$

$$= \$24{,}000 \div 0.07$$

$$= \$342{,}857 \ (V_L)$$

40. a

$$\text{Income } (I_B) = \text{Value } (V_B) \times \text{Capitalization rate } (R_B)$$

$$= (\$200 \times 2{,}800) \times 0.10$$

$$= \$560{,}000 \times 0.10$$

$$= \$56{,}000 \ (I_B)$$

LESSON 6: Graphic Analysis

TREND ANALYSIS USING GRAPHIC ANALYSIS

As we have learned earlier, within a specific market, the appraiser must analyze information gathered during the general data collection process and determine which unit or units of comparison accurately depict the expectations of the market participants. The use of statistics allows us to do just that. In addition to measures of variability, such as the **coefficient of variance (COV)**, which compares various units of comparison to determine which is the most reliable indicator of value, we can use correlation and linear regression to determine trends. Review Lesson 3 of Appendix A for a brief introduction to plotting points on a graph as well as an introduction to the various types of graphs.

DEPENDENT AND INDEPENDENT VARIABLES

The words *independent* and *dependent* can sometimes be confusing when the discussion involves statistics. It may not be clear what it is exactly that a variable is dependent upon. An **independent variable** is the hypothesized influence on a **dependent variable.** An *analyst* (someone who is skilled at analyzing data) seeks to ascertain whether values of the independent variable determine values of the dependent variables.

For example, an appraiser would be interested to determine if square feet (independent variable) actually determines or affects the sales price (dependent variable).

> The independent variable is the presumed cause, while the dependent variable is the presumed effect of the independent variable.

When graphing data, the dependent variable goes on the y-axis and the independent variable goes on the x-axis. The sales price represents the dependent variable, and it is placed on the vertical axis (y-axis). The square footage is the independent variable, and it is placed on the horizontal axis (x-axis). (See Figure 1.15.)

Simply stated, the sales price *depends* upon the gross living area of the home, but the gross living area of the home does *not depend* upon the sales price.

FIGURE 1.15
Square Feet vs. Sales Price

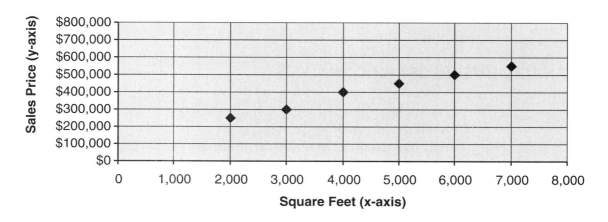

CORRELATION

Correlation is a statistical technique that shows whether pairs of variables are related, and if so, how strongly. When there is such a relationship between two variables, the relationship can be measured. Complete correlation between two variables is measured as either positive or negative. If one variable increases as the other variable increases, the result is positive. If one variable decreases as the other variable increases, the result is negative. If there is no correlation, the result is 0.

Positive and Negative Relationships

Looking at Figure 1.15, it is obvious that the points on the scatter plot follow a linear trend. There is a linear relationship, a correlation, between the

FIGURE 1.16
Square Feet vs. Sales Price with Trend Line

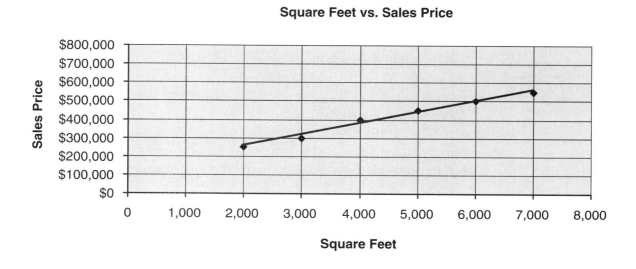

FIGURE 1.17
Negative Relationship

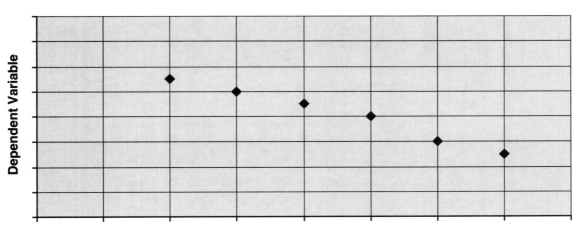

two variables. In this case, there is a *positive* relationship between the square feet and the sales price. In other words, as the square footage increases, so does the sales price.

Adding a trend line to Figure 1.15 makes it easy to identify the positive relationship between square feet and sales price (see Figure 1.16).

Negative Relationship   Figure 1.17 indicates a *negative* relationship between the independent variable and the dependent variable.

FIGURE 1.18
Sales Price per Square Foot vs. Size of Home (Negative Relationship)

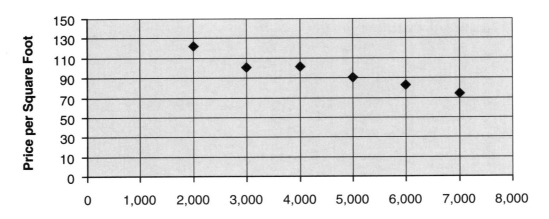

FIGURE 1.19
Sales Price per Square Foot vs. Size of Home (Negative Relationship) with Trend Line

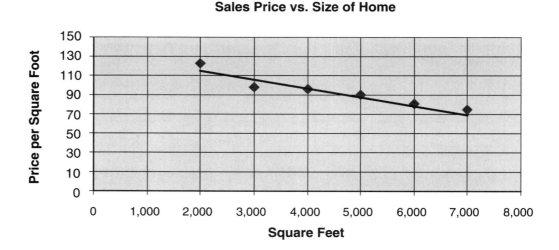

Using the same information as in the example above, but comparing the square feet to the price per square foot, we can see a *negative relationship*. Figure 1.18 indicates a *negative* relationship between the independent variable and the dependent variable. In other words, as the number of square feet increases, the sales price per square foot decreases.

Adding a trend line to Figure 1.18 makes it easy to identify the negative relationship between square feet and sales price (see Figure 1.19).

In Figure 1.20, a trend line cannot be plotted because the data is so scattered. In other words, the two variables appear to be uncorrelated.

FIGURE 1.20
Uncorrelated Data

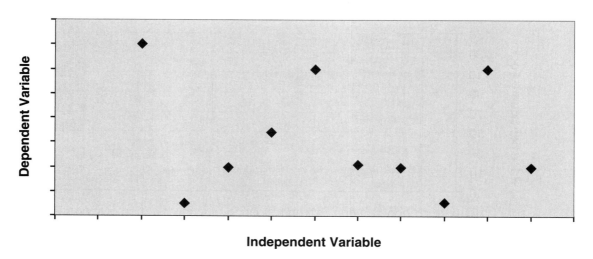

FIGURE 1.21
Square Feet vs. Sales Price to Estimate Sales Price

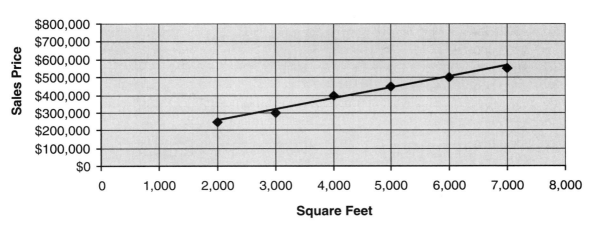

In a market where the variables do not correlate, graphic analysis is not possible because there is no trend or basis to support the analysis.

Interpolation and Extrapolation

Interpolation is a prediction made *between* known values of data (see Figure 1.21). It is obvious that there is a pattern when comparing the square feet to the sales price. Using the pattern established by the trend line, choosing any amount between 2,000 and 7,000 square feet allows us to estimate the sales price.

FIGURE 1.22
Interpolation—Estimated Price for 3,500 Square Feet

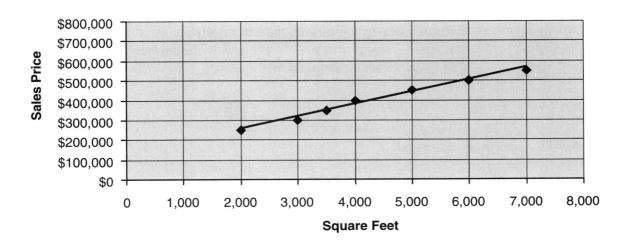

FIGURE 1.23
Extrapolation—Estimated Sales Price for 7,500 Square Feet

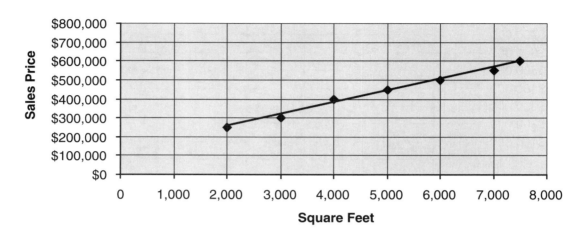

For example, using the trend line as a guide, the sales price can be estimated for 3,500 square feet. By locating 3,500 on the x-axis and locating the
point on the trend line that is in line with the y-axis, we can conclude that
the sales price would be $350,000 (see Figure 1.22).

Extrapolation is any prediction made *beyond* known values of data.

By using the pattern established by the trend line, the sales price can be
estimated by choosing any square feet amount beyond 7,000 square feet.

For example, extending the trend line in Figure 1.21 allows the estimation
of the sales price for 7,500 square feet. By locating 7,500 on the x-axis and
locating the point on the trend line that is in line with the y-axis, we can
conclude that the sales price would be $600,000 (see Figure 1.23).

Extrapolation is more risky than interpolation because it assumes that the
same pattern will continue past the known data range. This might result in
an unsupportable assumption.

REGRESSION

In statistics, **linear regression** is a method of estimating the variable y given
the value of variable x.

When points on a scatter plot appear to follow a linear trend, this relationship can be modeled by a linear function. A straight line depicts a linear

FIGURE 1.24
Slope = +1

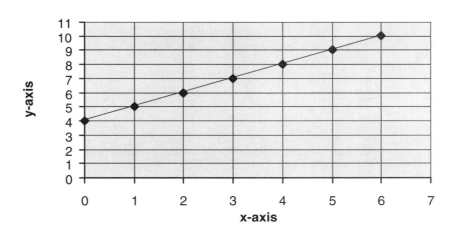

trend in the data. A **regression line** is a way to depict visually the relationship between independent and dependent variables. **Simple linear regression** is used when there is only one independent variable, and the relationship can be expressed in terms of a straight line.

Any line can be described in terms of its *slope* and *intercept.*

Slope

The **slope** of a line is the steepness of a line. The slope is measured as a change in *y*, called the **rise,** associated with a change in *x*, called the **run.** Figure 1.24 shows a slope of +1. In other words, a positive change of 1

FIGURE 1.25
Slope = −1

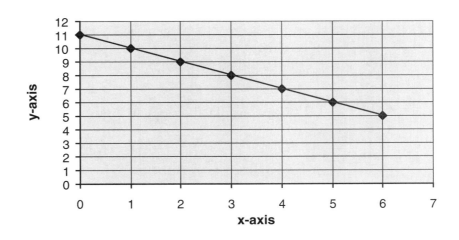

FIGURE 1.26
Slope = 0

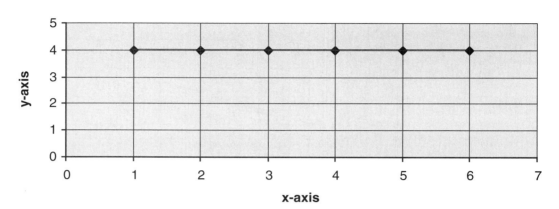

Slope = 0

on the **x-axis** has a positive change of 1 on the **y-axis.** For example, as x changes from 1 to 2, y changes from 5 to 6. With a positive slope, the line slopes uphill.

Figure 1.25 shows a slope of –1. In other words, a positive change of 1 on the x-axis has a negative change of 1 on the y-axis. For example, as x changes from 1 to 2, y changes from 10 to 9. With a negative slope, the line slopes downhill.

Figure 1.26 displays a slope of 0. If the slope = 0, then the line is horizontal.

The slopes in Figures 1.24 and 1.25 can be expressed as:

$$\text{slope} = \text{rise} \div \text{run}$$

The rise is calculated by picking two different points on the y-axis (y_2 and y_1) and the x-axis (x_2 and x_1):

$$\text{rise} = y_2 - y_1$$

$$\text{run} = x_2 - x_1$$

For example, the slope in Figure 1.24 would be calculated as:

$$\text{rise} \div \text{run} = (y_2 - y_1) \div (x_2 - x_1)$$

$$= (6 - 5) \div (2 - 1) = 1 \div 1 = 1$$

The slope in Figure 1.25 is calculated as:

$$\text{rise} \div \text{run} = (y_2 - y_1) \div (x_2 - x_1)$$

$$= (9 - 10) \div (2 - 1) = \text{-}1 \div 1 = \text{-}1$$

Intercept

The **intercept** is the point at which a line crosses an axis. The point at which the line crosses the y-axis is known as the *y-intercept*. The **y-intercept** of a line is the height of the line (rise) when $x = 0$. For example, in Figure 1.24 the y-intercept is 4, denoted as (0,4). In Figure 1.25, the y-intercept is 11, denoted as (0,11).

■ **In Practice**

Find the slope and y-intercept for the line in the graph below.

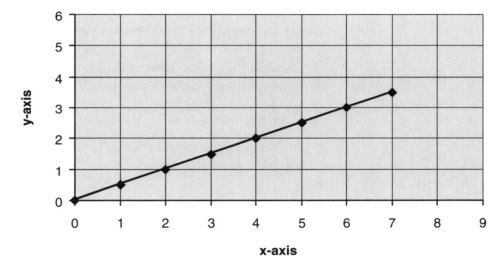

Solution:

Using any two points on the line:

$$\textbf{slope} = \textbf{rise} \div \textbf{run}$$

$$= (y_2 - y_1) \div (x_2 - x_1)$$

$$= (1 - 0.5) \div (2 - 1) = 0.5 \div 1 = 0.5$$

$$\textbf{y-intercept} = \textbf{0}$$

An Algebraic Equation for a Line

As mentioned earlier, a straight line depicts a linear trend in the data. If a linear relationship exists for a given set of data, the data can be plotted and a best-fit straight line can be drawn through the data. The equation for a straight line is:

$$y = mx + b$$

Where y = dependent variable

m = slope of the line; rise ÷ run; $(y_2 - y_1) \div (x_2 - x_1)$

x = independent variable

b = y-intercept

For example, suppose we want to estimate the sales price for a 3,500-square-foot home. We accomplished this earlier through interpolation by plotting and drawing a trend line (see Figure 1.22). It is not necessary to plot data in order to determine the constants m and b.

Looking at Figure 1.27, the sales price (y variable) at 3,500 can be estimated by applying the formula for a straight line.

■ First, select two comparable sales that bracket the subject.

In this case, we would choose the data points representing a 3,000- and a 4,000-square-foot home.

FIGURE 1.27
Square Feet vs. Sales Price

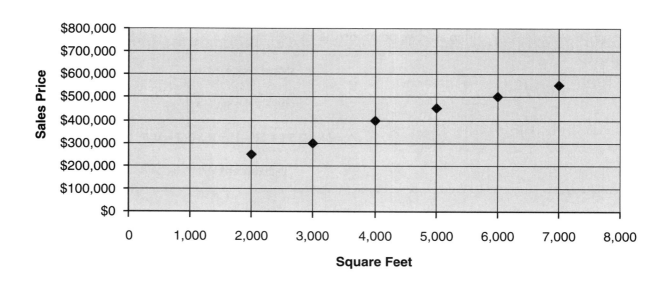

Square Feet vs. Sales Price

- Next, calculate the slope using the information from the selected x and corresponding y variables:

$$\text{slope} = \text{rise} \div \text{run}; (y_2 - y_1) \div (x_2 - x_1)$$

$$= (400{,}000 - 300{,}000) \div (4{,}000 - 3{,}000)$$

$$= 100{,}000 \div 1{,}000 = 100$$

- Next, chose any of the two x variables and the corresponding y variable and enter into the formula for a straight line in order to calculate b (y-intercept at $x = 0$):

$$y = \text{m}x + \text{b}$$

$$400{,}000 = 100\,(4{,}000) + \text{b}$$

- Using algebra techniques discussed in Appendix A, isolate the unknown variable:

$$\text{b} = y - \text{m}x$$

$$\text{b} = 400{,}000 - 100\,(4{,}000)$$

$$\text{b} = 0$$

- Substitute the calculated m and b (slope and y-intercept values) into the formula, using the know value of the x to estimate y:

In this case, x equals the subject's square footage, 3,500 square feet.

$$y = \text{m}x + \text{b}$$

$$y = 100(3{,}500) + 0$$

$$y = 350{,}000$$

- Therefore, the estimated sales price for a 3,500-square-foot home = $350,000.

Graphing the data points and using interpolation yields the same result.

◼ In Practice

Using the constants provided, estimate the sales price of a 2,800-square-foot home.

Solution:

$$y = \text{m}x + \text{b}, \text{ where } \text{b} = 0, \text{m} = 100, x = 2{,}800$$

$$y = 100\,(2{,}800) + 0$$

$$y = 280{,}000$$

FIGURE 1.28
Sales Price per Square Foot

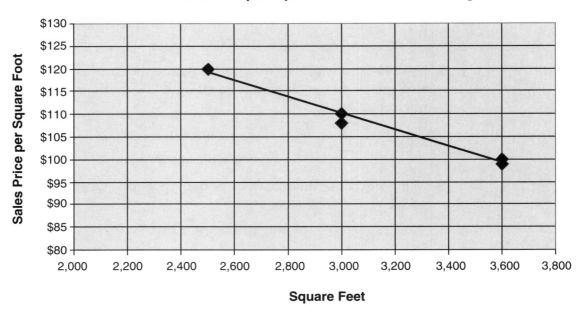

Sales Price per Square Foot vs. Size of Building

Therefore, the estimated sales price for a 2,800-square-foot home is $280,000.

It should be noted that results will differ depending on which two sets of bracketing variables are chosen and if the result was calculated using a financial calculator.

TABLE 1.8
Sample of Five Commercial Retail Buildings

Sale Number	Sales Price	Gross Building Area (sq. ft.)	Sales Price per Square Foot (rounded)	Number of Units	Sales Price per Unit
1	$300,000	2,500	$120	2	$100,000
2	$325,000	3,000	$108	7	$81,250
3	$330,000	3,000	$110	4	$82,500
4	$358,000	3,600	$99	5	$71,600
5	$360,000	3,600	$100	7	$72,000

FIGURE 1.29
Sales Price per Unit

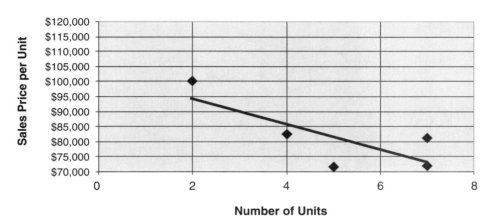

GRAPHIC ANALYSIS IN PRACTICE

A useful tool for determining the reliability of data is known as the coefficient of variance (COV). As discussed in Lesson 3 of Appendix A, the COV is the ratio of the standard deviation to the mean. It is a dimensionless number (i.e., has no physical unit associated with it) that can be used to compare the amount of variance between populations or samples. The COV measures the reliability of data by measuring the degree to which a set of data points vary. The *larger* this number, the *greater* is the variability in your data. When assessing precision, the *smaller* the COV, the *better* the precision, thus the more reliable predictor of the *dependent variable*.

This can be represented graphically by plotting the various units of comparison and noting that the COV closest to zero will have the least scattered data. Highly scattered data points on a graph indicate that the data points are far from the central tendency. Without actually calculating the COV, we can plot the two different units of comparison—price per square foot and price per unit—from the information in Table 1.8.

When we compare both graphs, it is apparent that the COV of the price per unit is higher than the COV of the price per square foot because the data points are more scattered on Figure 1.29. Therefore, the price per square foot is the most reliable indicator of value.

■ **In Practice**

Suppose your assignment is to estimate the market value of a vacant industrial parcel of land. After reviewing the following graphs of the sales price per front foot (lot width) and the sales price per square foot, determine which unit of comparison appears to be the most reliable indicator of value for the subject.

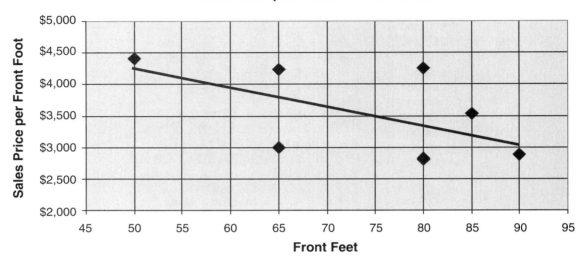

Sales Price per Front Foot vs. Front Feet

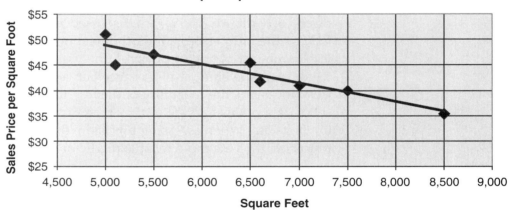

Sales Price per Square Foot vs. Area of Parcel

Solution:

It is clear that the sales price per square foot is the most reliable indicator of value because the data points are less scattered. This is an indication that there is less deviation from the central tendency, which results in a COV that is closest to zero when compared to the COV of the sales price per front foot.

■ **In Practice**

Using the grid below, calculate and plot the various units of comparison and indicate which unit of comparison is the most reliable. *(Hint:* Round calculations to the nearest one.)

Sale Number	Sales Price	Gross Building Area (sq. ft.)	Sales Price per Square Foot (rounded)	Number of Units	Sales Price per Unit	Number of Bedrooms	Sales Price per Bedroom
1	$490,000	6,800		11		16	
2	$580,000	7,000		12		12	
3	$550,000	7,000		8		14	
4	$560,000	7,500		11		14	
5	$475,000	6,500		8		15	
6	$550,000	6,800		9		9	
7	$600,000	7,500		12		12	

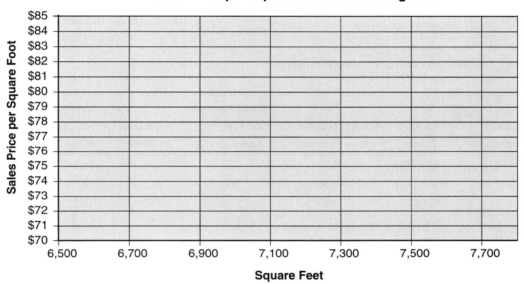

Sales Price per Square Foot vs. Building Size

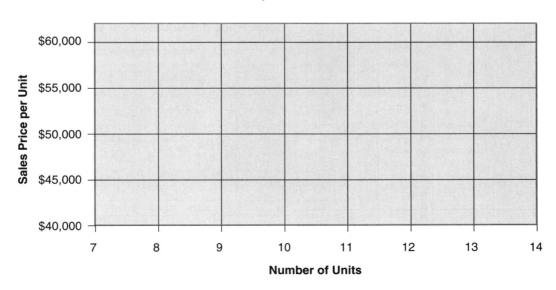

Sales Price per Unit vs. Number of Units

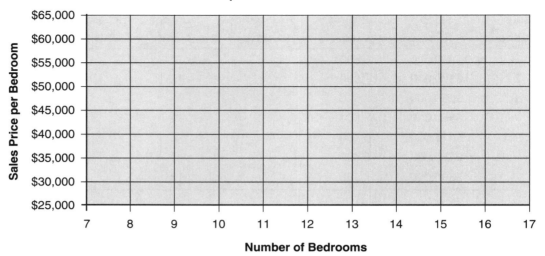

Sales Price per Bedroom vs. Number of Bedrooms

Solution:

Sale Number	Sales Price	Gross Building Area (sq. ft.)	Sales Price per Square Foot (rounded)	Number of Units	Sales Price per Unit	Number of Bedrooms	Sales Price per Bedroom
1	$490,000	6,800	$72	11	$44,545	16	$30,625
2	$580,000	7,000	$83	12	$48,333	12	$48,333
3	$550,000	7,000	$79	8	$68,750	14	$39,286
4	$560,000	7,500	$75	11	$50,909	14	$40,000
5	$475,000	6,500	$73	8	$59,375	15	$31,667
6	$550,000	6,800	$81	9	$61,111	9	$61,111
7	$600,000	7,500	$80	12	$50,000	12	$50,000

Unit of Comparison: Sales Price per Square Foot

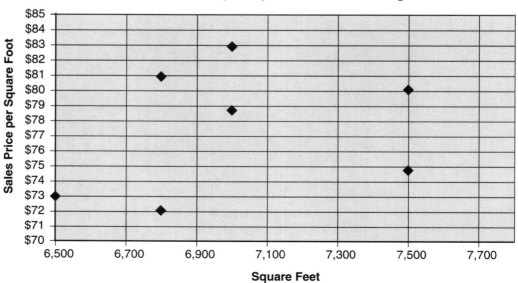

Sales Price per Square Foot vs. Building Size

Unit of Comparison: Sales Price per Unit

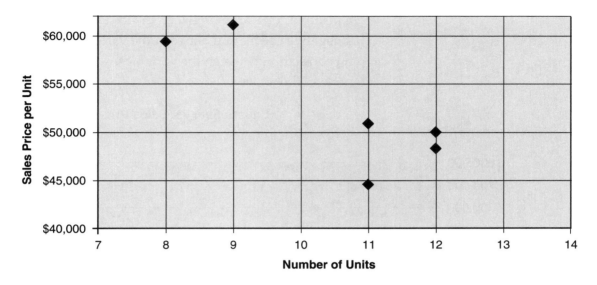

Sales Price per Unit vs. Number of Units

Unit of Comparison: Sales Price per Bedroom

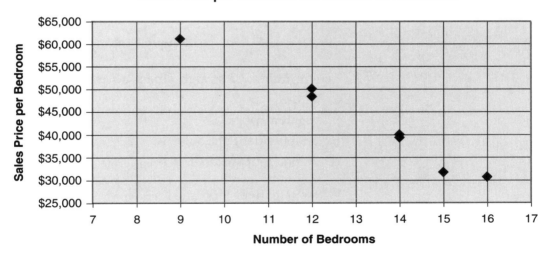

Sales Price per Bedroom vs. Number of Bedrooms

The sales price per bedroom has the least scattered data points; therefore, it is the most reliable predictor of value. If the COV for each unit of comparison were calculated, the sales price per bedroom would have the COV closest to zero because a trend can actually be identified.

LESSON 6 REVIEW QUESTIONS

1. The following graph indicates
   a. a positive correlation between the variables.
   b. a negative correlation between the variables.
   c. no correlation between the variables.
   d. none of the above.

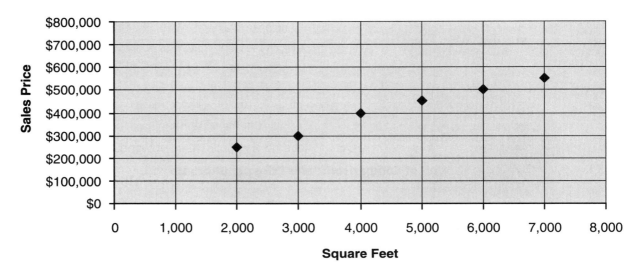

2. The formula for a straight line is $y = mx + b$, where m represents the
   a. slope.
   b. y-intercept.
   c. independent variable.
   d. dependent variable.

3. With a negative slope, the line
   a. slopes downhill.
   b. slopes uphill.
   c. is horizontal.
   d. does none of the above.

4. The formula for a straight line is
   a. $m = y + b$.
   b. $y = mx + b$.
   c. $y = mx \div b$.
   d. none of the above.

5. The formula to calculate the slope of a line is
   a. run ÷ rise.
   b. run × rise.
   c. rise ÷ run.
   d. all of the above.

6. The COV measures the reliability of data by measuring the degree to which a set of data points vary. The larger this number, the _____ the variability in your data.

7. Highly scattered data points on a graph indicate that the unit of comparison is a(n) _____ reliable indicator of value.

8. When assessing precision, the _____ the COV, the better the precision and, thus, the more reliable predictor of the dependent variable.

9. Calculate and plot the sales price per square foot and the gross building area (sq. ft.). (*Hint:* Round calculations to the nearest one.)

Sales Price	Gross Building Area (sq. ft.)	Sales Price per Square Foot (rounded)
$1,220,000	14,000	
$1,200,000	13,200	
$1,235,000	13,000	
$1,225,000	12,500	
$1,200,000	12,000	

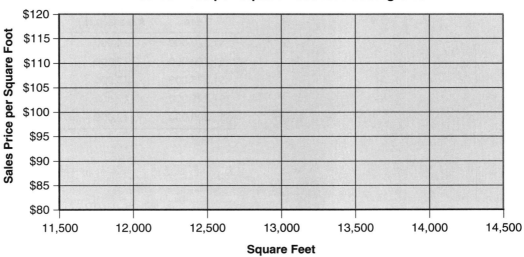

Sales Price per Square Foot vs. Building Size

10. Using the graph in question 9, the sales price per square foot for a 13,500-square-foot building can be estimated to be between
    a. $87 and $90.
    b. $95 and $100.
    c. $95 and $97.
    d. Cannot be determined

LESSON 6 REVIEW ANSWERS

1. a

2. a

3. a

4. b

5. c

6. greater

7. less

8. smaller

9.

Sales Price	Gross Building Area (sq. ft.)	Sales Price per Square Foot (rounded)
$1,220,000	14,000	$87
$1,200,000	13,200	$91
$1,235,000	13,000	$95
$1,225,000	12,500	$98
$1,200,000	12,000	$100

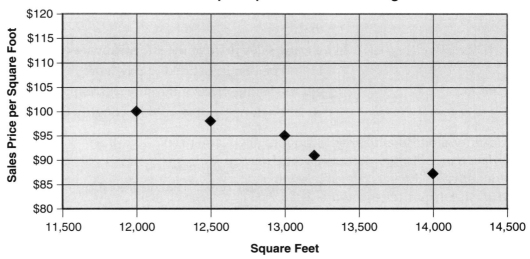

10. a

SECTION 1 REVIEW QUESTIONS

1. The principle of substitution as it applies to the cost approach states that
   a. the sales price of the subject must equal the cost.
   b. no person is justified to pay more than the cost new.
   c. the listing price of the subject should be less than the cost.
   d. the asking price should be roughly equal to the cost.

2. Which is a category of depreciation?
   a. Functional depreciation
   b. Economic or external depreciation
   c. Functional obsolescence
   d. Physical obsolescence

3. When there is a loss in value due to a poor layout, the property is said to suffer from
   a. physical depreciation.
   b. functional obsolescence.
   c. functional depreciation.
   d. layout depreciation.

4. A loss in value as a result of the market's negative response to something that is outside of the property lines is
   a. functional obsolescence.
   b. economic depreciation.
   c. physical depreciation.
   d. external obsolescence.

5. The cost approach includes
   a. the value of land as though vacant.
   b. an estimate of cost new.
   c. an estimate of accrued depreciation.
   d. all of the above.

6. Functional obsolescence that is a result of an overimprovement is referred to as a(n)
   a. hyperadequacy.
   b. overadequacy.
   c. superadequacy.
   d. none of the above.

7. The formula to calculate annual depreciation using the straight-line method is
   a. expected life ÷ cost new.
   b. cost new ÷ expected life.
   c. effective age ÷ total economic life.
   d. none of the above.

8. If the cost new is $200,000 and the estimated expected life is 50 years, what is the annual depreciation using the straight-line method?
   a. $3,000
   b. $2,000
   c. $4,000
   d. $25,000

9. The formula for the economic age-life method of depreciation is
   a. effective age ÷ remaining economic life.
   b. effective age ÷ effective age + remaining economic life.
   c. effective age ÷ total economic life.
   d. both b and c.

10. A home that was built 36 years ago and has an effective age of 30 years is said to have a chronological age of
    a. 30 years.
    b. 36 years.
    c. 66 years.
    d. none of the above.

11. Total economic life is
    a. remaining economic life minus effective age.
    b. actual age minus effective age.
    c. effective age plus remaining economic life.
    d. actual age minus remaining economic life.

12. The most detailed and comprehensive method of calculating depreciation is the
    a. age-life method.
    b. breakdown method or engineering method.
    c. unit-in-place method.
    d. straight-line method.

13. The most detailed method of estimating costs is the
    a. unit-in-place method.
    b. economic age-life method.
    c. quantity survey method.
    d. square-foot method.

14. A loss in value from all causes of depreciation is known as
    a. physical depreciation.
    b. functional obsolescence.
    c. external obsolescence.
    d. accrued depreciation.

15. A commercial building that was built 13 years ago and has an effective age of eight years is said to have an actual age of
    a. 10 years.
    b. 21 years.
    c. 8 years.
    d. none of the above.

16. Adjustments are always made to the
    a. sales price of the subject.
    b. sales prices of the comparable properties.
    c. listing price of the subject.
    d. listing prices of the comparables.

17. Which formula calculates a unit of comparison?
    a. Sales price ÷ Element of comparison
    b. Element of comparison ÷ Sales price
    c. Listing price ÷ Element of comparison
    d. Element of comparison ÷ Cost

18. If the subject does not have a particular amenity, and the market indicates that the particular amenity is worth an additional $3,500, the adjustment would be a
    a. positive $3,500 to the subject.
    b. negative $3,500 to the comparable sale.
    c. negative $3,500 to the subject.
    d. positive $3,500 to the comparable sale.

19. Which is *NOT* a unit of comparison?
    a. Price per square foot
    b. Price per bedroom
    c. Lot size
    d. Price per unit

20. Which is *NOT* an element of comparison?
    a. Square footage of building
    b. Number of bedrooms
    c. Number of units
    d. Price per unit

21. When there is an ample amount of sales of similar properties in an active market, the most reliable approach to value is the
    a. cost approach.
    b. income approach.
    c. sales comparison approach.
    d. quantity survey approach.

22. In which order should the adjustments be made to the first four elements of comparison when making percentage adjustments?
    a. Property rights conveyed, location, time, physical characteristics
    b. Property rights conveyed, financing, conditions of sale, market conditions (time)
    c. Lot size, market conditions, topography, soil conditions
    d. Lot size, topography, shape, financing

23. If an element of the comparable is *superior* to the subject, then a
    a. negative adjustment is made to the subject.
    b. positive adjustment is made to the subject.
    c. negative adjustment is made to the comparable sale.
    d. positive adjustment is made to the comparable sale.

24. If an element of the comparable is *inferior* to the subject, then a
    a. negative adjustment is made to the subject.
    b. positive adjustment is made to the subject.
    c. negative adjustment is made to the comparable sale.
    d. positive adjustment is made to the comparable.

25. A _____ adjustment is the sum of all positive and negative adjustments.
    a. gross
    b. net
    c. percentage
    d. lump-sum dollar

26. A _____ adjustment is the result of adding all of the adjustments for the comparables and ignoring the signs.
    a. gross
    b. net
    c. percentage
    d. lump-sum dollar

27. Which is considered to be a qualitative adjustment?
    a. Similar
    b. Superior
    c. Inferior
    d. All of the above

28. The types of income multiplier used for exclusively for residential properties are
    a. the potential gross income multiplier (PGIM) and effective gross income multiplier (EGIM).
    b. the gross rent multiplier (GRM) and gross monthly rent multiplier (GMRM).
    c. both a and b.
    d. neither a nor b.

29. Calculate the GRM for the comparable sales given the information in the following grid. (*Note:* round the calculated GRM to the nearest one.)

Sales Number	Value (sales price)	Gross Rent	GRM
1	$700,000	$48,947	
2	$695,000	$49,000	
3	$690,000	$47,000	
4	$689,000	$48,000	
5	$690,000	$47,500	

30. Using the information in question 29, if the subject, which is identical to comparable 2, has a projected monthly rent of $4,000, what is the indicated value of the subject using the GRM?

31. If potential gross income of a comparable property was $50,000 and the sales price was $645,000, what is the potential gross income multiplier (PGIM)?

32. If the subject has a potential gross income of $46,000, what is the indicated value using the multiplier calculated in question 31?

33. What is the EGIM of a property that sold for $456,000 and had potential gross income of $76,000, other income from coin-operated laundry machines of $5,000, and a vacancy and collection loss rate of 7 percent?

34. A single year's projected income for the subject property is converted directly into value using the _____.

35. If there is no correlation between variables, the correlation is
    a. 0.
    b. 1.
    c. 100.
    d. –1.

36. The following graph depicts a *positive/negative* relationship between the dependent and the independent variables.

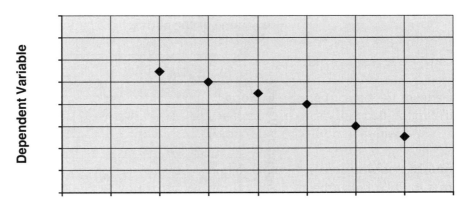

Independent Variable

37. _____ is any prediction made beyond known values of data.

38. _____ is a prediction made between known values of data.

39. The _____ variable is placed on the vertical axis (y-axis).

40. The _____ variable is placed on the horizontal axis (x-axis).

41. If the slope of a line is equal to 0, then the line
    a. slopes downhill.
    b. slopes uphill.
    c. is horizontal.
    d. does none of the above.

42. The formula to calculate the slope of a line is
    a. $(y_2 - y_1) \div (x_2 - x_1)$.
    b. rise ÷ run.
    c. change in y ÷ change in x.
    d. all of the above.

43. The formula for a straight line is
    a. $y = mx + b$.
    b. $b = y - mx$.
    c. both a and b.
    d. neither a nor b.

44. The following graph indicates
    a. a positive correlation between the variables.
    b. a negative correlation between the variables.
    c. no correlation between the variables.
    d. none of the above.

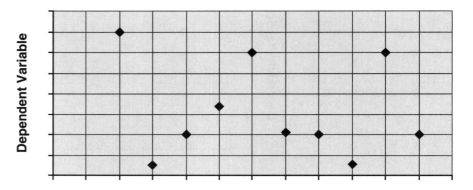

45. With a negative slope, the line
    a. slopes downhill.
    b. slopes uphill.
    c. is horizontal.
    d. does none of the above.

46. The formula for a straight line is $y = mx + b$, where b represents the
    a. slope.
    b. y-intercept.
    c. independent variable.
    d. dependent variable.

47. Use the information below to plot the sales price per square foot and the gross building area (sq. ft.).

Sales Price	Gross Building Area (sq. ft.)	Sales Price per Square Foot (rounded)
$300,000	2,500	$120
$336,000	3,200	$105
$330,000	3,000	$110
$345,000	3,400	$101
$342,000	3,600	$95

Sales Price per Square Foot vs. Size of Building

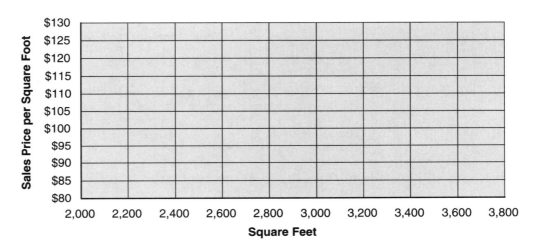

48. Using the graph in question 47, the sales price per square foot for a 2,800-square-foot building can be estimated to be between
    a. $100 and $105.
    b. $110 and $120.
    c. $105 and $110.
    d. $95 and $110.

49. Using the grid below, calculate and plot the various units of comparison. (*Hint:* Round calculations to the nearest one.)

Sale Number	Sales Price	Gross Building Area (sq. ft.)	Sales Price per Square Foot (rounded)	Number of Units	Sales Price per Unit	Number of Bedrooms	Sales Price per Bedroom
1	$1,200,000	11,000		18		48	
2	$1,500,000	12,000		14		22	
3	$1,000,000	11,500		20		40	
4	$1,600,000	14,000		21		30	
5	$1,650,000	14,500		28		20	

Sales Price per Square Foot vs. Building Size

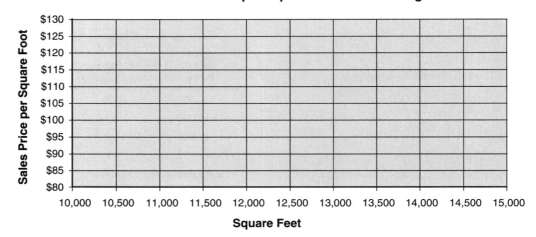

Sales Price per Unit vs. Number of Units

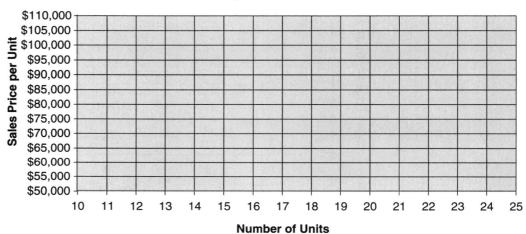

Sales Price per Bedroom vs. Number of Bedrooms

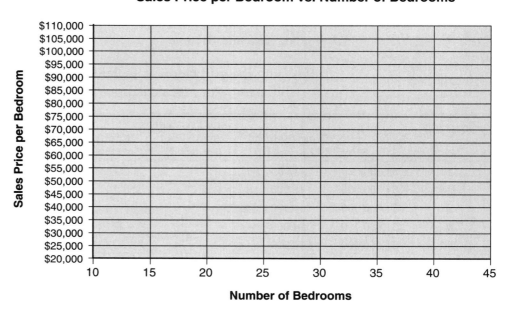

50. Using the grids in question 49, which unit of comparison is the most reliable (data points are less scattered and indicate a trend)?
    a. Sales price per square foot
    b. Sales price per unit
    c. Sales price per bedroom
    d. Cannot determine

51. Using the grids in question 49, which unit of comparison has the COV closest to zero?
    a. Sales price per square foot
    b. Sales price per unit
    c. Sales price per bedroom
    d. Cannot determine

DEVELOPING AND COMMUNICATING THE RESULTS

section two

LESSON 1: Problem Identification, Scope of Work, and Managing the Assignment

PROBLEM IDENTIFICATION

Your client, First Central Bank of Anytown, has asked you to determine the current market value of the fee simple property rights of a 2,400-square-foot three-bedroom, two-bath, single-family home located at 1813 S. 49th Avenue in Hometown, USA 60114. Hometown is a suburb of Metropolis, USA. Your client, the intended user, is located at 6400 W. Cermak Road, Anytown, USA 60123. First Central Bank of Anytown plans on using this appraisal for mortgage consideration.

The subject, built 25 years ago, has a living room, kitchen, dining room, two bathrooms, and three bedrooms. The home and the 22' × 24' detached two-car brick garage are all situated on a 50' × 155' lot. This one-story brick home does not have a basement. The subject is currently owner occupied; however, because Hometown is a college town with a major university nearby, many single-family properties similar to the subject property rent on an annual basis to university students. Further, the subject is to be appraised "as is" without any extraordinary assumptions or hypothetical conditions. Your standard statement of assumptions and limiting conditions are as follows:

1. The appraisal was based on the assumption that the title to the subject property is held in fee simple interest and is marketable and the property is free of and clear of all liens and encumbrances, except as noted.

2. No liability is assumed for matters that are legal or environmental in nature. Ownership and management are assumed to be in competent and responsible hands.

3. The valuation was prepared for the purpose stated and should not be used for any other purpose.

4. All direct and indirect information supplied by the client, its agents, or others concerning the subject property are assumed to be true and accurate. No responsibility is assumed for information supplied by others although any such information cited is believed to be reliable and correct.

5. Possession of this report or a copy thereof, or any part thereof, does not carry with it the right of publication, nor may it be used by anyone

but the party for whom it has been prepared without the prior written consent and approval of the authors of this report.

6. Any sketches in this report may show approximate dimensions and are included only to assist the reader in visualizing the property. Any maps and exhibits found in this report are provided for reader reference purposes only. No guarantee as to accuracy is expressed or implied unless otherwise stated in this report. No survey of the property has been made for the purpose of this report.

7. This report is intended to be read and used as a whole and not in parts. Separation of any section or page from the main body of the report is expressly forbidden and invalidates the report.

8. Where the property being considered is part of a larger parcel or tract, any values reported relate only to the portion being considered and should not be construed as applying with equal validity to other portions of the larger portion or tract.

9. It is assumed that the utilization of the land and improvements is within the boundaries of property lines of the property described and that there is no encroachment or trespass unless noted within the report.

The value sought for this property is market value, defined in *Basic Appraisal Principles* (Cengage Learning 2007) as the most probable price that a property should bring in a competitive and open market under all conditions requisite to a fair sale, with the buyer and the seller each acting prudently and knowledgeably, and assuming the price is not affected by duress or other such undue stimulus. Implicit in this definition are the consummation of a sale as of a specified date and the passing of title from seller to buyer under the following conditions:

1. Buyer and seller are *typically motivated*.

2. Both parties are *well-informed* or well-advised and acting in what they consider their best interests.

3. A *reasonable time* is allowed for exposure in the open market.

4. Payment is made in terms of *cash* in U.S. dollars or in terms of financial arrangements comparable thereto.

5. The price represents the *normal consideration* for the property sold unaffected by special or creative financing or sales concessions granted by anyone associated with the sale.

Since the assignment is to determine the current market value of the subject, the effective date will not be retrospective or prospective. Public records indicate that the current owner of the subject property is the borrower, Mrs. Grace. The subject property was transferred to Mrs. Grace ten years ago.

No other transactions for the subject were recorded. The subject has not sold, nor has it been listed for sale during the past ten years.

In Practice

Using the preceding information, identify the following:

The client and other intended users of the report

_____

The intended use of the report and the appraiser's opinions and conclusions

_____

The type and definition of value and the source of the definition

_____

The effective date of the appraiser's opinion and conclusions

_____

The description and location of the real estate

_____

The property rights to be valued

_____

The characteristics that are relevant to the type of value and the intended use of the appraisal along with the limiting conditions or limitations of the appraisal (the scope of work).

_____

Solution:

The client and other intended users of the report

First Central Bank of Anytown, 6400 W. Cermak Road, Anytown, USA 60123

The intended use of the report and the appraiser's opinions and conclusions

Mortgage funding

The type and definition of value and the source of the definition

Market value, _Basic Appraisal Principles_ (Cengage Learning, 2007)

The effective date of the appraiser's opinion and conclusions

Current

The description and location of the real estate

Single-family home located at 1813 S. 49th Avenue in Hometown, USA 60114

The property rights to be valued

Fee simple

The characteristics that are relevant to the type of value and the intended use of the appraisal along with the limiting conditions or limitations of the appraisal (the scope of work)

No special assignment conditions other than the standard assumptions and limiting conditions listed previously

SCOPE OF WORK

After engaging the assignment, your *preliminary* scope of work is generalized as follows:

1. The subject property and surrounding will be personally inspected by you and legally identified from data supplied by the property owner and public records.

2. A description of the site was based on personal inspection by you and from public records. An examination of zoning maps, ordinances, and other governmental restrictions, where applicable, will be made.

3. These general and specific data will be analyzed to determine the subject property's highest and best use as if the land were vacant and as if it were improved. Any trends in the subject property and the surrounding area will be considered in the analysis. The three commonly used approaches to value will be considered: the cost approach, the sales comparison approach, and the income capitalization approach.

4. The cost approach requires the collection of data regarding construction costs from one or more cost manuals and/or local contractors. Estimates of depreciation were derived from available data. The cost approach is most applicable when the subject is newer and/or reflects little or no depreciation.

5. The income capitalization approach requires the collection of data to ascertain market rent, vacancy, expenses, and capitalization rates for

similar properties. The sales comparison approach utilizes comparable sales data obtained from the buyer, real estate agents, public records, data gathering services, and other appraisers. In addition, a survey of market trends will be determined by discussion with real estate owners, brokers, and leasing agents active in the subject property area. Sales will be verified by examination of records.

6. All of the above data will be tempered by your experience and judgment. The scope of the appraisal assignment is subject to all the assumptions and limiting conditions set forth within this report.

■ In Practice

Would this scope of work be used for all appraisal assignments? Explain.

_____

_____

Provide a specific scope of work determination using the information garnered from your conversation with your client. Hint: What issues would support your scope of work determination?

_____

_____

Solution:

No, the scope of work varies depending upon the problem identification and the assignment conditions.

Important issues that determine the scope of work include:

The subject is an owner occupied single-family home; however, the subject is located in a college town near a university and can be rented on an annual basis. Therefore the income approach to value will be considered along with the cost and sales comparison approaches.

Market data will be analyzed and used in the sales comparison approach to value.

Replacement cost new will be determined once the physical attributes of the subject are determined.

There are no extraordinary assumptions or hypothetical conditions.

The appraisal is to be prepared "as is."

MANAGE THE ASSIGNMENT

After agreeing to take this assignment, you determine that you have the required competency to complete this assignment and you do not need assistance from another appraiser. You also estimate the completion date to be two weeks from the date of the order. You will begin the appraisal process by collection of general and specific data, once all of the pertinent problem identification information has been determined. While proceeding through the appraisal process, you will continually review and each step.

■ **In Practice**

Using the five management functions, identify how you will manage this assignment.

1. Plan: Determine the scope of work from the engagement process and what you know at this point about the assignment. To complete the appraisal assignment within _____.

2. Organize: Beginning with general and specific data and proceeding through the appraisal process, once the appraisal problem has been identified, list general and specific data requirements.

   General Data

   _____

   _____

   Specific Data

   _____

   _____

3. Staff: Determine your staff needs. Do you need any additional staff?

4. Direct: Once you proceed with this assignment, if you determine that the scope of work needs to change for any reason, you will proceed in a manner that will lead to the completion of credible results. What if a shift in the scope of work occurs, requiring the assistance of another associate?

5. Control: What is meant by control, and where is control applied?

   _____

   _____

Solution:

1. Plan: To complete the appraisal assignment within two weeks. Collect market data for all three approaches.

2. Organize: Beginning with general and specific data and proceeding through the appraisal process, once the appraisal problem has been identified.

   General Data:

   ■ Rental information

   ■ Sales prices and closing dates of comparable properties

   ■ Market data such as area market and location information

   Specific Data:

   ■ Real estate taxes for the subject

   ■ Property information such as size, utilities, condition, taxes, etc.

   ■ Plat of survey; blueprints or dimensions

   ■ Any special assessments

   ■ Physical characteristics

   ■ Legal description; property address

   ■ Confirm property rights and zoning

3. Staff: No, you do not need any additional staff since you have the competency to complete this assignment.

4. Direct: Once you proceed with this assignment, if you determine that the scope of work needs to change for any reason, you will proceed in a manner that will lead to the completion of credible results. What if a shift in the scope of work occurs, requiring the assistance of another associate? You would ensure that this associate has the competency to complete this assignment.

5. Control: Each step in the appraisal process will be reviewed throughout the entire process.

LESSON 2: Market Analysis Part 1: Data Collection, Highest and Best Use, and Land Value

DATA COLLECTION

You will recall from the market analysis section of this text we discussed the importance of providing relevant information to the client, and that "data dump," or information without analysis, is considered to be a major mistake in the appraisal profession. Much of what is written in the neighborhood analysis section of the report will come from relevant facts that should provide the client a comprehensive understanding of relevant issues concerning the subject, its location, and what drives value or use of the property being analyzed.

AREA, CITY, NEIGHBORHOOD, AND LOCATION DATA

The subject is located on 49th Avenue, which is south of Kimbark Road in Hometown, USA. Both 48th Avenue and Kimbark Road offer easy access to public transportation and employment. The area has residential and mixed-use commercial properties to support a viable economic community with most amenities located within the district. Hometown is located approximately seven miles southwest of the center of the Metropolis metropolitan area. Hometown is bounded on the north by Roosevelt Road, on the south by 39th Street, on the east by Jefferson Avenue, and on the west by Lombard Avenue. Hometown's northern and southern borders are skirted by major interstates Interstate Highways I-293 and I-56.

Hometown's location attracts many people to live here and businesses to locate in the area. Its world-class transportation links include exceptional rail service and close proximity to major interstates. It is just 30 minutes north of Big Wing International Airport and a 25-minute drive to the Municipal Airport. Hometown receives exceptional rail service from the Burlington, Illinois, Central Gulf, Metropolis and Pacific, and Manufacturer's Junction Railroads.

The majority of manufacturing firms in Hometown are privately owned and are highly sensitive to the needs of the community. Since its beginning in 1857, Hometown has been a community based on commercial success and growth. Dominated by 39th Street, Hometown's downtown commercial and retail districts have shown growth, adaptation, and revitalization. The commercial community is a blend of solid retail stores and service firms. Complementing this commercial sector are the business districts along Roosevelt Road, 14th Street, 25th Street, 26th Street, 35th Street, Hometown Avenue, Ogden Avenue, and the intersection of 31st Street and Laramie Avenue.

Demographics

The subject is located in the Census Bureau's Census Tract 998144. According to the file, the estimated 2006 median family income is for this tract is $65,827 while the 2000 median family income was $36,587. The population for this tract is 7,217. The total number of families for this tract is 1,642 and the total number of households is 2,061.

Sales Information for the Neighborhood of Hometown, USA

Start Date	End Date	No. of Units Sold	2007 Median Sales Price	2006 Median Sales Price
2/1/2007	4/30/2007	140	$535,500.00	$530,000.00
1/1/2007	3/31/2007	146	$535,000.00	$533,000.00
12/1/2006	2/28/2007	175	$535,000.00	$530,000.00
11/1/2006	1/31/2007	212	$535,000.00	$529,000.00
10/1/2006	12/31/2006	197	$540,000.00	$525,000.00
9/1/2006	11/30/2006	208	$540,000.00	$520,000.00
8/1/2006	10/31/2006	248	$540,000.00	$520,000.00
7/1/2006	9/30/2006	268	$539,000.00	$520,000.00
6/1/2006	8/31/2006	282	$539,000.00	$520,000.00
5/1/2006	7/31/2006	268	$531,000.00	$520,000.00
4/1/2006	6/30/2006	266	$534,500.00	$517,000.00
3/1/2006	5/31/2006	270	$530,000.00	$515,000.00
2/1/2006	4/30/2006	237	$530,000.00	$511,000.00

Sales Information for Four Nearby Neighborhoods in the Metropolis Metropolitan Area

City #1

Start Date	End Date	No. of Units Sold	2007 Median Sales Price	2006 Median Sales Price
2/1/2007	4/30/2007	131	$550,000.00	$550,000.00
1/1/2007	3/31/2007	131	$550,000.00	$550,000.00
12/1/2006	2/28/2007	155	$545,000.00	$550,000.00
11/1/2006	1/31/2007	207	$541,000.00	$550,000.00
10/1/2006	12/31/2006	227	$548,000.00	$555,000.00
9/1/2006	11/30/2006	246	$548,500.00	$553,000.00
8/1/2006	10/31/2006	253	$555,000.00	$550,000.00
7/1/2006	9/30/2006	232	$560,000.00	$548,000.00
6/1/2006	8/31/2006	248	$560,000.00	$546,000.00
5/1/2006	7/31/2006	247	$560,000.00	$546,000.00
4/1/2006	6/30/2006	265	$555,000.00	$548,000.00
3/1/2006	5/31/2006	257	$552,000.00	$545,000.00
2/1/2006	4/30/2006	219	$550,000.00	$538,000.00

City #2

Start Date	End Date	No. of Units Sold	2007 Median Sales Price	2006 Median Sales Price
2/1/2007	4/30/2007	64	$575,000.00	$565,000.00
1/1/2007	3/31/2007	59	$575,000.00	$565,000.00
12/1/2006	2/28/2007	64	$585,000.00	$561,000.00
11/1/2006	1/31/2007	66	$580,000.00	$554,000.00
10/1/2006	12/31/2006	68	$575,000.00	$550,000.00
9/1/2006	11/30/2006	79	$581,000.00	$560,000.00
8/1/2006	10/31/2006	102	$590,000.00	$560,000.00
7/1/2006	9/30/2006	109	$590,000.00	$559,000.00
6/1/2006	8/31/2006	115	$582,500.00	$560,000.00
5/1/2006	7/31/2006	106	$563,000.00	$557,500.00
4/1/2006	6/30/2006	101	$560,000.00	$555,000.00
3/1/2006	5/31/2006	88	$556,500.00	$550,000.00
2/1/2006	4/30/2006	79	$565,000.00	$543,000.00

City #3

Start Date	End Date	No. of Units Sold	2007 Median Sales Price	2006 Median Sales Price
2/1/2007	4/30/2007	41	$515,000.00	$525,000.00
1/1/2007	3/31/2007	54	$514,250.00	$525,000.00
12/1/2006	2/28/2007	59	$524,000.00	$530,000.00
11/1/2006	1/31/2007	77	$529,500.00	$530,000.00
10/1/2006	12/31/2006	70	$536,000.00	$535,000.00
9/1/2006	11/30/2006	63	$536,000.00	$530,000.00
8/1/2006	10/31/2006	55	$545,000.00	$537,000.00
7/1/2006	9/30/2006	60	$530,000.00	$532,000.00
6/1/2006	8/31/2006	76	$513,500.00	$527,000.00
5/1/2006	7/31/2006	79	$505,000.00	$517,000.00
4/1/2006	6/30/2006	75	$503,000.00	$505,000.00
3/1/2006	5/31/2006	64	$522,000.00	$521,000.00
2/1/2006	4/30/2006	49	$525,000.00	$518,000.00

City #4

Start Date	End Date	No. of Units Sold	2007 Median Sales Price	2006 Median Sales Price
2/1/2007	4/30/2007	17	$525,000.00	$527,000.00
1/1/2007	3/31/2007	18	$525,000.00	$523,000.00
12/1/2006	2/28/2007	23	$523,000.00	$525,000.00
11/1/2006	1/31/2007	38	$525,000.00	$525,000.00
10/1/2006	12/31/2006	40	$536,000.00	$530,000.00
9/1/2006	11/30/2006	42	$539,000.00	$525,000.00
8/1/2006	10/31/2006	35	$539,000.00	$536,000.00
7/1/2006	9/30/2006	25	$538,000.00	$230,000.00
6/1/2006	8/31/2006	28	$531,000.00	$530,000.00
5/1/2006	7/31/2006	37	$520,000.00	$525,000.00
4/1/2006	6/30/2006	44	$525,000.00	$517,500.00
3/1/2006	5/31/2006	44	$525,000.00	$493,000.00
2/1/2006	4/30/2006	34	$527,000.00	$492,000.00

If the appraiser were to simply insert the preceding nearby neighborhood tables into the appraisal report without further analysis or relevant reference, this would be an example of "data dump". Such information is most effective when it is provided with significant reference congruent with the scope of work for the assignment.

Recent Home Sales Information within Hometown, USA

Sale Number	Sales Price	Days on Market	Construction Quality/Condition	Home Size (GLA)	Configuration	Sales Price per Square Foot (Rounded)
1	$300,000	33	Average/average	1,400	2 bedroom, 1 bath	214
2	$322,000	32	Average/good	1300	2 bedroom, 1 bath	248
3	$333,000	21	Average/average	1,500	2 bedroom, 2 bath	222
4	$340.000	33	Average/good	1500	2 bedroom, 2 bath	227
5	$386,000	40	Average/average	1350	3 bedroom, 2 bath	286
6	$422,000	33	Average/good	1,800	3 bedroom, 1 bath	234
7	$433,000	25	Average/average	1,900	4 bedroom, 2 bath	228
8	$476,000	15	Good/good	2,000	4 bedroom, 2 bath	238
9	$498,000	33	Good/good	2,300	3 bedroom, 2 bath	217
10	$525,000	45	Good/good	2,400	3 bedroom, 2 bath	219
11	$545,000	23	Good/good	2,500	4 bedroom, 2 bath	218
12	$587,000	45	Good/good	2,800	4 bedroom, 2 bath	210
13	$595,000	60	Good/average	3,000	4 bedroom, 2 bath	198

■ In Practice

What can you deduce from the preceding information about the subject neighborhood home sales price per square foot and size (gross living area)?

Solution:

Generally, as the gross living area increases, the sales price per square foot decreases.

Housing

Most of the housing is post–World War II. Ranches, bungalows, and Georgians predominate. Condominiums and town homes are in abundance.

According to the census bureau, the total number of units for this tract is 2,289 and the median house age in years is 56, with the following breakdown:

One to four units	2,110
Owner-occupied units	1,003
Renter-occupied units	1,054

Owner-occupied one to four units	972
Vacant units	232

Schools   Elementary school children attend districts 194 and 196. Teenagers attend Theodore Roosevelt High School in district 1208.

TAXES AND ASSESSMENT DATA

According to the Hometown Recorder's records the real estate taxes (for tax year 2007) for the subject, PINs # 26-32-211-002-0000, are as follows:

Assessment Data

Land Assessment	Improvement	Total
$5,632	$9,380	$18,760
Real Estate Taxes:	$6,861.75	

Market Rental Information

Since the subject is located near a local university where single-family homes are rented on a monthly basis, rental information for the single-family homes was available. Three-bedroom, two-bath homes, like the subject, are in high demand since the typical renters are college students attending the local university. College students are more interested in bedroom and bath count versus the gross living area of the home. The following rental information was gathered from multiple sources, including local REALTORS® and the multiple listing service.

Sale Number	Sales Price	Effective Date of Data	Gross Monthly Rent	Gross Monthly Rent Multiplier (GMRM)	GLA	Configuration
1	$500,000	1 month prior	$2,000	250	1,800	2 bedroom, 1 bath
2	$523,000	1 year prior	$2,400	218	2,000	3 bedroom, 2 bath
3	$540,000	1 month prior	$2,500	216	2,700	3 bedroom, 2 bath
4	$545,000	1 week prior	$2,500	218	2,800	4 bedroom, 2 bath

Interest Rates

The present economy must be taken into account in this analysis, as must the difficulty of obtaining financing for real estate ventures. As of the date of this appraisal, typical mortgage financing term indicate the availability of an interest rate of approximately 6.25–7.00 percent for an 80 percent loan-to-value ratio based on a 15–30 year amortization schedule.

Additional Property Identification

According to the Commitment for Title Insurance, the Legal Description for the subject is as follows:

> THE NORTH ½ OF THE SOUTHEAST ¼ OF SECTION 5, TOWNSHIP 134 NORTH, RANGE 12 EAST OF THIRD PRINCIPAL MERIDIAN, WARREN PARK TOWNSHIP.

Site Improvements

The subject is located in an area where public utilities such as city water, sewer, and gas are available. The topography of the subject, slightly sloping, allows for proper drainage into the storm sewer system.

Special Assessments

There are no known changes to the site infrastructure in the near future that would result in special assessments.

HIGHEST AND BEST USE

Highest and Best Use: Land As Vacant and As Improved

Highest and best use is defined throughout this curriculum as the reasonable and probable use of land after considering all legally permissible, physically possible, and economically feasible uses. In arriving at a determination of highest and best use, all uses that physically and legally may be placed on the site, as well as the returns that these uses might generate, are considered.

Remember that the first natural assumption that we make as appraisal professionals concerning a knowledgeable property owner is that the owner will put the property to its highest and best use. Therefore, it is a given that the property must be appraised to its highest and best use; otherwise an extraordinary assumption must be made about the assignment. (Please refer to the current edition of the *Uniform Standards of Appraisal Practice*.)

The analysis of highest and best use is conducted on a property *as if vacant* and *as if improved*. This is done for several reasons. First, highest and best use as if vacant assumes that the property is vacant or can become vacant by razing (demolishing) the existing improvements. Analyzing the highest and best use of a property as if vacant allows the appraiser to identify which properties are truly comparable, and this process also helps identify the proper land value in the cost approach. Remember the consistent use theory calls for proper application of the land value to the use under which the property is being appraised.

The highest and best use analysis as if improved has a twofold purpose. First, it helps identify properties that are comparable to the subject; and second, it helps with the property management function of deciding which of the following should be done to the property:

1. Maintain the property and improvements as is

2. Renovate, convert, or modify the improvements

3. Repair the deferred maintenance and keep the improvements

4. Demolish the improvements

The conclusions section of the highest and best use analysis should specify who the likely purchaser of the property would be and summarize the analysis that preceded the conclusions. The highest and best use analysis should include a detailed description of each of the four tests that are conducted in a highest and best use analysis:

1. **Physically possible**—The *physically possible* test is much more than simply determining what improvements would physically fit onto a site. The physically possible question also asks, "What improvements would ideally be placed on the site?" or "What improvements take maximum advantage of the site given the current and future demand?" and "Can reasonable alterations be made, such as assemblage of surrounding properties, to accommodate a higher and better use?" This is what is meant by "appropriately supported." The market will dictate the alternative uses of a property.

2. **Legally permissible**—*Legal permissibility* has to do with current and future zoning laws and ordinances, and other such governmental influences. The test of legal permissibility helps the appraiser make a determination of the permitted uses under the law and expected changes in the law. Again, like physically possible, the question of alternate uses must be exhausted even if they do not initially pass the legal permissibility test. As an example, current zoning may not allow for a particular use, but the legal authority will entertain a zoning change if requested. After conducting a thorough investigation the appraiser finds that the legal authority would in fact allow for a change in use. Under this example, there is appropriate support for considering the affects of this potential change in use on the property value and the potential to change the highest and best use of the property.

3. **Financially feasible**—Simply because the property meets the physically possible test and legally permissible test does not mean that it will be financially feasible to put the property to that particular use. *Financial feasibility* asks, "Is it worth pursuing this option over another?" The question of feasibility is similar to the question of curability. The decision is made based on the market's support for the alternative use and whether it meets or exceeds the relative risk and cost of completing the option. Again, the question of appropriate support plays a huge role in determining financial feasibility.

4. **Maximally productive**—Remember that all four tests are performed on the property under the two considerations, as if vacant and as if improved. The final test of maximum productivity is actually conducted throughout the first three processes of physically possible, legally permissible, and financially feasible because each test is always working towards the ultimate test—"What is maximally productive under this test?" Often what is maximally productive within one test might not meet the same criteria within another, or sometimes a particular use as if vacant might not match the existing use as if improved.

Subject Site Data

The subject site, which is rectangular in shape, has an area of 7,750 +/– square feet or 0.18 acres. In addition, the site, which is surrounded by residential uses, is fairly level and at street grade, with no apparent soil problems.

There is nothing in the public records reviewed that would indicate that there are any adverse easements or encroachments, etc. The only known easements that exist are the typical utility easements. You have found no evidence of any limitations on ownership rights such as deed restrictions, etc.

Access to the site is from 49th Avenue. The site has 50 feet of frontage on 49th Avenue.

The street is improved with concrete curbs and gutters and asphalt surface. Public utilities of water, sewer, and electricity are connected to the site.

The site is level at street grade and drainage appears adequate. The subject site does not appear to be located in a special flood hazard area. According to FEMA Map # 1710XY 483F, dated 11/06/2000, the subject is in Zone X, a minimal flooding area.

The site is zoned for residential use, R-1, Residential District, by the Hometown Building and Zoning Department. Any use of the property would be required to conform to zoning restrictions for that category. Under this zoning the subject's current use conforms to this zoning. According to the Hometown zoning official, Mr. Cosentino, the permitted uses under the R-1 zoning include detached single-family dwelling and one- to four-unit dwellings. The minimum lot size requirement is 4,375 feet for a single family dwelling and 6,250 feet for one- to four-unit dwellings. The minimum lot width is 35 feet for single-family dwellings and 50 feet for one- to four-unit dwellings. The setback requirement for both single-family dwellings and one- to four-unit dwellings is 25 feet.

■ In Practice

List the physical characteristics of the subject site determined thus far.

Site dimensions & area

_____

Site shape

_____

Site utilities

_____

Site frontage

_____

Site topography

_____

Easements and encroachments

_____

Zoning

_____

Flood zone

_____

Solution:

Site dimensions & area

50' × 155', area = 7,750 square feet

Site shape

Rectangular

Site utilities

Public water, gas, sewer

Site frontage

50 feet

Site topography

Slightly sloping toward storm sewer system

Easements and encroachments

Only typical utilities easements; no known encroachments

Zoning

R-1, Residential District

Flood zone

FEMA Map # 1710XY 483F, dated 11/06/2000, the subject is in Zone X, a minimal flooding area

■ **In Practice**

Answer the following highest and best use as if vacant and improved questions for the subject:

What uses are physically possible on the subject given by the physical characteristics revealed by property analysis?

_____

_____

_____

_____

_____

_____

_____

_____

Are there any known private and public restrictions? Is the current use of the subject legally permissible?

_____

_____

_____

_____

_____

_____

_____

_____

What are the land uses in the immediate and nearby surrounding area? What is the most feasible use of the subject property?

_____

_____

_____

_____

_____

_____

_____

What is the most profitable use that conforms with current zoning of the site as if vacant?

_____

_____

_____

_____

_____

_____

_____

Solution:

What uses are physically possible on the subject given by the physical characteristics revealed by property analysis?

With an area of 7,750 +/– square feet or 0.18 acres the subject site has flexibility for improvement. In addition, the site is fairly level and at street grade, with no apparent soil problems.

Are there any known private and public restrictions? Is the current use of the subject legally permissible?

The only known restrictions affecting title are public restrictions of zoning and utility easements. The subject's current use is legally permissible since the minimum standards according to the Hometown building and zoning department are fulfilled.

What are the land uses in the immediate and nearby surrounding area? What is the most feasible use of the subject property?

Residential uses surround the subject property. This fact, coupled with the zoning designation, supports a residential use as the most feasible use of the property.

What is the most profitable use that conforms with current zoning of the site as if vacant?

The most profitable use of the site as if vacant would be the development of some type of residential use as currently being used. This would conform with current zoning.

■ **In Practice**

Highest and Best Use—Conclusion

What is your highest and best use conclusion?

Solution:

The subject property is an existing improved property with adequate functional utility and is in compliance with current zoning. The present economy must be taken into account in this analysis, as must the difficulty of obtaining financing for real estate ventures. The current single-family improvement is a viable and contributing use of the property and clearly adds to the value of the site above the value of the land alone. Therefore, by the above criteria, the current use fulfills the definition of highest and best use as a single-family residence.

LAND VALUE

There are no comparable vacant land sales within the subject's neighborhood; however, there are comparable sales of improved properties similar to the subject. These sales are all three-bedroom, two-bath, single-story homes without basements. Accrued depreciation for existing improvements of the properties similar to the subject in age, size, condition, and appeal is estimated to be 15 percent.

Sale 1 sold for $540,000 and has 2,300 square feet of gross living area. The estimated replacement cost new for this sale is $182 per square foot. The home is located on a site with dimensions of 50' × 150'.

Sale 2 sold for $526,000 and has 2,400 square feet of gross living area. The estimated replacement cost new is $170 per square foot. The home is located on a site with dimensions of 55' × 155'.

Sale 3 sold for $529,000 and has 2,450 square feet of gross living area. The estimated replacement cost new is $174 per square foot. The home is located on a site with dimensions of 53' ×152'.

Sale 4 sold for $520,000 and has 2,500 square feet of gross living area. The estimated replacement cost new is $161 per square foot. The home is located on a site with dimensions of 50' ×150'.

Use the following table to estimate the value of the subject site as though vacant using the extraction method.

Note: round the mean of the land values to the nearest $10,000.

Sale Number	Sales Price	Cost of Improvements (RCN)	Accrued Depreciation	Depreciated Cost of Improvements	Land Value
1					
2					
3					
4					
Mean					

Solution   The typical land/site value = $177,000.

Sale Number	Sales Price	Cost of Improvements (RCN)	Accrued Depreciation	Depreciated Cost of Improvements*	Land Value*
1	$540,000	$418,600	$62,790	$355,810	$184,190
2	$526,000	$408,000	$61,200	$346,800	$179,200
3	$529,000	$426,300	$63,945	$362,355	$166,645
4	$520,000	$402,500	$60,375	$342,125	$177,875
Mean					**$177,000, rounded**

*Calculate the depreciated cost of the improvements by deducting the estimated accrued depreciation percentage (15%) from the RCN. Calculate land value by subtracting depreciated cost of improvements from the sales price.

LESSON 3: Market Analysis Part 2: The Approaches to Value, Graphic Analysis, and Reconciliation

THE APPROACHES TO VALUE

Cost Approach

From your inspection notes, you have detailed the following information about the subject:

Exterior Detail

Construction	Masonry
Foundation	Concrete
Elevation	One-story built on a slab
Roof	Low-pitch asphalt; good condition

Interior Detail

Floors	Carpet/hardwood/ceramic
Walls	Plaster
Ceiling	Plaster
Windows	Double hung

Mechanical Systems

Electrical service	Adequate
Heating	Gas-forced air
Air-conditioning	Central air
Plumbing	Eight fixtures

Composition

First floor	Three bedrooms, two baths, living room, dining room, kitchen, laundry room

Gross Living Area   2,400 square feet

General Condition & Utility

The improvements have an estimated total economic life of 75 years. The actual age of the improvements is 25 years and the quality of construction is good. After visiting the subject, you estimate that the subject has a remaining economic life of 60 years. Both baths have recently been remodeled and the kitchen has been gut rehabbed, similar to new construction, last year.

The subject's interior walls are 8 feet high and the exterior walls are 8.5 feet high. The subject, a rectangular-shaped one-story home, has dimensions 25' by 96'. The estimated cost of site improvements is $9,000.

The floor plan is typical for this type of property in this market and you observe that that are no obvious superadequacies; therefore, your subject does not suffer from any functional obsolescence. No external obsolescence is observed.

Recall that the site value was calculated earlier to be $177,000.

Using a cost guide, you found the unit-in-place costs listed below. Hint: round square footage to the nearest one, and cost to the nearest tenth. (See Appendix A, Lesson 1 for discussion on rounding.)

Foundation	Concrete walls and footing at $165 per linear foot
Floor framing	$7.50 per sq. ft. of floor area
Roof	$7.25 per sq. ft. of roof area
Interior finishes	Ceiling, partition walls, interior painting $18,000;
	floor covering $15,000;
	cabinets, fixtures $30,000

Front and rear exterior walls	Face brick on concrete block at $65.75 per sq. ft. of wall area (25' × 8.5');
	each side has one entrance door, 3' × 6'8" at $400;
	each side has one 4' × 6' window @ $350
Side exterior walls	Face brick on concrete block at $65.75 per sq. ft. of wall area (96' × 8.5');
	windows on 20% of wall area @ $20.25 per sq. ft.
Wall framing	$132.00 per linear foot of building perimeter
Electrical	$29.45 per sq. ft. of GLA
Heating/cooling	$20,000
Plumbing	$17.55 per sq. ft. of GLA
Garage	$32 per sq. ft.

■ In Practice

What is the replacement cost new of the improvements (home and garage)?

Foundation	Concrete walls and footing at $165 per linear foot
Floor framing:	$7.50 per sq. ft. of floor area
Roof	$7.25 per sq. ft. of roof area
Interior finishes	ceiling, partition walls, interior painting $18,000;
	floor covering $15,000;
	cabinets, fixtures $30,000

_____

_____

Front and rear exterior walls   face brick on concrete block at $65.75 per sq. ft. of wall area (25' × 8.5');

each side has one entrance door, 3' × 6'8'' at $400;

each side has one 4' × 6' window @ $350

_____

_____

_____

Side exterior walls   face brick on concrete block at $65.75 per sq. ft. of wall area (96' × 8.5');

windows on 20% of wall area @ $20.25 per sq. ft.

_____

_____

_____

_____

_____

Wall framing $132.00 per linear foot of building perimeter

_____

Electrical $29.45 per sq. ft. of GLA

_____

Heating/cooling $20,000

_____

Plumbing $17.55 per sq. ft. of GLA

_____

Garage $32 per sq. ft.

_____

Total replacement cost new (RCN) $_____

Solution:

RCN using unit-in-place costs:

Subject gross living area = 2,400 sq. ft. (25' × 96')

Foundation:

Perimeter (2 × 25) + (2 × 96) = 242 linear ft.

242 ft. @ $165.00	$39,930.00

Floor framing:

2,400 sq. ft. @ $7.50	$18,000.00

Roof:

2,400 sq. ft. @ $7.25	$17,400.00

Interior finishes:

Ceiling, partition walls, and interior painting:	$18,000.00
Floor covering:	$15,000.00
Cabinets and fixtures:	$30,000.00

Front and rear exterior walls:

25' × 8.5' = 212.5 sq. ft × 2 = 425 sq. ft.

− 40 sq. ft. for doors (20 sq. ft. × 2)

<u>− 48 sq. ft. for windows (24 sq. ft. × 2)</u>

337 sq. ft. @ $65.75		$22,158.00
2 doors @ $400	$800	
2 windows @ $350	<u>$700</u>	$23,658.00

Side exterior walls:

2 (96' × 8.5') = 1,632 sq. ft. − 326 sq. ft. (20% for windows)

= 1,306 sq. ft. @ $65.75		$85,869.50
326 sq. ft. @ $20.25	<u>$6,601.50</u>	$92,471.00

Wall framing:

Perimeter $(2 \times 25') + (2 \times 96') = 242$ ft.

242 ft. @ $132.00 $31,944.00

Electrical:

2,400 sq. ft. @ $29.45 $70,680.00

Heating/cooling: $20,000.00

Plumbing:

2,400 sq. ft. @ $17.55 $42,120.00

Total RCN for home   **$419,203.00**

Garage:

528 sq. ft. @ $32 $16,896

Total RCN   **$436,099.00**

■ **In Practice**

Using the effective age-life method:

What is the percentage of physical depreciation?

_____

What is the total physical depreciation amount?

_____

What is the indicated value of the subject using the cost approach? (Hint: round your final calculation to the nearest 10,000)

_____

Solution:

Because the estimated total economic life of the improvements is 75 years, and there is an estimated remaining economic life of 60 years, the effective age is 15 years (75 – 60).

$$\frac{\textbf{Effective age}}{\textbf{Total economic life}} = \textbf{\% of depreciation}$$

$$= \textbf{15} \div \textbf{75} = \textbf{0.20 or 20\%}$$

$$\text{Physical depreciation} = \text{RCN} \times \% \text{ of depreciation}$$

$$= \$436,099.00 \times 0.20 = \$87,219.80$$

	$436,099.00	**Replacement cost new (RCN)**
−	87,219.80	**Physical depreciation**
−	0	**Functional obsolescence**
−	0	**External obsolescence**
	$351,879.20	**Depreciated cost of improvements**
+	$177,000.00	**Site value**
+	$9,000.00	**Site improvements**
	$537,879.00	**Indicated value using the cost approach, *rounded***

SALES COMPARISON APPROACH

After performing the inspection, you determine that the subject has a good location and is in good condition; comparable sales, which were all arm's-length sales of fee simple ownership rights, were obtained from the market; and all pertinent information is summarized below:

Sale 1

Sale 1 is a one-story 25-year-old frame constructed home of 2,500 square feet of gross living area has three bedrooms, two baths, and a two-car garage. At the time this home sold, six weeks ago, it was in average condition. The sales price of this sale, located at 3701 S. 61st Court, was confirmed at $510,000. This property was sold without special financing and has a good location.

Sale 2

This one-story 26-year-old frame home has 2,450 square feet of gross living area, three bedrooms, and one bath. This sale does not have a garage. At the time this home was sold, three months ago, it was in good condition. The sales price of this home, located at 704 Kensington, was confirmed at $500,000. This home, which sold without special financing, has a location that is considered good.

Sale 3

This one-story 20-year-old brick retail building has 2,400 square feet of gross living area, three bedrooms, two baths, a two-car garage, and a street frontage of 50 feet. At the time this home was sold, six months ago, it was in good condition. The sales price of this home, located at 418 Kent Road, was confirmed at $530,000. This home, which sold without special financing, has a location that is considered good.

Sale #4

This one-story 25-year-old frame home has 2,500 square feet of gross living area, four bedrooms, two baths, and a two-car garage. At the time this building was sold, six months ago, it was in good condition. The sales price of this sale, located at 6205 Garfield, was confirmed at $555,000. This home, which sold without special financing, has a location that is considered good.

■ **In Practice**

Using the given information, complete the sales grid using paired sales analysis.

	Subject	Sale #1	Adjust	Sale #2	Adjust	Sale #3	Adjust	Sale #4	Adjust
Sales Price									
Property Rights									
Financing Concessions									
Conditions of Sale									
Market Conditions (time)									
Location									
Bedrooms									
Baths									
GLA (sq. ft.)									
Age (yrs.)									
Condition									
Quality of Construction									
Garage									
Porch/Deck/Patio									
Net Adjust (%)									
Gross Adjust (%)									
Indicated Value									

Comparison	Element Difference	Difference in Sales Price
vs.		
vs.		
vs.		

Note: The size adjustment can be determined using the price per square foot unit of comparison; however, adjustments are not necessary for differences in GLA of 100 feet or less.

Solution:

	Subject	Sale #1	Adjust	Sale #2	Adjust	Sale #3	Adjust	Sale #4	Adjust
Sales Price	N/A	$510,000		$500,000		$530,000		$550,000	
Property Rights	Fee Simple	Fee Simple		Fee Simple		Fee Simple		Fee Simple	
Financing Concessions	N/A	None		None		None		None	
Conditions of Sale	Arm's-length	Arm's-length		Arm's-length		Arm's-length		Arm's-length	
Market Conditions (time)	N/A	6 wks prior		3 months prior		6 months prior		6 months prior	
Location	Good	Good		Good		Good		Good	
Bedrooms	3	3		3		3		4	−$40,000
Baths	2	2		2		2		2	
GLA (sq. ft.)	2,400	2,400		2,450		2,400		2,500	
Age (yrs.)	25	25		26		25		25	
Condition	Good	Good		Good		Good		Good	
Quality of Construction	Brick	Frame	+$10,000	Frame	+$10,000	Brick		Frame	+$10,000
Garage	2-car garage	2-car garage		none	+$10,000	2-car garage		2-car garage	
Porch/Deck/Patio									
Net Adjust (%)			$10,000 (2.0%)		$20,000 (4.0%)		$0 (0%)		−$30,000 (−5.5%)
Gross Adjust (%)			$10,000 (2.0%)		$20,000 (4.0%)		$0 (0%)		$50,000 (9.0%)
Indicated Value			$520,000		$520,000		$530,000		$520,000

1 vs. 4	Bedrooms	$40,000
1 vs. 2	2-car garage	$10,000
2 vs. 3	Quality of construction	$10,000*

*Calculated after adjusting sale 2 for garage (+$10,000), then taking the difference in the sales prices of sale 2 and sale 3. ($530,000 – $510,000).

■ **In Practice**

Reconcile within the sales comparison approach to value.

Solution:

Subject value using the sales comparison approach: $525,000

Rationale: Sale 3 has the least amount of gross adjustments; however, the next sale with the fewest adjustments is sale 1. Therefore it is reasonable to assume that the concluded value is between the adjusted sales prices of sale 1 and sale 3.

INCOME APPROACH

■ **In Practice**

From the market rental information collected earlier, estimate the gross monthly rent for the subject.

Solution:

From the market rental information collected earlier and placing greatest weight on sales 3 and 4, it is reasonable to project to a gross monthly rent of $2,500.

■ **In Practice**

Rental information gathered from the four sales used in the sales comparison approach information is detailed below. Calculate the GMRM for all four sales. (*Note:* round the calculated multiplier to the nearest one.)

Sale Number	Value (sales price)	Monthly Rent	GMRM
1	$510,000	$2,400	

2	$500,000	$2,300
3	$530,000	$2,500
4	$550,000	$3,000

Solution:

Sale Number	Value (sales price)	Monthly Rent	GMRM (value ÷ monthly rent)
1	$510,000	$2,400	212
2	$500,000	$2,300	217
3	$530,000	$2,500	212
4	$550,000	$3,000	183

■ **In Practice**

Conclude to an income approach to value by using the GMRM.

Solution:

The estimated value of the subject using the GMRM = $530,000 [$2,500 × 212].

Rationale: Since sales 1 and 3 were found to be most similar to the subject, it is reasonable to use a GMRM of 212.

GRAPHIC ANALYSIS

As we discussed earlier in Section 1, **linear regression** is a method of estimating the value of variable y given the value of variable x.

The following two graphs depict the sales price per square foot and GLA and the sales price per bedroom vs. the number of bedrooms. This information was gathered during the data collection of Hometown market sales.

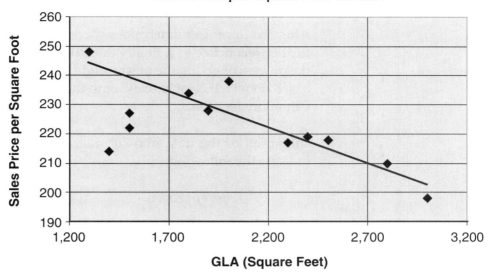

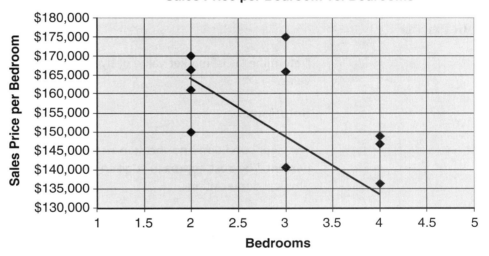

■ **In Practice**

Determine which unit of comparison, the sales price per bedroom or the sales price per square foot, would be the most reliable, and then estimate a value range of the subject market value.

Solution:

The sales price per square foot is the more reliable indicator of value since the graph indicates a discernible trend.

RECONCILIATION

After the appraiser determines the value under each approach, he or she further reconciles to a final value conclusion. This **final reconciliation** is the process of giving the most weight to a particular approach over another based on which is most relevant to the problem in order to conclude a final valuation decision.

Taking all of the data into consideration, the three approaches to value indicate the following:

Cost approach	$534,676
Sales comparison approach	$525,000
Income capitalization approach	$530,000

■ In Practice

Determine "as is" market value of by reconciling between the three approaches to value.

Solution:

The age, condition and location necessitate utilizing a depreciation factor of 20 percent. The cost approach is given limited weight since the subject suffers from physical depreciation.

The sales comparison approach indicates what knowledgeable purchasers are willing to pay for properties that are similar in major characteristics to the subject.

Of the three approaches to value, the sales comparison approach is considered the most conclusive and is given the most weight in determining the final estimate of value.

The income capitalization approach is concerned with the present worth of future benefits. Single-family homes of this type generally are purchased by an occupant rather than an investor. Therefore, the production of income is not often the primary factor in the buyer or seller's mind. In the case of the subject, the income approach has limited applicability, as the income is not the primary motivation of the participants. Accordingly, the income capitalization approach to value was given the limited weight in this value conclusion.

The "as is" market value of the subject property is therefore estimated to be $525,000.

LESSON 4: Communicate the Results

REPORTING

To *communicate the results* is to report the results of the appraisal process. This last step in the appraisal process is somewhat erroneously referred to as the "appraisal" because the results are generally written in a physical report with a concluded value known as an appraisal. In truth the **appraisal** is a *process* of developing an opinion of value; or the opinion of value itself. In other words, the physical report does not in and of itself make an appraisal. It is the process and the value conclusion that makes up an appraisal, while the report is simply a communication of the results. It is worth noting that an appraiser must be careful not to communicate results in a misleading manner, as required under Standard 2 of the *Uniform Standards of Professional Appraisal Practice* (**USPAP**).

Communication is another term that society identifies as something that we do daily and all of the time, something so commonplace that it does not need to be formally studied. Many people seem to believe "Communication is waiting for someone to finish talking so that I can begin to speak," or at least that is what they seem to believe based on their actions.

Speaking is one thing, and listening is quite another, but communication is not simply putting the two together and hoping for the best. *Communication* is a skill that must be honed and constantly developed to be truly effective. **Communication** is the sharing of knowledge between sender and receiver through messages. To communicate *effectively* means communication with an audience in mind, with the intention of having some sort of effect on that audience. **Effective communication** is therefore the sharing of knowledge with an audience in mind. We will investigate effective communication further, but first let's look at the communication process.

THE COMMUNICATION PROCESS

Because we come from such varied backgrounds and education, each of our ability to "communicate," whether we are a sender or receiver of messages, is constantly in question. Therefore, there is no way to know precisely how any person will react to what we communicate or if we have spoken in terms that they can truly understand. We might share a common

FIGURE 2.1
The Communication Process

language and come from similar backgrounds, and yet the words that we use and how we use them might communicate an unintended message to the receiver.

In virtually any environment we are constantly bombarded with messages. Verbal, written, visual, audio, tactile, and nonverbal messages are all around us. We send and receive messages in so many forms throughout the day that one would think that we would all become very proficient in this skill set early in life. In truth, communication can break down relatively easily, even in its simplest form. The following is an outline of how communication takes place:

- The sender must begin with a notion or a thought, which is translated to a message within the sender's mind.

- The message is transferred to a medium such as a written document, an oral statement, or some other such form.

- The message is delivered to the receiver.

- The receiver must decipher or translate the message to the best of his or her ability based on the interpretation of the message.

- If required, a reaction or response is then manufactured in the mind of the receiver.

While this system seems elementary and oversimplified, we can easily see several places where communication can break down. From the genesis of the sender's thought to the acceptance and understanding in the mind of the receiver, much can happen.

The Effective Communication Process

The communication process is quite simple and yet there are several areas of potential pitfalls that can take place within the process. Indeed we would agree that communication takes place on a continuum in most people's lives throughout the day. But effective communication is something altogether different. Effective communication starts with an appeal to a specific audience and ends with a response from the audience that the sender wishes to accomplish. In effective communication strategy there are four general steps:

- Establish the objective for your communication
- Identify the target audience
- Choose the most effective communication medium for your needs
- Create and communicate the message

In the case of appraisal report writing, our objective is to transfer the knowledge that has been uncovered in the appraisal process. Further, the report must reach answers, opinions, and conclusions to the question outlined in the problem identification step, and gain the assent of the audience. How is this done? Well, using the four steps of effective communication strategy, consider the following steps in the effective communication process for reporting and appraisal assignment:

1. Establish the objective for your communication
    a. Problem identification within the appraisal process
    b. Scope of work
2. Identify the target audience
    a. Assess the target audience
    b. Develop an appeal for the audience
3. Choose the most effective communication medium for your needs
    a. Oral report
    b. Narrative report
    c. Form report
4. Create and communicate the message
    a. Understand the content of the message
    b. Organize thoughts in the message
    c. Write the message
    d. Revise, edit, and proofread the message

Effective communication is no different from report writing. In fact, the word *report* can be substituted for the word *message* in the above steps. The balance of this lesson will be spent on considering the audience and the best method of appealing to the audience.

The Audience

As appraisal professionals, we have an ethical obligation to draft reports that are not misleading. How then do we ensure that our thoughts are precisely understood and interpreted as we intended? Further, how do we influence or persuade the client or intended user of our report that we are correct in our analysis and opinions, that we have fulfilled the burden of proof of supporting our claims with evidence and reason, and that therefore we deserve the assent of the reader?

We have alluded to the importance of considering the audience so that we might more effectively communicate our thoughts. Aristotle understood this phenomenon all too well when he wrote the following passage from the *Rhetoric*:

> "Persuasion may come through the hearers when the speech stirs their emotions. Our judgments when we are pleased and friendly are not the same as when we are pained and hostile."

You will note that not only does Aristotle identify a need to strike the emotion of the listener, but he also identifies something basic to human nature: we respond better to words, presentations, and arguments that please us. Indeed, sometimes it is impossible to please a reader who has discovered through your work that there is some sort of problem or some negative issue concerning a property or its value. But in truth, the reader should be pleased with the manner in which the information has been transferred.

The concept of striking the audience's emotion to gain some level of persuasion is what Aristotle referred to as *pathos*. **Pathos** refers to the ability of the speaker to connect with the feelings, wishes, desires, fears, and passions of the audience. We use the Greek derivative of this word *pathos* in our own language with words such as sym*path*y and em*path*y.

In pleasing the audience we can persuade the reader to find agreement with our argument. So how then does one connect with the audience or communicate so that the reader will be pleased? The answer is fairly simple, but it is consistently overlooked in report writing. It is generally a matter of keeping the audience in mind throughout the reporting process. Ask questions such as:

- What would I want to know about this if I were the reader?
- How would I like to be presented with this information?
- Does this make sense?
- Does the content of this report flow well?
- Have I reached the truth of the matter, and will this have an effect on the reader?

In the words of the great Roman statesman and orator Cicero, "If you wish to persuade me, you must think my thoughts, feel my feelings, and speak my words." This statement is so profoundly true that we must break it down for analysis.

"If you wish to persuade me…"

To persuade anyone of anything requires an appeal to his or her judgment whereby you wish to influence his or her behavior, attitude, or thoughts. In the context of appraisal report writing you are attempting to gain the assent of the reader towards your argument; to persuade the reader into adherence with your opinions and conclusions using solid evidence and reasoning.

Very well, we understand the goal, but how do we do this? It seems that Cicero has provided us the answer to this question as well.

"…you must think my thoughts"

One cannot be more absolute than using the word *must*. In the first point we must think like the audience. Understand what the audience is hoping to discover from your report. Ask yourself the obvious first question: "What does my audience want to know; why have my services been engaged?"

It is vital that we develop our persuasive arguments from the critical reader's perspective. Keep in mind that the assumption here is that "the critical reader" is to be the client and the intended user. We shall see in the next lesson that the style of our writing is with the reader, *any* reader in mind. But when we refer here to the *critical* reader, our intention is to emphasize the knowledgeable reader for whom the report is drafted and read. The critical reader, like the critical listener in argumentation, is someone who will apply the critical thought process to our claims, opinions, and conclusions.

"…feel my feelings"

To feel someone's feeling is akin to empathizing with them; to be able to relate to their needs and wants. Note the word *empathize* includes the Greek root *pathos*. This is also vital to gaining the assent of the audience, because no reaction is possible without some sort of emotional connection; albeit, the connection here is on a very primitive and almost subconscious level.

It must resonate with the audience that you truly understand the issues and that you further understand and have identified with their needs here. This is a very powerful thing! You cannot fake this part of the equation. Your writing must reflect that you have given thought to the situation and that you recognize the important issues at hand and how the issues affect that with which the reader is concerned.

There is no substitute for the truth, and that is what you must emphasize within your report. This is what we mean when we refer to maintaining credibility throughout the process. We are not committing ourselves to a touchy-feely approach to reporting—not at all. We are saying that no matter how our opinions and conclusions affect the reader, our job is to be truthful and professional. Because our argument is sound and based on logical connections to the truth of the matter, our attempts to gain the reader's agreement should be received with the same professional and informative spirit in which it is being projected.

After considering the claims made and opinions presented along with the evidence that has been provided, the critical reader should either accept the resolution or reject the argument and shift the presumption by providing other evidence in support of another viewpoint that supports that shift. In other words, the critical reader should either accept the supported argument or challenge the argument with evidence that provides for a different conclusion. Once a supported claim is made, it is not appropriate for the critical reader to simply disagree because he or she does not like the results.

The reader might not like the answer, but the point is that it is the true answer to this problem. Further, it should be presumed that the writer has developed the assignment results in accord with the standard of practice using recognized methods and techniques and relevant information that has been verified. If this is not shown to be the case, then the case itself should be rejected, and it is well within the rights of the critical reader to demand more explanation, evidence, support, etc.

"…and speak my words."

This simply means "Talk to me in a language I understand." Do not use confusing words, acronyms, jargon, or incomplete thoughts in your description of the case. Be direct and clear by choosing words that are not ambiguous! Your words should be accurate and not subject to multiple interpretations.

While your explanations might seem simple enough to you, they might be a bit lofty for the reader. Report writers almost always overestimate the level of understanding of their clients. One reason is that our terminology, methods, techniques, technology, and services have become so commonplace and familiar to us that it seems easy to understand. We see this particularly in consulting assignments where the client knows what is needed from the appraiser, yet the client is unfamiliar with the nuances of valuation methods, principles, and techniques. Of course the appraisal professional will mistakenly assume that the client is far better versed in all aspects of valuation because of the level of intelligence shown in engaging the assignment.

Most clients will seldom tell us that they don't understand something. This is because there is an intimidation factor that forces the client to think, "Should I know this? I should know this, right? Why don't I know this? Well, let's just proceed as if I know this." And the sad part of it all is that you have unknowingly missed an opportunity to become even more valuable to your client.

How does one avoid this? Evaluate the reader and the reader's experience level, and of course remain consciously aware of the reader. If you are writing for multiple people with different experience levels, then you must write for the least knowledgeable first. Consider the audience and the four expertise possibilities:

1. The **uninformed** audience

2. The **acquainted** audience

3. The **informed** audience

4. The **expert** audience

Let's look at how our writing should appeal to each level of expertise.

The Uninformed Audience

This does not mean generally ignorant or uneducated—it means informed about what it is that we do. The great American folk comedian Will Rogers used to say, "Everyone is ignorant, just on different subjects."

This point is well stated when speaking of the uninformed audience. It could be that your reader is an Ivy League–educated CEO of a major corporation and just does not understand the appraisal process or some of the routine methods and techniques that are used in valuation.

A reader in this audience is likely to be a one-time user of your services. The uniformed audience is likely to be someone who carefully reads your cover letter (letter of transmittal), skims through the rest of the report for content, and again reads with care the areas of analysis or conclusions, such as the sections containing reconciliation. Further, the uniformed reader is looking for graphics or other such visuals to help explain the information is a manner that is more palatable. The details and more technical information will be left for a colleague or employee with experience in those areas to critique. Here are some suggestions for writing for the uninformed reader:

■ Keep the cover letter short, businesslike, and precisely to the point. Avoid words or terms that require explanation, such as acronyms or specialized definitions. Sometimes definitions are unavoidable, as in a case when you are performing an analysis that requires a hypothetical condition or an extraordinary assumption (See current edition of *USPAP*). In such cases, provide a precise definition that is quoted directly from the source.

- In your opening sentences, keep your focus on the specific functionality that will allow the reader to understand what is about to take place. This way if the material requires specialized knowledge or a higher level of expertise to interpret, the reader can scan past it or ask for clarity from a more knowledgeable colleague or some other similar source.

- This reader is subject to *information overload*. **Information overload** is when the reader becomes confused because there is too much information, particularly when the information is specialized. Provide only the information that the reader needs. Do not confuse the reader with too much information, especially that of a technical nature.

- Keep the writing very basic. Short is better than long; simple is always better than complex. Focus the attention on what this means to the reader, rather than how this works.

- Use illustrations. There are two main methods of illustration: *visual illustration* and *verbal illustration*. **Visual illustrations** are graphs, maps, photos, outlines, and charts. **Verbal illustrations** are famous quotes, metaphors, anecdotes, comparisons, and analogies. By making your point concrete and equating it to something that everyone can understand, you have moved far closer to connecting with the audience having pulled the reader through the fog and clutter of words. As always, keep the illustrations simple for this audience.

- Always avoid industry jargon. It makes the reader feel like an outsider, and that is intimidating. Have you ever talked to an IT guy about your AV or why the CRT is not working on your PC? We have our own acronyms such as *USPAP (Uniform Standards of Professional Appraisal Practice)* and GFWA (gas-forced warm air), to name a couple. If you must use them, at least define each acronym the first time you use it before repeating it throughout your writing.

- Avoid referencing resources that are commonly used only within appraising. This level or reader will not use such resources or will likely not have access to them. If you must refer to information taken from such a resource, provide a copy in an appendix section of the report.

- Describe all procedures or processes in an easy step-by-step manner. Allow the reader to understand how the processes work and what is significant about the results.

- Always highlight your main points and make all transitions obvious. Reinforce your messages with typography, borders, boldface, color, and anything else that makes the main points jump off of the page.

The Acquainted Audience

A reader in this category is likely to be someone who reads appraisals often. This audience is acquainted with your profession and aware of what you should provide and will likely be more responsive to your opinions, recommendations, and conclusions. But with this higher level of understanding comes a greater level of critical analysis on the part of the reader.

Most of the typical users of appraisal services fall into this category. The acquainted audience understands methods and techniques, but might not understand the appropriateness of using them.

All of the guidelines for the uninformed audience are appropriate for the acquainted audience, with some additional liberties allowed. Some general jargon and familiar acronyms are acceptable, but just like with the uniformed audience these should be defined the first time they are used. Some suggestions for the acquainted audience follow:

- More complex graphics are acceptable at this level, provided, of course, that they are clear and accurate.

- Generally known terms or jargon can be used, but in a context that is easy discern their meaning.

- Resources should be accessible to this level; if not, the information should be provided in an appendix, not simply referenced.

The Informed Audience

The informed audience has extensive knowledge of your field, although they might not expressly practice as an appraisal professional. Many underwriters fall into this category. The reader in this audience is looking for anything that establishes links between the familiar and the new. While the reader in this category has specialized knowledge of your field, there might be a lack of understanding in complex cases or events that are outside of the norm. Most of your reports are critiqued by the informed reader. Some suggestions for the informed audience follow:

- Highlight those issues that are beyond the norm. This reader is so familiar with the norm that anything that falls outside of it will be found out and scrutinized. Better to gain the confidence of this reader by being upfront with any peculiar issues or concerns.

- This reader also likes to see technically sound reports using recognized methods and techniques.

- This reader is pretty good at recognizing flimsy arguments and usually understands the appropriateness of the methods and techniques used.

- To persuade this reader you must stay focused and centered, keeping the transitions in thought logical and rational.

- This reader will reject the *data dump* or *information dump*. **Data dump** and **information dump** are slang terms for either including too much irrelevant information in your writing or including information without analysis. In report writing this is called *fluff*, and it leads to poor report writing. What's worse, fluff is easy to spot and implies that the writer has nothing important to say. Give this reader too much irrelevant information or data without analysis and your report will immediately lose credibility.

The Expert Audience

A reader in this category knows as much about your field as you do. The expert is likely to be an appraiser and would also likely qualify as an appraisal peer. An appraiser's peer is an appraiser who has expertise and competency in a similar type of assignment. An expert audience not only has an extensive knowledge of your field, but also has detailed knowledge and familiarity with the latest methods, techniques, resources, and applications. An expert audience is well versed in the appropriateness of the information, methods, and techniques presented in the report. The guidelines noted for the acquainted reader are all in force with the expert reader, with some additional cautions:

- The use of jargon and acronyms are more acceptable for this reader but be judicious. Even an "expert's" eyes will gloss over with the use of too much insider language or too many acronyms.

- Provide technical background in a manner that is not too elementary.

- Keep details of math, equations, statistics, and other technical information in the body of the report and in areas where they are expected to be placed.

- And, as always, maintain your objectivity and use a professional tone. Be familiar, but do not slip into casual familiarity with the reader. You are, after all, making an argument for your opinions and conclusions.

The Appeal

Once the expertise level of the audience is assessed, the appeal to the audience can begin. Knowing the audience is only the beginning point to knowing the best way to speak to the audience. The most effective communicators are those who strike the emotion, address the important issues, support all claims with evidence, and argue on relevant grounds.

Remember the audience is composed of critical readers. Ensuring that the message is understood is undoubtedly the most crucial concern of a report writer. Sometimes a form report is adequate to transfer information; other times the situation simply cannot be addressed with a checked box on a form. The great American general George S. Patton once said, "Fixed fortifications are monuments to the stupidity of man." While the good general was speaking about military installations such as forts or ramparts, his point works well with respect to report writing. If you allow a form to dictate what you are allowed to say, you might find yourself in trouble when you are faced with a need to say more. Never let a form or lack of time limit what you absolutely have an obligation to report.

Effective communication also means that you have truthfully and accurately covered the relevant issues of the case. In form reporting, if there is simply not enough room for the explanation that is required, an addendum is needed. Be sure to recount throughout the report that there is an attached addendum. Otherwise, sometimes such documents might "mysteriously" be removed from the report, especially if the information contained within the addendum is less than desirable for the client to have in the file. Hey, it happens!

The point here is that you are the captain of your ship, which means that you have a responsibility to report credible results in a manner that is NOT misleading. Sometimes the information can easily be transferred in a form report, and other times a narrative report is required.

In effective communication the term *narrative* means something akin to storytelling. The point about narrative is well captured in the following passage.

The Importance of Narrative

Everyone loves a good story! Hollywood has built a multi-billion-dollar empire upon good stories. Indeed, some of America's greatest speakers have been proficient storytellers. Mark Twain, Will Rogers, and Ernest Hemingway were all great narrators. Something about the way they speak rivets us to their words, and the sound of their written voice soothes us. But is their voice what endears them to us, or is it something more? It is something unspoken yet ever-present. The sense of an immortal work carries with it an almost simplistic quality that allows the masses to identify with the piece. This symbiotic relationship between storyteller and listener is what elevates the writer to immortal status. What reader cannot identify with the simple Mississippi River charm of Twain's characters or the pain Hemingway describes as the embattled old man struggles with his enormous catch? And when Will Rogers says, "You know I just don't understand politicians," what CEO or dockworker can't identify with that statement? Their words bring us to a commonality that transcends all levels of intellect, education, and professional status. Their words speak to the human condition with which we all can identify.

Narration will always be the best way to identify with people, and vice-versa. Narration helps to explain the details of our case in a manner that is clear and logical. We are curious creatures and we all love a good story—just keep it informative and interesting.

The point of the previous passage is to show that sometimes the best way to say something is to just say it! While it is likely possible to set a matrix of boxes to check that would describe the important points of the passage, this does not allow for a connection between writer and reader. Narratives should be used whenever possible and particularly when extraordinary issues require explanation.

Sometimes, the use of narrative is not recommended and a verbal illustration is more appropriate. Of the two formats that follow, which would you rather read?

> **Capitalization Method and Rate**
>
> The loan-to-value ratio is based on a 70/30 with an annual interest rate of 7% and a rate to the equity of 9%. The amortization term is 20 years with a three- to five-year balloon. The calculated annual loan constant is therefore set at 0.093036. The mortgage component is calculated at 0.065125 and the equity component is 0.027000 for an overall capitalization rate of 9.3% using the band of investments method.

Or

> **Capitalization Method and Rate**
>
> The salient factors that have been applied to the subject are shown below:
>
> | | |
> |---|---|
> | Ratio of Loan to Value: | 70 percent |
> | Equity Ratio: | 30 percent |
> | Equity Requirement: | 9 percent |
> | Interest Rate: | 7 percent |
> | Amortization: | 20-year term |
> | Balloon: | 3 to 5 years |
> | Annual Constant: | 0.093036 |
>
> Calculation of Overall Rate:
>
> | | |
> |---|---|
> | $0.70 \times 0.093036 =$ | 0.065125 |
> | $0.30 \times 0.090000 =$ | <u>0.027000</u> |
> | | 0.093125 |
>
> Weighted Average (Basic Rate): 0.093125 percent; as rounded, 9.3%
>
> | | |
> |---|---|
> | Overall Rate | 9.3% |

The answer should be quite obvious. While there will always be a delicate balance between what the reader needs to know and how to present the information to the reader, a good rule of thumb is to use your own judgment and ask the fundamental question:

"How would I like to have to read this report?"

LESSON 4 REVIEW QUESTIONS

1. _____ illustrations are famous quotes, metaphors, anecdotes, comparisons, and analogies.

2. Effective communication starts with an appeal to a specific _____.

3. _____ dump or _____ dump are slang terms for either including too much irrelevant information in your writing or including information without analysis.

4. To persuade this reader you must stay focused and centered, keeping the transitions in thought _____ and rational.

5. Keep details of math, equations, statistics, and other technical information in the body of the report and in areas where they are _____ to be placed.

6. The narration will always be the best way to _____ with people and vice-versa.

7. In effective communication the term _____ means something akin to storytelling.

8. An appraiser's peer is an appraiser who has expertise and _____ in a similar type of assignment.

9. Do not confuse the reader with too much information, especially that of a _____ nature.

10. _____ is when the reader becomes confused because there is too much information, particularly when the information is specialized.

LESSON 4 REVIEW ANSWERS

1. Verbal

2. audience

3. Data; information

4. logical

5. expected

6. identify

7. narrative

8. competency

9. technical

10. Information overload

COMPLEX PROPERTIES

CASE STUDY

The Engagement

A lending officer from a local bank, ABC Bank, that provides home loans telephones you and requests an appraisal of a single-family home located at 325 W. 31st Street. The lending officer further states that the bank wants to provide the homeowner with a mortgage on the property and that you should perform the assignment according to the current guidelines for appraisals used for lending purposes. Because of the current lending and housing environment, the bank compliance officer has asked you to provide a market study concerning the subject market. The market study should be provided in a SWOT analysis format and the focus should contain a three-fold purpose with conclusions. First to familiarize the client with the nuances of subject market, secondly to address the "fit" of the subject property within the market, and finally to identify any notable risks, hidden risks, or other such considerations. The conclusion section should provide an "insightful" understanding of the subject market addressing future prospects and potential for the subject property. The lender provides you with the borrower's information and requests that you perform an inspection the day after tomorrow because the property owner and resident, Mrs. Grey, is available then, and she will have the necessary documents such as blueprints, tax bills, and a plat of survey. You and the lender agree on payment arrangements and the delivery date of the report.

The Inspection

Upon arrival at the Grey residence you immediately note that 31st Street has been recently widened from a quiet two-lane street to a busy four-lane road and that the speed limit has increased from 30 mph to 45 mph. During the inspection of the property, Mrs. Grey has also told you that some of her neighbors have recently moved and that their properties have been converted to such retail uses as a hair salon, a boutique, a flower shop, and a real estate sales office. After further conversation with Mrs. Grey, you note that she lightheartedly complained about the university students that are renting the house next door. Her exact statement was, "They seem like nice kids, but let me tell you that it gets pretty crazy around here on the weekends." You inquire about other properties in the area, and Mrs. Grey informs you that there are several houses along her street that are rented to college students because of the "proximity to the University campus."

Mrs. Grey provides you with a copy of the tax bill that confirms that the property has a single-family use, an old set of blueprints that confirms the subject as being a brick ranch-style dwelling of 1,200 square feet, and the plat of survey. Your inspection confirms the accuracy of the documents and that the subject has three bedrooms, one-and-a-half baths, a living room, a dining room, and a kitchen, on a full unfinished basement with a two-car detached garage. Your inspection also notes a gas-forced hot air furnace with a central air-conditioning unit and a 40-gallon hot water heater, with a standard 200 amp circuit breaker electric panel, all appearing to be in good working condition. Your completed inspection reveals a well-maintained property with typical utilities and landscaping, with no deferred maintenance required. You would rate the subject as average for the market area.

Walking around the immediate area you note that several properties have been recently converted (within the past two years) to commercial uses. You further note fraternity and sorority emblems affixed on the upper façade of some of the homes along 31st Street, and that the campus boundary for the University is less than two blocks away. These same properties seem to be generally maintained aside from the occasional cracked window, broken screen door, or hanging side-yard gate.

Data Collection

After performing a thorough inspection of the property and the immediate environs, you note the following from data collection:

The village in which the subject is located has indeed recently rezoned the block on which Mrs. Grey's property is located. The zoning official has confirmed that Mrs. Grey's property is considered to be legal nonconforming; however, the subject would be allowed to continue the residential use "even if the improvements burned down." The same official states that the property could easily be changed to commercial/retail use. The village is allowing either a commercial/retail or residential use along 31st Street. Further, the village would allow the property to be sold and maintained as a residential property, should Mrs. Grey choose to sell. Upon measuring the subject site, you have confirmed the subject lot dimensions to be 105' × 175'.

After speaking with real estate agents in the area, you learn that several houses are rented to college students on an annual gross-rent basis. The entire year's rent is typically paid up front at the start of each fall semester, and is terminated at the end of each 12-month period. Rent renewals are typically negotiated in mid-May which is approximately 90 days prior to the close of most lease terms ending mid-August. You have been able to collect copies of four current leases of properties similar to the subject. One real estate agent projects a 3% increase for most leases in the coming year, which is confirmed as "typical" for the area according to the campus housing director. The same campus housing director provided you with two properties that were recently purchased by the University for renting to two new adjunct professors. The same housing director told you that the campus is "always interested in acquiring more housing properties for renting to their expanding educational staff."

Because the subject is available for change in use to a commercial/retail use, you explored the possibility of converting the property with a standard build-out. The cost to perform this build-out is estimated at $35,000. Under this new use you estimate the expense to be 30 percent. You also estimate that the property as converted would rent for $18 per square foot with 3 percent market-derived vacancy. You have also determined that a fireplace is worth $3,000 in this market.

The University currently has an enrollment of 18,000 students of which 14,500 students reside on campus in dormitories and university-owned apartment facilities. On-campus housing is fully occupied with limited potential to develop more dormitory facilities on the immediate campus grounds. The University has begun renovation and expansion of existing classroom facility to accommodate two newly developed degree programs that will be implemented beginning with next year's fall term.

Picking up a campus newspaper you learn that recently the University was ranked within the top 5 universities nationally for *"student quality of life"* by a national rating service. The newspaper also contained an article concerning a wealthy benefactor that has donated several acres adjacent to the university, and noted that annexation proceedings are underway. The article further speculates that some of the land granted to the university would be reserved for future dormitory and campus housing expansion, but the article also stated that this was "pure speculation at this time." Within the same paper, a poll of students attending this University revealed that while many students are happy with the quality of life on campus, there was a significant amount of students that preferred to be living off campus but close to the University.

Nationally, there is an increasing trend in the unemployment numbers across all job sectors, with blue collar workers in industrial sectors increasing faster than any other employment group. Median household income levels have remained in line with inflation figures for the past two years. At this time inflation has remained under 2% per year, but the uncertainty of a slowing economy has some economists projecting a future increase in inflation.

The national housing market has slowed dramatically over the past two quarters, with new construction being hit hardest. According to the National Association of REALTORS®, sales of existing homes are down 7% on average over the past three quarters, and sales have been slipping over the past two years. The Home Builders Association has put the downtrend in new construction sales at over 10% below last year, which was down 2% from the previous year.

Because of the slowing economy and scarcity of jobs, college and university enrollment is up 6% on average over the past two years from the prior decade. Nationally, community colleges have seen an increase of 8% over the same period. More and more higher education institutions have electronic curriculum or some form of distance learning system, and the trend is expected to increase steadily as demand for enrollment continues to grow. This means that fewer students will be required to live on or near the campus of the university in which they have matriculated, as class attendance is just a computer terminal away. This could have a profound impact on campus housing across the country.

You have gathered the following comparable sales:

Property A

This property sold one month ago for $148,000 and has 1,250 square feet of gross living area, a room count of six rooms, three bedrooms, and one-and-a-half baths, with a full unfinished basement and a two-car detached garage. The property also has central air and heat and is considered to be in average condition, but has a fireplace. The home is located on the same block of 31st Street as Mrs. Grey's, with lot dimensions of 100' x 180'. The zoning is similar to Mrs. Grey's, and would allow for either a residential or commercial use; however, a conversation with the selling broker has confirmed that the property is going to continue with the residential use.

Property B

This property sold three months ago for $169,000 and has 1,250 square feet of gross living area, a room count of six rooms, three bedrooms, and one-and-a-half baths, with a full unfinished basement and a two-car detached garage. The property also has central air and heat and is considered to be in average condition, but has a fireplace. The home is located on a quiet cul-de-sac behind the subject, with lot dimensions of 105' × 175'. The zoning is strictly residential use, and the property is rented for $17,000 per year under a gross rent lease.

Property C

This property sold two months ago for $163,000 and has 1,200 square feet of gross living area, a room count of six rooms, three bedrooms, and one bath, with a full unfinished basement and a two-car detached garage. The property also has central air and heat and is considered to be in average condition. The home is located along a quiet residential street with lot dimensions of 100' x 180'. You are able to estimate a depreciation level for this sale at 27 percent and a replacement cost of $171,500 for the improvements. The zoning is strictly residential use.

Property D

This property originally sold one year ago for $143,000, and rented to college students for $15,000 per year under a gross rent lease. At the time of the sale the property had 1,200 square feet of gross living area, a room count of six rooms, three bedrooms, and one-and-a-half baths, with a full unfinished basement and a two-car detached garage. The property also has central air and heat and is considered to be in average condition. This sale was converted to a boutique and resold for $210,000 and rents for $18 per square foot with a 30 percent expense ratio. Occupancy in this building is similar to the market occupancy estimated at 97 percent.

Property E

This property just sold last week for $215,000 and has 1,300 square feet of area. The property is directly next door to the subject and is a conversion to a real estate office. You find that the building rents for $1,275 per month with the tenant paying the expenses, taxes, and property insurance. The property also has central air and heat, with a lot dimension of 100' × 180'. In verifying the information you befriend the REALTOR® involved with the sale, and he suggests that there are two other sales of similar properties that have been converted along the same roadway. Both sales are provided below as Properties F and G.

Property F

This commercial property rental is 1,300 square feet and is leased for $15.50 per square, has an expense ratio of 25 percent, and recently sold for $209,000. This property is also along 31st Street in the same district.

Property G

This rental is getting $15,500 per year net operating income. The property recently sold after conversion for $215,000 and is 1,600 square feet. The property has an expense ratio of 33 percent and is in average condition but is limited in use based on its location in the same district as the subject.

Property H

This commercial site sale is 110' x 170' and recently sold for $112,500. The site is comparable to the subject in location and use as if converted.

Property I

You discover from your investigation of the market that an older single-family property in poor condition along the same street as the subject was sold eight months ago for $90,000 with a cost to raze the property of $12,000. The site dimensions are 98' x 175' and the site is considered to have similar location and utility as the subject.

Property J	You have found a dental office in the area that recently sold for $320,000. The depreciated cost of the improvements is estimated at $190,000. The site dimensions are 120' x 185'.
Property K	This site is located adjacent to Property B on the cul-de-sac with a dimension of 80' x 180' x 110' x 180' and closed three months ago for $35,000.
Property L	This residential site sale is located adjacent to a water tower and overhead power-line facility, and sold two weeks ago for $38,000 with lot dimensions of 120'x 180'.
Property M	This residential property was recently purchased by the University for $150,000 and is currently rented to an adjunct professor for $15,000 per year on a gross rent basis. Included in the sales price was $5,000 towards relocation expenses to the seller. This property appears to be similar to the subject in size, appeal, location, condition, and utility.
Property N	This residential property was recently purchased by the University for $154,500 and is currently leased to an adjunct professor for $16,000 per year on a gross rent basis. This property appears to be similar to the subject in size, appeal, location, condition, and utility.

THE ANALYSIS

In the area below, identify the scope of work and provide a *preliminary* survey of the property and the management of the assignment.

The client and other intended users of the report

_____

_____

_____

The intended use of the report and the appraiser's opinions and conclusions

_____

_____

_____

The type and definition of value and the source of the definition

_____

_____

_____

The effective date of the appraiser's opinion and conclusions

_____

_____

_____

HIGHEST AND BEST USE AS IF VACANT

In the area below determine the highest and best use of the site as if vacant and put to either a single-family use or as a commercial/retail use. Reconcile between the two uses.

Site Estimate Single-Family Use

Property	Sales Price	Cost of Improvements (RCN)	Accrued Depreciation	Depreciated Cost of Improvements	Site Value
C					

Property	Site Value	Lot Square Footage	Price per Square Foot
C			
K			
L			

Site Estimate Commercial/Retail Use

Property	Sales Price	Cost to Raze the Building	Total Site Value
I			

Property	Sales Price	Depreciated Cost of Improvement	Site Value
J			

Property	Site Value	Lot Square Footage	Price per Square Foot
H			
I			
J			

Reconciliation

_____

_____

_____

_____

_____

Based on the values of the site as if vacant, which is more valuable: single-family or commercial/retail use?

_____

_____

_____

Sales Comparison   Conduct a sales comparison for the single-family use with the following information and reconcile to a value conclusion.

Description	Subject	Sale A	Adjustment	Sale B	Adjustment	Sale C	Adjustment
Sales Price	N/A	$148,000				$163,000	
Location	Busy street		-0-	Resident			
Rooms	6	6	-0-	6	-0-	6	-0-
Bedrooms	3	3	-0-	3	-0-	3	-0-
Baths	1.5	1.5	-0-	1.5	-0-	1	
Garage	2	2	-0-	2	-0-	2	-0-
A/C	Yes	Yes	-0-	Yes	-0-	Yes	-0-
Fireplace	No	Yes		Yes		Yes	
Basement	Full/ Unfinished	Full/ Unfinished	-0-	Full/ Unfinished	-0-	Full/ Unfinished	
Conclusion			$		$		$

Reconcile

_____

_____

_____

_____

The Income Approach

Determine property value using the direct capitalization method and reconcile a value conclusion for the commercial/retail use:

Property	Value (Sales Price)	NOI	Capitalization Rate
D			
E			
F			
G			

Reconcile

_____

_____

_____

_____

_____

Determine the property value using VIM and reconcile the value conclusion for the residential rental use.

Property	Value (Sales Price)	Gross Income	Multiplier
B			
D			
M			
N			

Reconcile

_____

_____

_____

_____

_____

Entrepreneurial Incentive and Entrepreneurial Profit

Determine the entrepreneurial incentive for converting the subject property from a single-family to a commercial/retail use. If the property is actually converted and the entrepreneurial incentive is actually acquired from the proceeds, what is the entrepreneurial profit on a percentage basis?

Entrepreneurial Incentive

Cost of Property As Is	(+) Cost of Conversion	(=) Total Cost of Investment	Value as Converted	(–) Total Cost of Investment	Entrepreneurial Incentive
	$35,000				

Entrepreneurial Profit

_____

_____

_____

What is the highest and best use as improved? Why?

_____

_____

_____

Has the highest and best use analysis changed the scope of work?

_____

_____

_____

How should this property be valued?

_____

_____

_____

Can the subject be valued NOT to its highest and best use? If so, what precautions should the appraiser take?

_____

_____

_____

Which approaches to value are likely to receive the greatest weight if the subject is valued as:

A single-family property?

_____

_____

A commercial/retail property?

_____

_____

The scope of the SWOT analysis is to have a three-fold purpose:

1) to familiarize the client with the nuances of the subject market
2) to analyze how the subject property "fits" into the market
3) to identify any notable risks, hidden risks, or other such considerations.

Strengths:

_____

_____

_____

_____

_____

_____

_____

_____

_____

_____

_____

Weaknesses:

_____

_____

_____

_____

_____

_____

_____

_____

_____

_____

Opportunities:

_____

_____

_____

_____

_____

_____

_____

_____

_____

_____

_____

_____

Threats:

_____

_____

_____

_____

_____

_____

_____

_____

_____

_____

_____

_____

Conclusions:

_____

_____

_____

_____

_____

_____

_____

_____

_____

_____

_____

_____

SOLUTION

In the area below, identify the scope of work and provide a *preliminary* survey of the property and the management of the assignment.

The client and other intended users of the report:

ABC Bank

The intended use of the report and the appraiser's opinions and conclusions:

For mortgage consideration

The type and definition of value and the source of the definition:

Market value (See definition in *Basic Appraisal Principles*)

The effective date of the appraiser's opinion and conclusions:

The date of inspection (which is the day after tomorrow's date in this case).

Highest and Best Use As if Vacant

In the area below determine the highest and best use of the site as if vacant and put to either a single-family use or as a commercial/retail use. Reconcile between the two uses.

Site Estimate: Single-Family Property

Property	Sales Price	Cost of Improvements (RCN)	Accrued Depreciation	Depreciated Cost of Improvements	Site Value
C	$163,000	$171,500	27%	$125,195	$37,805

Property	Site Value	Lot Square Footage	Price per Square Foot
C	$37,800	18,000	$2.10
K	$35,000	17,100	$2.04
L	$38,000	21,600	$1.75

Site Estimate: Commercial/Retail Use

Property	Sales Price	Cost to Raze the Building	Total Site Value
I	$90,000	$12,000	$102,000

Property	Sales Price	Depreciated Cost of Improvements	Total Site Value
J	$320,000	$190,000	$130,000

Property	Site Value	Lot Square Footage	Price per Square Foot
H	$112,500	18,700	$6.01
I	$102,000	17,150	$5.95
J	$130,000	22,200	$5.85

Reconciliation

The estimated value of the subject site for single-family use may be reasonable at $2.00 per square foot rounded. It makes sense that Sale L is less than the concluded values in the market as it has undesired conditions (water tower and overhead power lines) associated with the property. Of course the subject site as if vacant and ready to be put to its highest and best use, which is the commercial/retail use, is $6.00 per square foot.

Although the single-family vacant land grid indicated a value of $2.00 per square foot for the subject site, in reality, to a single-family user the subject site would likely sell less than the $2.00 per square foot value as a single-family residential site because of its busy street location, as if there were no other use available to the subject property. But in this case, if the site was vacant it would sell as a commercial/retail site for $6.00 per square foot under the theory of highest and best use, as this is the "maximum productive" use of the subject site.

To determine the value of the subject site under a single-family residential use for the cost approach, a downward percentage adjustment could be applied to the market-derived highest and best use value of the site as if vacant of $6.00 per square foot. From this $6.00 per square foot figure the appraiser would apply a market-derived functional obsolescence attributable to the single-family residential improvements.

If, however, the commercial/retail highest and best use was not allowable for the subject property, then the single-family site would be the highest and best use as if vacant, and the cost approach to a single-family user might be on the $2.00 per square foot value derived from the single-family properties located in a residential neighborhood. There would be an adjustment required, however, for the busy street location of the subject. In practice, this adjustment is typically removed from the subject site prior to conducting the cost approach, and placed in the cost approach as something less than the $2.00 per square foot. To determine the location adjustment for the busy street, please refer to the Sales Comparison approach for residential use in this case.

Because the subject property is an interim use as a single-family residential use, the Consistent Use Theory must be considered. Remember the "Consistent Use Theory" holds that land cannot be valued on one use while the improvements are valued based on another. It would therefore appear that the Consistent Use Theory precludes the use of the $6.00 per square foot figure in conducting a cost approach to value for the subject property as a single-family use. However because the improvements as a single family do contribute to the value of the property beyond the value as if vacant and ready to be put to a commercial retail/use, this is not a violation of the Consistent Use Theory.

Note:

The subject site is 75' × 175' or 13,125 square feet. This figure multiplied by the $6.00 per square foot amount equates to $78,750. This concluded value of the subject as if vacant and ready to be put to its highest and best use (commercial/retail) is less than the $145,000 concluded value as a residential use. Therefore the improvements have contributory value beyond the net value (after demolition) of the subject land as if vacant.

Many property improvements are not the ideal improvements for the land under highest and best use, but they may clearly create increments of value above the value of the land alone. While it may appear to be a violation of the Consistent Use Theory to pair the residential improvements within this example with the highest and best use as if vacant figure of $6.00 per square foot for commercial/retail use, it is actually a reflection of the fact that the market simply acknowledges that the current residential improvements with the land have a value beyond the vacant commercial/retail land value alone.

Based on the values of the site as if vacant, which is more valuable: single-family or commercial/retail use?

Commercial/retail use is $6.00 per square foot, while single-family use in this market is estimated at $2.00 per square foot and even less for the subject because of the busy street location.

SALES COMPARISON APPROACH

Conduct a sales comparison for the single-family use.

Description	Subject	Sale A	Adjustment	Sale B	Adjustment	Sale C	Adjustment
Sales Price	N/A	$148,000		$169,000		$163,000	
Location	Busy Street	Busy Street	-0-	Resident	-$21,000	Resident	-$21,000
Rooms	6	6	-0-	6	-0-	6	-0-
Bedrooms	3	3	-0-	3	-0-	3	-0-
Baths	1.5	1.5	-0-	1.5	-0-	1	+$6,000
Garage	2	2	-0-	2	-0-	2	-0-
A/C	Yes	Yes	-0-	Yes	-0-	Yes	-0-
Fireplace	No	Yes	-$3,000	Yes	-$3,000	Yes	-$3,000
Basement	Full/ Unfinished	Full/ Unfinished	-0-	Full/ Unfinished	-0-	Full/ Unfinished	
Conclusion			$145,000		$145,000		$145,000

Reconciliation

The subject has an "as is" (single-family) indicated value under the sales comparison approach of $145,000, as indicated.

THE INCOME APPROACH

Determine property value using the direct capitalization method for the commercial market:

Sale	Value (Sales Price)	NOI	Capitalization Rate
D	$210,000	$14,666	0.06984
E	$215,000	$14,841	0.06903
F	$209,000	$14,659	0.07014
G	$215,000	$15,500	0.07209

Reconciliation

Based on the commercial sales found in the market, it is reasonable to conclude the capitalization rate at 7 percent.

Applying a market-derived vacancy rate of 3 percent and a rental of $18 per square foot using an estimated expense ratio of 30 percent, the concluded value using the direct capitalization method is $210,0000 (1,200 x $18.00 = $21,600 x 0.97 = $20,952 x 0.70 = $14,666 ÷ 0.07 = $209,520 or $210,000 as rounded).

*Remember, Sale M included $5,000 in moving costs that are considered to be sales concessions and would require an adjustment to the sales price of $150,000.

Therefore:

$150,000 – $5,000 = $145,000 (adjusted sales price).

Property	Value (Sales Price)	Gross Income	Multiplier
B	$169,000	$17,000	9.94
D	$143,000	$15,000	9.53
M	$145,000*	$15,000	9.66
N	$154,500	$16,000	9.66

Reconcile

The range of multipliers is fairly tight from 9.5 to 9.9. Because sales D, M, and N are most similar, a concluded multiplier of 9.6 is reasonable.

ENTREPRENEURIAL INCENTIVE AND ENTREPRENEURIAL PROFIT

Determine the entrepreneurial incentive for converting the subject property from a single-family to a commercial/retail use. If the property is actually converted and the entrepreneurial incentive is actually acquired from the proceeds, what is the entrepreneurial profit on a percentage basis?

Entrepreneurial Incentive

Cost of Property As Is	(+) Cost of Conversion	(=) Total Cost of Investment	Value as Converted	(–)Total Cost of Investment	Entrepreneurial Incentive
$145,000	$35,000	$180,000	$210,000	$180,000	$30,000

Entrepreneurial Profit

Approximately 16.7% ($30,000 ÷ $180,000)

What is the highest and best use as improved? Why?

The highest and best use as improved is clearly a commercial/retail use. The value of the property as if vacant and as improved are both maximized under the commercial/retail use.

Compare:

- $2 vs $6 as if vacant

- $145,000 to $210,000 (with 16.7 percent profit) as if improved

Has the highest and best use analysis changed the scope of work?

Yes; the client has requested an analysis of the single-family property, yet the market conditions applied to highest and best use have altered the scope to appraise the property to its highest and best use as a commercial/retail property.

How should this property be valued?

The property should be valued to its highest and best use. One of the natural assumptions that we make as appraisers concerning the knowledgeable owner of real estate is that the owner will put the property to its highest and best use. This is the basis of market value as well ("knowledgeable buyer"). Therefore it is natural to assume the property should be valued to its highest and best use, unless requested otherwise. If this is the case, then the appraiser must consider the fact that the request (a client-imposed assignment condition) has the potential to produce an appraisal report that is misleading. This is not to say that the appraiser cannot fulfill the request; it simply means that some further discussion is required to complete the assignment. (See also the next question.)

Can the subject be valued NOT to its highest and best use? If so, what precautions should the appraiser take?

Yes. This assignment does have the potential to be misleading, and therefore the appraiser *must* take precautions to ensure credible results and not to mislead the reader of the report.

The client should be notified that the property has a highest and best use that coincides with a commercial/retail use and therefore should be appraised under that scope of work. This is called a *re-engagement*, and it is the basis of why we say that scope of work has a four-step process (determination, **confirmation**, performance, and disclosure) and not just a three-step process (determination, performance, and disclosure).

Suppose that after being notified of the situation concerning highest and best use, the client continues to request the appraisal as a single-family use, stating, "We don't care about the property's hypothetical value. Mrs. Grey is a longtime bank customer who is not going to move and we will keep this loan in-house, so please appraise it as a single-family residence." Then the appraiser is allowed to continue provided that the client is made aware that an *extraordinary assumption* must be made in order to complete the assignment. The extraordinary assumption would read something along the lines of:

> "This appraisal assumes that the property owner would maintain a single-family use, which is contrary to the highest and best use of the property. This is known as an extraordinary assumption..."

Or

> "Because the client's request is to value the property contrary to the highest and best use of the real estate, an extraordinary assumption is being placed on this analysis that a property owner would actually purchase and maintain the property as a single-family use, which is contrary to the market supported highest and best use currently noted within the market."

Finally, the resulting appraisal report would have to be drafted as a *restricted use* report as defined within the current edition of the *Uniform Standards of Professional Appraisal Practice (USPAP)*.

Which approaches to value are likely to receive the greatest weight if the subject is valued as:

A single-family property?

The sales comparison approach

Commercial/retail property?

The income approach

The scope of the SWOT analysis is to have a three-fold purpose:

1) to familiarize the client with the nuances of the subject market
2) to analyze how the subject property "fits" into the market
3) to identify any notable risks, hidden risks, or other such considerations.

Strengths:
- Market allows for residential and commercial use.
- Current use allowed "even if the improvements burned down."
- Residential properties may be rented in this market.
- There is a demand for residential leasing.
- Residential leases are typically paid 1 year in advance.
- University is "always interested in acquiring housing properties."
- Campus boundary is less than 2 blocks away.
- Conversion to commercial/retail use has attractive return.
- Currently inflation is low.

Weaknesses:
- As in any interim use market, housing along 31st Street might fall out of favor, and commercial/retail might become saturated before the subject would be converted.
- Slowing economic conditions might lead to a recession whereby commercial/retail development is thwarted.

Opportunities:
- University is expanding educational staff.
- University is expanding student enrollment.
- Nationally more people are pursuing higher education.
- Currently, on-campus housing is fully occupied, with limited development potential.

Threats:
- Distance learning might deplete a need for housing near the university campuses.
- More housing might be built because of land donation to the University.
- Many economists are predicting an increase in inflation.

Conclusions:

The nuances of the market with risks identified:

The proximity of the subject to the University makes this property attractive for either a residential or a commercial/retail use. As noted previously, the subject property is allowed to maintain the current residential use, should the bank be forced to foreclose. If the subject were to be rented as a single-family property, such leases are typically paid 1 year in advanced with escalations in line with current inflation figures.

As with all interim use properties, there is a risk of the subject falling out of favor for the single-family use because of the busy street location. Further, the threat of future student housing development on the recently granted land compiled with a growing distance learning curriculum could cause a drop in need for the subject as a residential lease.

In an area with interim use properties that have conversion potential, such as the subject market, there is always the potential for market saturation with too many similar commercial/retail uses near the University. As an example: too many coffee shops. This combined with a slowing economy might stunt the development potential as a commercial/retail property for the subject some time in the future.

Subject "fit" with risks identified:

Currently and for some time into the future, the subject can be rented to either college students or possibly rented to adjunct faculty if an arrangement could be worked out with the university, making it attractive as an investment property. The subject could also be quickly marketed to the University as they are always looking to acquire residential property in the area.

As a commercial/retail conversion, the subject has attractive return potential to a developer or investor wishing to rent to a commercial/retail merchant provided market saturation is not noted.

As stated previously the threats of new on-campus housing and distance learning curriculum might eliminate a need for leasing the subject to students, but some students believe that there are advantages to living just off campus.

APPRAISAL MATH AND STATISTICS

LEARNING OBJECTIVES

By the end of this appendix, participants will be able to

- explain the order of operations;

- add, subtract, multiply, and divide negative numbers;

- calculate percentages and convert them into decimals;

- understand reciprocals;

- round numbers;

- understand exponents;

- understand problem-solving techniques;

- comprehend basic algebra concepts;

- understand interpolation and extrapolation;

- understand units of comparison;

- calculate area and volume;

- distinguish between gross living area (GLA), gross building area (GBA), gross leasable area (GLA), and net leasable area (NLA);

- convert various units of measure;

- understand the difference between population and sample;

- understand measures of central tendency;
- calculate the mean, median, and mode of an array of numbers;
- understand measures of variability;
- calculate range, variance, and standard deviation;
- calculate weighted averages;
- define statistics;
- identify the different sampling techniques;
- understand outliers and how to deal with them;
- calculate the coefficient of variance (COV);
- be familiar with bar charts, scatter plots, and histograms;
- plot x-coordinates and y-coordinates;
- understand frequency distributions;
- understand skewness of distribution;
- understand the properties of a normal curve;
- understand normal distribution;
- define the empirical rule and when it can be used;
- define correlation and correlation coefficient;
- understand the financial principle of the time value of money;
- distinguish between simple interest and compound interest;
- understand each of the six functions of a dollar;
- use the various methods to compute each of the six functions of a dollar; and
- calculate a mortgage payment.

KEY TERMS

above grade area

additive inverse

algebraic expression

annuity

area

array

bar chart

bias

bimodal

Cartesian coordinate
system

class frequency

class interval

cluster sampling

coefficient of variance
(COV)

compounding

compounding period

cubic units

data set

decomposition

depth

digit

discounting

discount rate

division rule

Ellwood tables

empirical rule

exponent

extrapolation

frequency histogram

frontage

front foot

front footage

future value

future value of $1

future value annuity of
$1 per period

gross building area
(GBA)

gross leasable area
(GLA)

gross living area

interpolation

least common
denominator (LCD)

linear measurement

mean

measures of central
tendency

measures of variability

median

mixed-sign rule

mode

multiplication rule

multiplicative inverse

negative number

net leasable area (NLA)

nominal data

normal distribution

order of operations

outliers

parameter

payment to amortize
$1

percent/percentage

perimeter

place value

population

positive number

present value

present value of $1

present value annuity
of $1 per period

prism

qualitative

quantitative

random sample

range

reciprocal

reversion

rounding digit

rounding off

same-sign rule

sample

sampling frame

scatter plot

simple random sample

sinking fund factor

six functions of a dollar

skewness

square

square root

standard deviation

statistic

statistics

stratified sampling

stratum

systematic sampling

time value of money

unit of comparison

variance

volume

weighted average

width

x-axis

x-coordinate

y-axis

y-coordinate

LESSON 1: Basic Mathematical Functions

An appraiser needs to have an overall understanding of basic mathematics. Mathematics is necessary for all types of analyses where the solution involves a *quantitative* technique. A **quantitative** technique involves something that is measured and expressed as a quantity. A measurement that is not expressed as a quantity is referred to as **qualitative.**

In appraisal assignments, all three approaches to value involve quantitative techniques. Appraisal assignments involve many computations, including fractions, percentages, decimal equivalents, conversions of units of measure, area calculations, volume calculations, and distance calculations. Additional computations within appraisal assignments involve statistical techniques discussed in Lesson 3 of this appendix as well as financial techniques discussed briefly in Lesson 4 of this section. Advanced appraisal courses discuss these techniques, and a thorough understanding of them is necessary in order to produce a credible appraisal report.

ORDER OF OPERATIONS

It is extremely important to understand and perform the order of operations correctly. The **order of operations** refers to which mathematical function is performed first, second, and so on in a math problem with multiple functions. The following is the order of operations needed to conclude to a correct answer:

1. Calculate operations in enclosures (parentheses, brackets, or braces) first, working from the innermost enclosure first to the outermost enclosure

2. Raise the terms to the exponents (powers) and roots

3. Perform all multiplication and division operations, whichever comes first, from left to right

4. Perform all addition and subtraction operations, whichever comes first, from left to right

For example, operations in parentheses are performed before exponents.

Correct	Incorrect
$(6 + 3)^2$	$(6 + 3)^2$
$= (9)^2$	$= 6^2 + 3^2$
$= 81$	$= 45$

For example, exponents are performed before multiplication.

Correct	Incorrect
6×3^2	6×3^2
$= 6 \times 9$	$= 18^2$
$= 54$	$= 324$

■ In Practice

Work from the innermost enclosure first to the outermost enclosure and remember the order of operations within all enclosures. For example, simplify and solve the following problem listing each step taken:

$$7 \times [(6 \times 3)^2 + (20 \div 5 + 5)]$$

Solution:

■ Calculate the innermost enclosure first, remembering the order of operations, and then plug the results into the equation:

$$7 \times [(18)^2 + (4 + 5)]$$

■ Calculate the next innermost enclosure, remembering the order of operations, and then plug the results into the equation:

$$7 \times [(18)^2 + (9)]$$

■ Calculate the next innermost enclosure, remembering the order of operations, and then plug the results into the equation:

$$7 \times (324 + 9)$$

■ Calculate the next innermost enclosure, remembering the order of operations, and then plug the results into the equation:

7 × (333)

■ Calculate the final outermost enclosure, and then plug the results into the equation and solve the equation:

7 × 333 = 2,331

For example: Calculate multiplication and division from left to right, whichever comes first.

Correct	Incorrect
$6 \times 9 \div 27$	$6 \times 9 \div 27$
$(6 \times 9) \div 27$	$6 \times (9 \div 27)$
$= 54 \div 27$	$= 6 \times 0.33$
$= 2$	$= 1.98$

WHAT ARE NEGATIVE AND POSITIVE NUMBERS?

Negative numbers are numbers that have a minus sign (-) in front of them, meaning that the number is less than zero. **Positive numbers** are numbers that have a plus sign (+) in front of them, meaning that the number is greater than zero. Usually, a positive number is expressed without a sign in front of it. In other words, +16 is the same as 16.

To simplify, suppose you have $1,000 in a checking account. Your bank balance would read +$1,000. Now you decide to withdraw $1,000. Your bank balance now reads $0. You then write a check for $1,000, causing an overdraft of $1,000. Your balance now reads -$1,000; in other words, $1,000 less than zero.

To perform mathematical calculations with negative and positive numbers, you must understand the same-sign rule, the mixed-sign rule, subtracting and adding negative numbers, and multiplying and dividing negative numbers.

Same-Sign Rule

The **same-sign rule** is: When combining numbers with the same sign, keep the sign and then add.

$$(+a) + (+b) = +(a + b)$$

$$(-a) + (-b) = -(a + b)$$

To simplify, take the following steps:

1. First, determine if the numbers are positive or negative.

$$(+a) + (+b) = ? \text{ or } (-a) + (-b) = ?$$

2. Place the sign of the numbers in front of a set of parentheses.

$$+(\quad) \text{ or } -(\quad)$$

3. Write the numbers inside the parentheses and place a plus sign (+) between them.

$$+(a + b) \text{ or } -(a + b)$$

4. Add the numbers and remove the parentheses.

■ **In Practice**

Solve the following:

$$+11 + 17 = ?$$

Solution:

$$+11 + 17 = ?$$

$$= +(11 + 17)$$

$$= +28$$

■ **In Practice**

Solve the following:

$$-11 - 17 = ?$$

Solution:

$$-11 - 17 = ?$$

$$= -(11 + 17)$$

$$= -28$$

■ **In Practice**

Solve the following:

$$-3 - 10 - 6 = ?$$

Solution:

$$-3 - 10 - 6 = ?$$

$$= -(3 + 10 + 6)$$

$$= -19$$

Mixed-Sign Rule

The **mixed-sign rule** is not quite as simple as the same-sign rule. When combining two numbers with different signs, take the following steps:

$$+a - b = ? \text{ or } -a + b = ?$$

1. Ignoring the signs, determine which of the two numbers is larger and place the sign of that number in front of a set of parentheses.

$$+(\quad) \text{ or } -(\quad)$$

2. Inside the parentheses, subtract the smaller number from the larger number.

■ **In Practice**

Solve the following:

$$+10 - 2 = ?$$

Solution:

■ Ignoring the signs, determine which of the two numbers is larger and place the sign of that number in front of a set of parentheses.

$$+(\quad)$$

■ Inside the parentheses, subtract the smaller number from the larger number.

$$= +(10 - 2)$$

$$= +(8)$$

$$= +8$$

■ In Practice

Solve the following:

$$-10 + 2 = ?$$

Solution:

1. Ignoring the signs, determine which number is larger and place the sign of that number in front of a set of parentheses.

$$-(\quad)$$

2. Inside the parentheses, subtract the smaller number from the larger number.

$$= -(10 - 2)$$

$$= -(8)$$

$$= -8$$

■ In Practice

Solve the following combining the same-sign rule and the mixed-sign rule.

$$-3 + 8 - 8 + 11 + 6 - 9 = ?$$

Solution:

1. Group the positive and negative numbers separately.

$$+8 + 11 + 6 \qquad -3 - 8 - 9$$

2. Apply the same-sign rule on each group, by placing the sign of each group number in front of a set of parentheses, writing the numbers inside the parentheses, and placing a plus sign (+) between them.

$$+(8 + 11 + 6) - (3 + 8 + 9)$$

3. Apply the mixed-sign rule by determining the sign of the larger number, placing it outside the parenthesis, and subtracting the smaller number from the larger number.

$$+ (25) - (20)$$

$$= +(25 - 20)$$

$$= +5$$

ADDING AND SUBTRACTING NEGATIVE NUMBERS

Adding a Negative Number

Some equations have two signs next to each other with no numbers between them.

$$5 + (-9)$$

To add a positive and a negative number:

1. Ignore the signs and find the positive difference between the numbers.

2. Attach the sign of the original larger number.

■ **In Practice**

Solve the following:

5 + (-9) = ?

Solution:

1. Ignore the negative sign and find the positive difference between 5 and 9.

    9 – 5 = 4

2. Attach the sign of the original larger number (9), which is a minus sign (–). Therefore:

    5 + (-9) = -4

Subtracting a Negative Number

All negative numbers have a positive counterpart known as its additive inverse. An **additive inverse** is a number that when added to another number equals zero. For example, the additive inverse of -10 is +10. Adding -10 to its additive inverse (+10) results in zero. Therefore, adding a negative number is the same as subtracting its positive counterpart (additive inverse) and subtracting a negative number is the same as adding its positive counterpart (additive inverse).

■ **In Practice**

Solve the following:

8 – (-3) = ?

Solution:

$$8 - (-3) = ?$$

$$= 8 + (+3) = 11$$

MULTIPLYING AND DIVIDING NEGATIVE NUMBERS

Multiplication Rule

The **multiplication rule** states that when multiplying two numbers with the same sign, the result is positive, and when multiplying two numbers with different signs, the result is negative.

For example:

$$8 \times (-6) = -48$$

$$2 \times 2 = 4$$

$$-12 \times (-2) = 24$$

Division Rule

The **division rule** states that when dividing two numbers with the same sign, the result is positive, and when dividing two numbers with different signs, the result is negative.

For example:

$$45 \div (-3) = -15$$

$$100 \div 20 = 5$$

$$-30 \div -5 = 6$$

■ **In Practice**

Solve the following equation using the multiplication and division rules, remembering the order of operations.

$$12 \times (-3) \div 2 = ?$$

Solution:

$$12 \times (-3) \div 2 = ?$$

$$(-36) \div 2 = -18$$

PERCENTAGES AND DECIMALS

Denoted by a percent sign (%), **percent** means divided by 100, per 100, or per 100 parts (100 parts = 1 whole). For example, 25% means 25 ÷ 100 or ¼, which translates into 0.25.

■ To convert a percentage to a decimal, just divide by 100, or just move the decimal point two places to the left, adding zeros if needed, and remove the percent sign (%).

For example, to convert 60% to a decimal, move the decimal point to the left two spaces, and drop the percent sign (%). The result is 0.60.

■ To convert a decimal to a percentage, multiply by 100, or just move the decimal point two spaces to the right, and add a percent sign.

For example, to convert 0.0875 to a percentage, multiply 0.0875 by 100, or move the decimal point to the right two spaces, and add a percent sign (%). The result is 8.75%.

■ **In Practice**

Convert the following percentages to decimals:

1. 74%

2. 14%

3. 16.5%

4. 0.01%

5. 8¾%

Solution:

Simply move the decimal point two spaces to the left and remove the percent sign, or divide by 100.

1. 74% = 74 ÷ 100 = 0.74

2. 14% = 14 ÷ 100 = 0.14

3. 16.5% = 16.5 ÷ 100 = 0.165

4. 0.01% = 0.01 ÷ 100 = 0.0001

5. 8¾% = 8 + (3/4)% = 8 + (3 ÷ 4)% = 8 + 0.75% = 8.75% = 8.75 ÷ 100 = 0.0875

■ **In Practice**

Convert the following decimals to percentages.

1. 0.01

2. 0.99

3. 0.0066

4. 0.50

5. 0.0001

Solution:

Simply move the decimal point two spaces to the right and add a percent sign or multiply by 100.

1. $0.01 = 0.01 \times 100 = 1\%$

2. $0.99 = 0.99 \times 100 = 99\%$

3. $0.0066 = 0.0066 \times 100 = 0.66\%$

4. $0.50 = 0.50 \times 100 = 50\%$

5. $0.0001 = 0.0001 \times 100 = 0.01\%$

PERCENTAGE PROBLEMS

To find a percentage of a number, just convert to a decimal and multiply.

■ **In Practice**

What is 50 percent of 700?

$$50\% \times 700 = ?$$

Solution:

First, convert the percentage to a decimal, and then multiply by 700.

$$50\% \times 700 = ?$$

$$= (50 \div 100) \times 700$$

$$= 0.50 \times 700$$

$$= 350$$

There are three variables used to solve percentage problems:

- Percent (rate)
- Total
- Part

Using the preceding problem:

$$Percent\ (rate) = 50\%$$

$$Total = 700$$

$$\textbf{Part = 350}$$

State the problem as follows:

$$\textbf{Part} = Percent \times Total$$

Because there are three variables in this problem, at least two variables must be known. The Percent and the Total represent the known (given) variables in the preceding example. We solve for the unknown variable (Part).

As with all mathematical formulas, the unknown variable will vary; therefore, we can express the previous formula three different ways depending on which of the three variables are known (given).

$$\textbf{Part} = Percent \times Total \qquad\qquad \textbf{350} = 0.50 \times 700$$

or

$$\textbf{Percent} = \frac{Part}{Total} \qquad\qquad \textbf{0.50} = \frac{350}{700}$$

or

$$\textbf{Total} = \frac{Part}{Percent} \qquad\qquad \textbf{700} = \frac{350}{0.50}$$

The mixture of unknown variables and known variables determines which equation is used to solve the problem.

■ In Practice

$60,000 represents what percent of $100,000?

Solution:

$$\text{Percent (rate)} = ?$$

$$\text{Total} = \$100,000$$

$$\text{Part} = \$60,000$$

$$\text{Percent} = \frac{\text{Part}}{\text{Total}} = \frac{\$60,000}{\$100,000}$$

$$= 0.60 = 0.60 \times 100 = 60\%$$

■ **In Practice**

120 represents 50 percent of what number?

Solution:

$$\text{Percent (rate)} = 50\% \text{ or } 0.50$$

$$\text{Total} = ?$$

$$\text{Part} = 120$$

$$\text{Total} = \frac{\text{Part}}{\text{Percent}} = \frac{120}{0.50} = 240$$

■ **In Practice**

If you paid $90 for an item that was discounted by 10%, what was the original price?

Solution:

Because $90 is the result after an item is discounted by 10%, it represents 90% (100% – 10%) of the original price. Remember, 90% converted into a decimal is expressed as 0.90.

$$\text{Total} = \frac{\text{Part}}{\text{Percent}}$$

$$\text{Total} = \frac{\$90}{0.90} = \$100$$

Therefore, the original price was $100.

■ In Practice

If a recent 8% price increase resulted in a sales price of $750,000, what was the price before the recent increase?

Solution:

■ First, recognize that $750,000 represents some number that was increased by 8%. In other words, it is the result of a number being increased by 108%.

$$\text{\$750,000} = \text{price before increase} \times \text{(1.08)}$$

Percent (rate) = 108% or 1.08

Total = price before increase

Part = $750,000

$$\text{Total} = \frac{\text{Part}}{\text{Percent}} = \text{Price before increase} = \frac{\text{\$750,000}}{\text{1.08}}$$

$$= \text{\$694,444}$$

Therefore, the price before the increase was $694,444.

PERCENTAGE INCREASES AND DECREASES

Always calculate percentage increases and decreases with respect to the value before the change took place. For example, suppose a home sold for $450,000 in January of 2006 and resold in January of 2008 for $560,000. What is the percentage increase in the sales price?

1. Calculate the actual difference (the increase or decrease) in the sales price from January of 2006 to January of 2008.

$$\$560,000 - \$450,000 = \$110,000$$

2. Then calculate the percentage increase with respect to the original sales price.

$$\$110,000 \div \$450,000 = 0.244 \times 100 = 24.4\%$$

In appraisal problems, use the actual percentage increase or decrease calculation when determining a market condition (time) adjustment in the sales comparison grid.

It could be determined from the previous example, that the property value increased approximately 12.2 percent per year. The actual distribution of the 24.4 percent increase throughout the 24-month period is difficult to determine. In other words, the majority of the increase in value could have taken place within the six months prior to January of 2008, or perhaps a 1 percent escalation per month took place.

Place Values

A **digit** is a symbol that is used in the system of numbers. A digit can be one of ten symbols: 0, 1, 2, 3, 4, 5, 6, 7, 8, or 9.

For example, the number 345 has three digits: 3, 4, and 5.

Each digit of a number has a different **place value**, the name of a place or location of a digit. Place value is determined by its position as a number. Determine the value of a digit by its position in a number.

For example, each digit in the number 345 has a different place value.

> 345
>
> ones place value (5 ones)
>
> tens place value (4 tens)
>
> hundreds place value (3 hundreds)

Larger numbers have more place values. For example, the number 562,345 has six digits and therefore six place values.

> 562,345
>
> 1s: ones place value (5 ones)
>
> 10s: tens place value (4 tens)
>
> 100s: hundreds place value (3 hundreds)
>
> 1,000s: thousands place value (2 thousands)
>
> 10,000s: ten-thousands place value (6 ten-thousands)
>
> 100,000s: hundred-thousands place value (5 hundred-thousands)

Decimal numbers also have place values. The first digit after the decimal point is the tenths (1/10s) place value; the next digit to the right is the hundredths (1/100s) place value; the next digit to the right is the thousandths (1/1,000s) place value; the next digit is the ten-thousandths (1/10,000s) place value; and so on.

For example, each digit after the decimal point in the number 0.6785, has a different place value.

0.6785

1/10,000s: ten-thousandths place value (5 ten-thousandths)

1/1,000s: thousandths place value (8 thousandths)

1/100s: hundredths place value (7 hundredths)

1/10s: tenths place value (6 tenths)

ROUNDING

The process of **rounding off** expresses a rounded number as an expression of an exact number. Rounding makes numbers easier to work with and is used when numbers do not have to be exact. It is a form of estimating. To round a number, you must first determine the **rounding digit,** which is the digit that occupies the place value you are rounding to.

Rounding Whole Numbers

- **Rule 1**—Determine the rounding digit and look to the right of it. If the digit is less than 5 (0, 1, 2, 3, or 4), do not change the rounding digit. Change all the digits to the right of the rounding digit to 0.

- **Rule 2**—Determine the rounding digit and look to the right of it. If the digit is 5 or greater (5, 6, 7, 8, or 9), round the rounding digit up by one number. Change all the digits to the right of the rounding digit to 0.

Rounding Decimal Numbers

- **Rule 1**—Determine the rounding digit and look to the right of it. If the digit is less than 5, just drop all the digits to the right of it.

- **Rule 2**—Determine the rounding digit and look to the right of it. If the digit is 5 or greater, round the rounding digit up by one number and drop all digits to the right of it.

Rounding Numbers to the Nearest 10

- Round numbers that end in 1 through 4 down to the next lower number that ends in 0. For example, 93 rounded to the nearest ten is 90.

- Round numbers that end in 5 or more up to the next higher even ten. For example, 67 rounded to the nearest ten is 70.

Rounding Numbers to the Nearest 100

- Round numbers that end in 1 through 49 down to the next lower number that ends in 00. For example, 523 rounded to the nearest hundred is 500.

- Round numbers that end in 50 or more up to the next higher even hundred. For example, 889 rounded to the nearest hundred is 900.

Rounding Numbers to the Nearest 1,000

- Round numbers that end in 001 through 499 down to the next lower number that ends in 000. For example, 4,433 rounded to the nearest thousand is 4,000.

- Round numbers that end in 500 or more up to the next even thousand. For example, 7,989 rounded to the nearest thousand is 8,000.

Rounding Numbers to the Nearest 10,000

- Round numbers that end in 0001 through 4,999 down to the next lower number that ends in 0000. For example, 64,328 rounded to the nearest ten-thousand is 60,000.

- Round numbers that end in 5,000 or more up to the next even ten-thousand. For example, 87,689 rounded to the nearest ten-thousand is 90,000.

Rounding Numbers to the Nearest 100,000

- Round numbers that end in 00001 through 49,999 down to the next lower number that ends in 00000. For example, 5,447,867 rounded to the nearest hundred-thousand is 5,400,000.

- Round numbers that end in 50,000 or more up to the next even hundred-thousand. For example, 5,555,999 rounded to the nearest hundred-thousand is 5,600,000.

Rounding Decimals to the Nearest Hundredth (0.01)

- If the thousandths place of the decimal is 4 or less, drop it and leave the hundredths place as it is; do not change it. For example, 0.742 rounded to the nearest hundredth is 0.74.

- If the thousandths place is 5 through 9, the hundredths place is increased by 1. For example, 0.637 rounded to the nearest hundredth is 0.64.

Rounding Decimals to the Nearest Tenth (0.1)

- If the hundredths and thousandths places are 49 or less, drop them and leave the tenths place as it is; do not change it. For example, 0.742 rounded to the nearest tenth is 0.7.

- If the hundredths and thousandths places are 50 or more, increase the tenths place by 1. For example, 0.867 rounded to the nearest tenth is 0.9.

  For example, 845.2791 becomes:

  1,000 when rounding to the nearest thousand (1,000)

  800 when rounding to the nearest hundred (100)

  850 when rounding to the nearest ten (10)

845 when rounding to the nearest one (1)

845.3 when rounding to the nearest tenth (0.10)

845.28 when rounding to the nearest hundredth (0.01)

845.279 when rounding to the nearest thousandth (0.001)

■ **In Practice**

669.3459 becomes:

_____ when rounding to the nearest thousand (1,000)

_____ when rounding to the nearest hundred (100)

_____ when rounding to the nearest ten (10)

_____ when rounding to the nearest one (1)

_____ when rounding to the nearest tenth (0.10)

_____ when rounding to the nearest hundredth (0.01)

_____ when rounding to the nearest thousandth (0.001)

Solution:

669.3459 becomes:

1,000 when rounding to the nearest thousand (1,000)

700 when rounding to the nearest hundred (100)

670 when rounding to the nearest ten (10)

669 when rounding to the nearest one (1)

669.3 when rounding to the nearest tenth (0.10)

669.35 when rounding to the nearest hundredth (0.01)

669.346 when rounding to the nearest thousandth (0.001)

EXPONENTS

An **exponent** indicates how many times a base number is to be used as a factor. For example, 8^3 means 8 raised to the third power, or 8 cubed.

$$8^3 = 8 \times 8 \times 8 = 512$$

The base number is 8 and the exponent is 3. The base can be a whole number, a decimal number, or a fraction. Some rules for using exponents:

- **Rule 1**—A base number that is raised to the power of 1 equals the base number itself.

$$n^1 = n$$

- **Rule 2**—With the exception of 0, any base number raised to the power of zero equals 1.

$$n^0 = 1$$

- **Rule 3**—When multiplying two powers with the same base, simply add the exponents.

$$a^3 \times a^2 = a^{3+2}$$

■ In Practice

Solve the following:

1. $7^3 = ?$

2. $5^5 = ?$

3. $6^3 = ?$

4. $(0.30)^4 = ?$

5. $10^1 = ?$

6. $3^3 \times 3^2 = ?$

7. $23^0 = ?$

8. $(1/2)^3 = ?$

Solution:

1. $7^3 = 7 \times 7 \times 7 = 343$

2. $5^5 = 5 \times 5 \times 5 \times 5 \times 5 = 3{,}125$

3. $6^3 = 6 \times 6 \times 6 = 216$

4. $(0.30)^4 = 0.30 \times 0.30 \times 0.30 \times 0.30 = 0.0081$

5. $10^1 = 10$

6. $3^3 \times 3^2 = 3^{3+2} = 3^5 = 3 \times 3 \times 3 \times 3 \times 3 = 243$

7. $23^0 = 1$

8. $(1/2)^3 = (0.50)^3 = (0.50) \times (0.50) \times (0.50) = 0.125$

SQUARES AND SQUARE ROOTS

The **square** of a number, n, is that number multiplied by itself.

$$n^2$$

For example,

$$\text{square of } 5 = 5^2 = 5 \times 5 = 25$$

$$\text{square of } 2 = 2^2 = 2 \times 2 = 4$$

$$\text{square of } 4 = 4^2 = 4 \times 4 = 16$$

$$\text{square of } 3 = 3^2 = 3 \times 3 = 9$$

The **square root** of a number, n, is the number that gives n when multiplied by itself.

$$\sqrt{n}$$

For example,

$$\text{square root of } 25 = 5, \text{ because } 5 \times 5 = 25$$

$$\text{square root of } 4 = 2, \text{ because } 2 \times 2 = 4$$

$$\text{square root of } 16 = 4, \text{ because } 4 \times 4 = 16$$

$$\text{square root of } 9 = 3, \text{ because } 3 \times 3 = 9$$

FRACTIONS

Reciprocals

All numbers, except 0, have a **reciprocal** or **multiplicative inverse**, which is a number that when multiplied by n results in 1.

$$\text{Reciprocal of } n = \frac{1}{n}$$

$$\textit{Proof: } n \times \frac{1}{n} = \frac{(n \times 1)}{n} = 1$$

For example, the reciprocal of 8 = 1/8

$$\textit{Proof: } 8 \times \frac{1}{8} = \frac{(8 \times 1)}{8} = 1$$

The reciprocal of a fraction is the fraction inverted.

$$\text{Reciprocal of } a/b = b/a$$

$$\textit{Proof: } a/b \times b/a = \frac{a \times b}{b \times a} = 1$$

For example, the reciprocal of 3/4 = 4/3.

$$\textit{Proof: } 3/4 \times 4/3 = \frac{3}{4} \times \frac{4}{3} = \frac{3 \times 4}{4 \times 3} = \frac{12}{12} = 1$$

■ **In Practice**

Find the reciprocal and show proof of the following:

1. 56

2. 6/7

3. 0.90

4. 1

5. 1/0.24

Solution:

1. 1/56;   Proof: $56 \times 1/56 = 56/56 = 1$

2. 7/6;   Proof: $6/7 \times 7/6 = 42/42 = 1$

3. 1/0.90;   Proof: $0.90 \times 1/0.90 = 0.90/0.90 = 1$

4. 1;   Proof: $1 \times 1/1 = 1$

5. 0.24;   Proof: $1/0.24 \times 0.24 = 0.24/0.24 = 1$

Adding and Subtracting Fractions

All fractions have a *numerator* and a *denominator*. The numerator is the number above the line in a fraction or the top number in a fraction. The denominator is the number below the line in a fraction or the bottom number in a fraction. To add or subtract fractions, all denominators must be the same. This is accomplished by finding the *least common denominator (LCD),* also referred to as the *least common multiple (LCM).* The **least common denominator** of two or more denominators, other than zero, is the smallest whole number that is divisible by each denominator.

To find the least common denominator:

■ First list all multiples of each denominator.

■ Then, look for the lowest number that is the same in all lists of denominators—the least (lowest) common denominator.

■ Use that number as the denominator for all of the fractions.

■ Finally, determine the new numerator for each fraction by first dividing the least common denominator (LCD) by the fraction's denominator and then multiplying that number by the numerator.

$$\text{New numerator} = \frac{\text{LCD}}{\text{Denominator}} \times \text{Numerator}$$

$$\text{New denominator} = \text{LCD}$$

For example:

$$\frac{3}{2} + \frac{5}{4} + \frac{3}{10} = ?$$

■ First, list all multiples of each denominator:

Multiples of 2:	2, 4, 6, 8, 10, 12, 14, 16, 18, 20, 22…
Multiples of 4:	4, 8, 12, 16, 20, 24, 28…
Multiples of 10:	10, 20, 30, 40, 50…

■ Then, look for the lowest number that is listed for each denominator.

Multiples of 2:	2, 4, 6, 8, 10, 12, 14, 16, 18, **20**, 22…
Multiples of 4:	4, 8, 12, 16, **20**, 24, 28…
Multiples of 10:	10, **20**, 30, 40, 50…

Because 20 is the lowest number that appears on all three lists, it is the least common denominator.

■ Finally, find the equivalents of each fraction using the least common denominator, which in this case is 20.

$$\frac{3}{2} + \frac{5}{4} + \frac{3}{10} = ?$$

$$\text{New numerator} = \frac{\text{LCD}}{\text{Denominator}} \times \text{Numerator}$$

New denominator = LCD

new numerator for $\frac{3}{2}$ = (20 ÷ 2) × 3 = **30**

new denominator = 20

Therefore, the equivalent fraction for $\frac{3}{2}$ is $\frac{30}{20}$

new numerator for $\frac{5}{4}$ = (20 ÷ 4) × 5 = **25**

Therefore, the equivalent fraction for $\frac{5}{4}$ is $\frac{25}{20}$

new numerator for $\frac{3}{10}$ = (20 ÷ 10) × 3 = **6**

Therefore, the equivalent fraction for $\frac{3}{10}$ is $\frac{6}{20}$

Now it is possible to calculate the sum of all three fractions because they all have the same denominator.

$$\frac{30}{20} + \frac{25}{20} + \frac{6}{20} = \frac{\textbf{61}}{\textbf{20}}$$

Therefore, to add and subtract fractions, first find the lowest common denominator. Convert each fraction to its equivalent value expressed using a common denominator.

Multiplying and Dividing Fractions

To multiply fractions, simply multiply the numerators and multiply the denominators.

For example:

$$\frac{4}{5} \times \frac{9}{10} = \frac{4 \times 9}{5 \times 10} = \frac{36}{50}$$

To divide fractions, multiply the first fraction (the *dividend*) by the reciprocal of the second fraction (the *divisor*).

For example:

$$(6/8) \div (3/5) = \frac{6}{8} \times \frac{5}{3} = \frac{30}{24}$$

■ **In Practice**

Solve the following:

1. $(7/8) - (3/4) = ?$

2. $(6/9) \div (4/5) = ?$

Solution:

1. $(7/8) - (3/4) = ?$

    The LCD $= 8$

    New numerator for $(7/8) = (8 \div 8) \times 7 = 7$

    New numerator for $(3/4) = (8 \div 4) \times 3 = 6$

    New denominator for both fractions $= 8$

    The problem is now restated as $\dfrac{7}{8} - \dfrac{6}{8} = \dfrac{1}{8}$

2. $(6/9) \div (4/5) = (6/9) \times (5/4) = \dfrac{6}{9} \times \dfrac{5}{4} = \dfrac{30}{36}$

PROBLEM-SOLVING STRATEGIES

Problem solving is basically the processes followed to solve a problem. Less complex mathematical problems require fewer steps to find a solution. Progressively, more complex mathematical problems require several steps to find a solution.

Solving Word Problems

All types of mathematical problems can involve word problems. Many word problems can be solved by breaking the problem down into smaller pieces and solving for each piece. The following is a general sequence of steps used to solve word problems:

1. **Determine what the problem is asking for.** Word problems can be especially frustrating at times mainly because it is difficult to ascertain just what they are asking.

2. **Identify all of the variables.** Determine the known and unknown variables. By determining the knowns and unknowns, any superfluous information (unnecessary information not relevant to the problem) can then be eliminated.

3. **Assign the symbols.** Assign symbols to variables that may be required in some formulas.

4. **Set up the formula or list the procedure.** With the given information, set up all possible formulas or list all possible procedures that will solve the problem.

5. **Substitute the symbols.** Substitute any symbols in the formula with all relevant variable information.

6. **Solve the formula.** Be consistent with the use of units. For example, change inches to feet or feet to yards, and so on.

7. **Is the problem answered? Is the answer reasonable?**

■ **In Practice**

Using word problem techniques, solve the following:

What is the capitalization rate if a property sold for $500,000 and had a net operating income of $60,000?

Solution:

1. **Determine what the problem is asking for:** Capitalization rate

2. **Identify all of the variables:**

    Net operating income = $60,000

    Value = $500,000

    Capitalization rate = ?

3. **Assign the symbols:**

    I = Net operating income = $60,000

    V = Value = $500,000

    R = ?

4. **Set up the formula or list the procedure:** The income capitalization formula (IRV) is expressed three ways:

    $$I = R \times V \quad \text{or} \quad R = I \div V \quad \text{or} \quad V = I \div R$$

    The unknown variable determines which formula to use. In this case, we are solving for the capitalization rate (R); therefore, the middle formula is used.

5. **Substitute the symbols:**

    R = $60,000 ÷ $500,000

6. **Solve the formula:**

    R = $60,000 ÷ $500,000 = 0.12 or 12%

7. **Is the problem answered? Is the answer reasonable?**

Solving Equations/ Algebraic Expressions

In mathematics, equations are statements indicating the equality of two quantities (*numerical equation*) or statements using symbols (**algebraic expressions**). For example: $2 + 2 = 4$ is a numerical equation, while $x + 6 = 8$ is an algebraic expression. The right side of an equation is equal to the left side separated by an equal sign ($=$). Solving an equation involves finding the value or values of a variable that satisfy the statement. Algebraic operations can be used to solve equations with numbers or symbols. There are several ways in which equations can be manipulated while still maintaining a true statement:

- **Rule 1**—Multiplying or dividing both sides of the equation by the same number or variable does not change the solution.

- **Rule 2**—Adding or subtracting both sides of the equation by the same number or variable does not change the solution.

- **Rule 3**—Raising both sides of the equation by the same exponent or taking the same root of both sides of the equation does not change the solution.

These rules, applied to true statements, can manipulate equations in order to solve them. The values of the variables making the equation true are referred to as *solutions*.

To solve equations with one variable:

- Add, subtract, multiply, or divide both sides of the equation by the same number.

- Once the variable is isolated on one side of the equation, the other side of the equation is the solution.

For example, in order to solve $x + 6 = 8$, we can isolate the unknown variable, x, and solve:

- Subtract 6 from both sides of the equation:

$$x + 6 - \mathbf{(6)} = 8 - \mathbf{6}$$

$$x + 0 = 2$$

$$x = 2$$

■ **In Practice**

Solve the equation:

$$3x + 2 = 20$$

Solution:

To isolate the *x*, first subtract 2 from both sides of the equation.

$$3x + 2 - 2 = 20 - 2$$

Which simplifies to:

$$3x = 18$$

Next divide both sides by 3:

$$\frac{3x}{3} = \frac{18}{3}$$

The value of the variable is now the solution:

$$x = 6$$

Interpolation and Extrapolation

Interpolation is a prediction made *between* known values of data. **Extrapolation** is any prediction made *beyond* known values of data.

For example, if a cost guide gives the per square foot costs to build a 2,200-square-foot home and a 2,400-square-foot home, but your subject is 2,300 square feet, you will need to interpolate the per square foot costs for the subject.

Good Quality

2,200 sq. ft.	2,400 sq. ft.
$92.00/sq. ft.	$88.00/sq. ft.

The difference in square feet between the two given values is 200 square feet (2,400 – 2,200). The difference in the dollars per square foot is $4.00 ($92.00 – $88.00). It is obvious that the larger the building, the lower the cost per square foot to build.

The difference in size, 200 square feet, represents two 100-square-foot increments. If we divide $4.00 by 2 we get the incremental cost per 100 square feet of size ($4.00 ÷ 2 = $2.00).

The subject is 2,300 square feet, which represents 1 scale distance of 100 feet from 2,400 square feet. Remembering that the larger the building, the less it costs per square foot, we can add $2.00 to the per square foot costs at 2,400 square feet.

This results in an estimated cost per square foot of $90.00 ($88.00 + $2.00).

Therefore, we can estimate that the cost to build a 2,300-square-foot building is $207,000 (2,300 sq. ft. × $90.00).

The same concept can be applied if the size of the subject was out of the known data range; in other words, larger than 2,400 square feet. If this were the case, extrapolation would be performed. Extrapolation is more risky than interpolation because it must be assumed that the same pattern will continue past the known data range.

LESSON 1 REVIEW QUESTIONS

1. $(8 + 1)^2 =$

2. $3 + (+9) =$

3. $10 - (-3) =$

4. $\{18 + [(12 - 2) \div 5]\} =$

5. $20 \times 4 \div 2 =$

6. $10 \div 5 \times 6 =$

7. $2{,}500 \div (-500) =$

8. $3 - 10 - 6 =$

9. What is 20% of 600?

10. A property sold for $300,000, which was 4.8% less than the list price. What was the property listed for, rounded to the nearest thousand?

11. The number of home listings for sale in a certain market area was 1,403 in 2006 and 1,104 in 2007. What was the percentage decrease?

12. Round 125 to the nearest ten.

13. Round 3.8099 to the nearest one-hundredth.

14. $17^1 =$

15. $87^0 =$

16. $(1/4)^4 =$

17. What is the reciprocal of 35?

18. What is the reciprocal of 1/23?

19. $(8/5) + (6/4) =$

20. $2x - 10 = 10, x =$

LESSON 1 REVIEW ANSWERS

1. $(8 + 1)^2 = (9)^2 = 81$

2. $3 + (+9) = 3 + 9 = 12$

3. $10 - (-3) =$

   $+10 - (-3) =$

   $+(10 + 3) =$

   13

4. $\{18 + [(12 - 2) \div 5]\}$

   $\{18 + [(10) \div 5]\}$

   $\{18 + [2]\} = 20$

5. $20 \times 4 \div 2 = 80 \div 2 = 40$

6. $10 \div 5 \times 6 = (10 \div 5) \times 6 = 2 \times 6 = 12$

7. $2{,}500 \div (-500) = -5$

8. $3 - 10 - 6 =$

   $+3 - 10 - 6$

   $+(3) - (10 + 6)$

   $+(3) - (16)$

   $-(16 - 3) = -(13) = -13$

9. $20\% \times 600 = ?$

   $(20 \div 100) \times 600 = 0.20 \times 600 = 120$

10. $300,000 is the result after the list price was reduced by 4.8%; therefore, it represents 95.2% (100% − 4.8%) of the list price. Remember, 95.2% converted into a decimal is 0.952.

$$\textbf{Total} = \frac{\text{Part}}{\text{Percent}}$$

$$\textbf{Total} = \frac{\$300{,}000}{0.952} = \$315{,}126, \text{ rounded to } \mathbf{\$315{,}000}$$

Therefore the list price was $315,000.

11. Calculate the actual difference (the increase or decrease) in the number of home listings from 2006 to 2007.

$$1{,}104 - 1{,}403 = -299$$

Then, calculate the percentage decrease with respect to the original year (2006):

$$(-299 \div 1{,}403) = -0.213$$

$$(-0.213) \times 100 = -21.3\%$$

12. 130

13. 3.81

14. $17^1 = 17$

15. $87^0 = 1$

16. $(1/4)^4 = (0.25)^4 = (0.25) \times (0.25) \times (0.25) \times (0.25) = 0.003906$

17. The reciprocal of $35 = 1/35$

    Proof: $35 \times 1/35 = 35/35 = 1$

18. The reciprocal of $1/23 = 23$

    Proof: $1/23 \times 23 = 23/23 = 1$

19. $(8/5) + (6/4) =$

    The LCD = 20

    New numerator for $(8/5) = (20 \div 5) \times 8 = 32$

    New numerator for $(6/4) = (20 \div 4) \times 6 = 30$

    New denominator for both fractions = 20

    The problem is now restated as $\dfrac{32}{20} + \dfrac{30}{20} = \dfrac{62}{20}$

20. $2x - 10 = 10$

    $2x - 10 + \mathbf{10} = 10 + \mathbf{10}$

    $2x = 20$

    $\dfrac{2x}{2} = \dfrac{20}{2}$

    $x = 10$

LESSON 2: Calculating Area

AREA AND VOLUME

As part of the specific and general data collection process, appraisers need to calculate the area (and volume where applicable) of buildings and sites.

A review of basic geometric formulas is in order to calculate *area* and *volume*. **Area** is the amount of space within a two-dimensional surface enclosed by a boundary. **Volume** is the amount of space within a three-dimensional object expressed in cubic units (cubic feet, inches, or yards).

Although a data source or builder may provide area information, the appraiser must verify that the information is correct.

The area of a site is usually expressed in terms of square feet (sq. ft.) or acres, whereas the area and volume of a building are generally expressed in terms of square feet (sq. ft.) or cubic feet (cu. ft.), respectively.

The symbol for inches is " and the symbol for feet is '. For example, 55' indicates 55 feet, while 67" indicates 67 inches.

Area

Rectangle   A rectangle is a figure that has pairs of opposite sides with equal length. The area of a rectangle is the product of its length and its width. All four sides meet at right angles (90 degrees) to each other.

w

l

Area = length × width

$A = l \times w$

For example, a rectangle with a length of 2 feet and a width of 1.5 feet calculates to an area of 3 square feet (2'× 1.5').

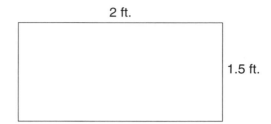

2 ft.

1.5 ft.

Square   A square is a rectangle with four sides of equal length that meet at right angles (90 degrees). The area of a square is the length of a side, *s*, squared.

s

$$Area = s \times s$$

$$A = s^2$$

For example, a square where the length of each of the four sides is 3 inches calculates to an area of 9 square inches (3^2).

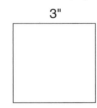

3"

Triangle   A triangle is a figure bounded by three lines that meet at three angles. The area of a triangle is equal to one-half of its base multiplied by its height. Any side of a triangle can be considered as the base; however, the height must be an imaginary line perpendicular (at a 90 degree angle) to the base. (See Figure A.1.)

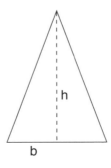

h

b

$$Area = \tfrac{1}{2}(base \times height)$$

$$A = \tfrac{1}{2}bh$$

FIGURE A.1
Calculating the Area of a Triangle

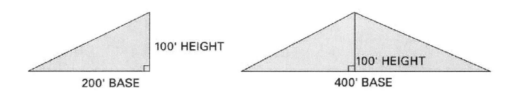

100' HEIGHT

200' BASE

0.5 x 200 (Base) x 100 (Height) = 10,000 Square Feet

100' HEIGHT

400' BASE

0.5 x 400 (Base) x 100 (Height) = 20,000 Square Feet

For example, a triangle with a base of 10" and a height of 14" calculates to an area of 70 square inches: ½ × (10"× 14").

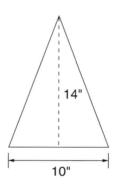

14"

10"

Irregular Figures   When the shape of a building or site is *irregular* (not an exact rectangle or triangle), calculate the area by the process of *decomposition*. **Decomposition** is the act of breaking down something into smaller parts. Break down irregular figures into a series of rectangles and triangles; then add together the calculated areas of each rectangle or triangle to obtain the total area. See Figure A.2 for an example of decomposition.

Volume

Volume is the amount of space within a three-dimensional object expressed in **cubic units** (cubic feet, inches, or yards) and is used to determine the capacity that an object occupies. For example, an appraiser may need to calculate volume when an appraisal assignment involves a warehouse that houses large equipment. (See Figure A.3.)

Calculate the volume of a rectangular box by multiplying the surface area of one side by the height.

$$\text{Volume} = \text{length} \times \text{width} \times \text{height}$$

$$V = lwh$$

FIGURE A.2
Calculating Total Area of Land and/or a House

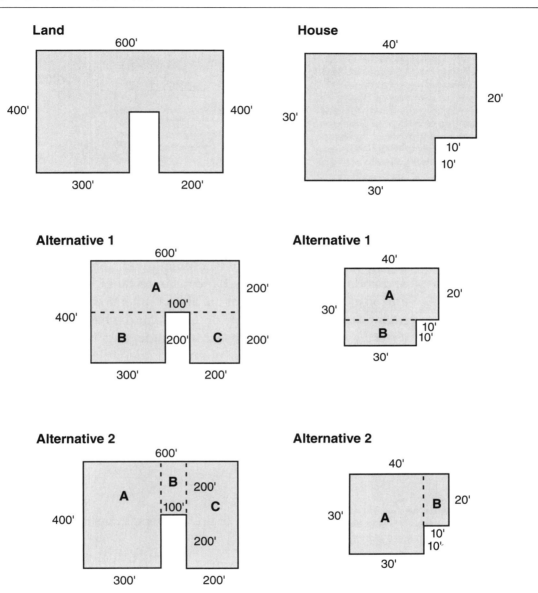

■ **In Practice**

Calculate the volume in cubic feet of a solid rectangle (rectangular prism) with the following dimensions:

length = 300'

width = 400'

height = 18'

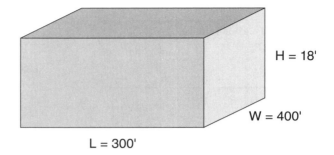

Solution:

Simply multiply the length by the width by the height (lwh).

Volume = 300' × 400' × 18' = 2,160,000 cubic feet

Volume of a Prism   A **prism** is a three-dimensional solid figure with bases and ends that are equal in shape (as in rectangular, circular, or triangular) and size. The bases and ends are also parallel to each other. The name of the prism depends on the shape of its base. If the base is a rectangle, then it is a *rectangular prism*; if the base is a triangle, then it is a *triangular prism.* The formula for calculating the volume of a triangular prism is:

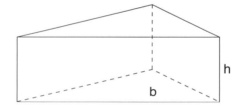

V = ½(base × height of line perpendicular to the base × width)

V = ½(bhw)

FIGURE A.3
Calculating Volume

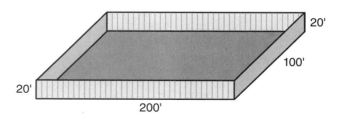

For example, a home is a combination of a rectangular prism and a triangular prism. To calculate the volume of a home, including attic area, divide the building into two different figures (decomposition). Then add together the two calculated volumes for each figure, resulting in the total building volume.

For example, to compute the volume of the following house, first divide the house into two shapes, S and T.

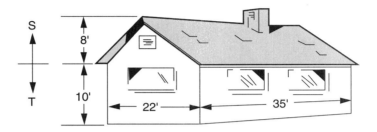

Find the volume of S.

$$V = ½(b \times h \times w) = ½ \times (22' \times 8' \times 35') =$$

$$½(6,160 \text{ cu. ft.}) = 3,080 \text{ cu. ft.}$$

Find the volume of T.

$$V = 22' \times 35' \times 10' = 7,700 \text{ cu. ft.}$$

Total volumes S and T.

$$3,080 \text{ cu. ft.} + 7,700 \text{ cu. ft.} = 10,780 \text{ cu. ft.}$$

Perimeter

The **perimeter** is the length of the boundary lines of a closed figure, generally expressed in terms of linear inches, linear feet, or linear yards. A **linear measurement**, also referred to as *lineal measurement,* is a single dimension relating to a line. Perimeter calculations come in handy when using cost manuals/software to determine reproduction and replacement costs used in the cost approach.

$$\text{Perimeter of a rectangle} = 2 \times \text{length} + 2 \times \text{width}$$

$$P = 2l + 2w$$

For example, the perimeter of a rectangle with a length of 20 feet and a width of 15 feet is 70 feet.

$$P = (2 \times 20) + (2 \times 15)$$

$$P = 40 + 30 = 70 \text{ feet}$$

The perimeter of a triangle is equal to the sum of the lengths of all three sides.

$$P = a + b + c$$

For example, the perimeter of a triangle with lengths of 7, 3, and 10 feet is 20 feet.

$$P = 7 + 3 + 10$$

$$= 20 \text{ feet}$$

Front Footage/Frontage

Front footage, or **frontage**, refers to the portion of land that faces a desirable feature, such as a street (access), a golf course, or a body of water. The length of frontage is a linear measurement expressed as front feet. A **front foot** is a strip of land 1 linear foot long. Calculating frontage is important when valuing retail properties or industrial properties as there may be a relationship between sales price and street access or a railroad siding.

Site dimensions include width and depth. The **width** of a site is the length from side to side, while the **depth** is the length from front to back.

Generally the side that faces the street is the first dimension listed; therefore, the width of a site is generally the frontage. For example, a site with dimensions of 160' × 400' has a width of 160', a depth of 400', and frontage of 160'.

Like Units of Measure

When calculating areas of a shape that has different units of measure (for example, inches, feet, and yards), it is important to convert all measurements into one unit of measure. To calculate areas properly, multiply feet by feet, multiply inches by inches, and multiply yards by yards. See Figure A.4 for a conversion chart.

FIGURE A.4
Conversion Chart for Inches, Feet, and Yards

12 inches = 1 foot 36 inches = 1 yard 3 feet = 1 yard	
To convert feet to inches, *multiply the number of feet by 12.*	(ft. × 12 = in.)
To convert inches to feet, *divide the number of inches by 12.*	(in. ÷ 12 = ft.)
To convert yards to feet, *multiply the number of yards by 3.*	(yd. × 3 = ft.)
To convert feet to yards, *divide the number of feet by 3.*	(ft. ÷ 3 = yd.)
To convert yards to inches, *multiply the number of yards by 36.*	(yd. × 36 = in.)
To convert inches to yards, *divide the number of inches by 36.*	(in. ÷ 36 = yd.)

FIGURE A.5
Conversion Chart for Square Inches, Square Feet, and Square Yards

To convert square feet to square inches, *multiply the number of square feet by 144.*	(sq. ft. × 144 = sq. in.)
To convert square inches to square feet, *divide the number of square inches by 144.*	(sq. in. ÷ 144 = sq. ft.)
To convert square yards to square feet, *multiply the number of square yards by 9.*	(sq. yd. × 9 = sq. ft.)
To convert square feet to square yards, *divide the number of square feet by 9.*	(sq. ft. ÷ 9 = sq. yd.)
To convert square yards to square inches, *multiply the number of square yards by 1,290.*	(sq. yd. × 1,290 = sq. in.)
To convert square inches to square yards, *divide the number of square inches by 1,290.*	(sq. in. ÷ 1,290 = sq. yd.)

■ **In Practice**

1. 6' × 5" = _____ square feet or _____ square inches

2. 1 yard × 5' = _____ square feet or _____ square yards

Solution:

1. 6' × 5" = **2.5 square feet** [6 × (5 ÷ 12)] square feet or
   360 square inches [(6 × 12) × 5] square inches

2. 1 yard × 5' = **15 square feet** [(1 × 3) × 5] square feet or
   1.67 square yards [1 × (5 ÷ 3)] square yards

The calculations to convert square inches, square feet, and square yards units of measure may also be necessary. For example, there are 144 square inches in a square foot (12" × 12"). See the conversion chart in Figure A.5.

■ **In Practice**

1. 7,200 square inches = _____ square feet

2. 243 square feet = _____ square yards

Solution:

1. 7,200 square inches = **50** square feet; (7,200 ÷ 144) square feet

2. 243 square feet = **27** square yards; (243 ÷ 9) square yards

The calculations to convert cubic inches, cubic feet, and cubic yards units of measure may also be necessary. For example, there are 1,728 cubic inches in a cubic foot (144" × 12"). See the conversion chart in Figure A.6.

FIGURE A.6
Conversion Chart for Cubic Inches, Cubic Feet, and Cubic Yards

To convert cubic feet to cubic inches, *multiply the number of cubic feet by 1,728.*	(cu. ft. × 1,728 = cu. in.)
To convert cubic inches to cubic feet, *divide the number of cubic inches by 1,728.*	(cu. in. ÷ 1,728 = cu. ft.)
To convert cubic yards to cubic feet, *multiply the number of cubic yards by 27.*	(cu. yd. × 27 = cu. ft.)
To convert cubic feet to cubic yards, *divide the number of cubic feet by 27.*	(cu. ft. ÷ 27 = cu. yd.)
To convert cubic yards to cubic inches, *multiply the number of cubic yards by 46,656.*	(cu. yd. × 46,656 = cu. in.)
To convert cubic inches to cubic yards, *divide the number of cubic inches by 46,656.*	(cu. in. ÷ 46,656 = cu. yd.)

■ **In Practice**

1. 8,640 cubic inches = _____ cubic feet

2. 1,620 cubic feet = _____ cubic yards

Solution:

1. 8,640 cubic inches = **5** cubic feet; (8,640 ÷ 1,728) cubic feet

2. 1,620 cubic feet = **60** cubic yards; (1,620 ÷ 27) cubic yards

Unit of Comparison

A **unit of comparison** is a per unit indicator. Within a specific market, the appraiser must analyze information gathered during the general data collection process and determine which unit or units of comparison accurately depict the expectations of the market participants. For example, use front footage when market data indicates a relationship between sales price and frontage. The use of statistics helps determine which unit of comparison to employ by using various indicators.

Common units of comparison for various property types follow:

■ **Units of Comparison for Vacant Land**
  ● Agricultural—price per acre, animal unit
  ● Residential—price per acre, square foot
  ● Multifamily—price per potential unit, square foot, acre
  ● Commercial—price per acre, square foot, front foot
  ● Industrial—price per acre, square foot, front foot

■ **Units of Comparison for Improvements**
  ● Farm—price per animal unit
  ● Residential—price per room, bedroom, square foot
  ● Multifamily—price per unit, room, bedroom, bath, square foot

- Commercial—price per square foot, unit
- Industrial—price per square foot, cubic foot

The preceding is a list of common units of comparison. For any given property type in any given market, there may be a relationship between sales price and a unit of comparison not listed.

■ **In Practice**

What is the purchase price per square foot of a vacant site with dimensions of 50' × 180', and a purchase price of $250,000?

Solution:

area of vacant site = 9,000 square feet (50' × 180')

purchase price per square foot = purchase price ÷ square footage of vacant site

$250,000 ÷ 9,000 = $28 per square foot, *rounded*

■ **In Practice**

Using the information from the preceding In Practice problem, calculate the purchase price per acre and per front foot. *Hint:* An acre contains 43,560 square feet.

Solution:

area of vacant site = 9,000 square feet (50' × 180')

acreage of vacant site = 9,000 ÷ 43,560 = 0.21 acre

purchase price ÷ acreage of vacant site = purchase price per acre

$250,000 ÷ 0.21 acre = $1,190,476 per acre

frontage of vacant site 50' × 180' site = 50'

purchase price ÷ frontage = purchase price per front foot

$250,000 ÷ 50' = $5,000 per front foot

Gross Living Area (GLA)

One of the most important aspects of the specific data collected about a property is the gross living area (GLA). **Gross living area** of a house is the *above grade area* enclosed by the outside walls. **Above grade area** is the portion of a building that is above ground level. Below grade areas include basements and subbasements. Also not included in GLA are areas of a building that are not heated or cooled, or areas that are not actually livable. These areas include garages, open porches, unfinished attics, and the second-floor area that does not actually have a floor in a two-story foyer entrance.

As mentioned earlier, a data source or builder may provide the square footage of land and gross living area information; however, the appraiser must verify that the information is correct. The use of proper measuring devices and techniques is extremely important. There are many measuring devices on the market to aid appraisers. The following steps help ensure the proper calculation of GLA:

- Draw a sketch of the footprint (foundation) of the building.

- Measure and record all the outside measurements.

- Measure the garage, whether attached or unattached. If it is an attached garage, the interior wall is considered an outside wall of the building.

- Measure any attached porches. The interior wall of a porch is considered to be an outside wall of the building.

- If the building has more than one story, check each story against the footprint of the building. Be sure to account for overhang areas (i.e., second-story areas cantilevered over the first floor). Conversely, subtract any notched-out areas in the second floor.

- Convert any measurements in inches to feet. For example, convert 12'6" to 12.5'.

- Double-check measurements for reasonableness and accuracy, and take many photos if necessary.

- Use decomposition to calculate areas of all floors. Do not include below-grade areas (basements or subbasements), garages, unheated and cooled areas, porches, and so on.

■ **In Practice**

Calculate the gross living area of the single-story home shown below.

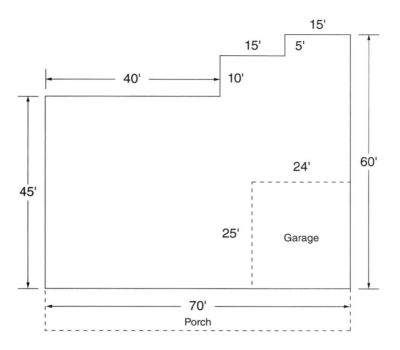

Solution:

GLA:

A = 5' × 15' =	75 sq. ft.
B = 10' × (15' + 15') = 10' × 30' =	300 sq. ft.
C = 24' × (45' − 25') = 24' × 20' =	480 sq. ft.
D = (70'− 24') × 45' = 46' × 45' =	2,070 sq. ft.
Total =	**2,925 sq. ft.**

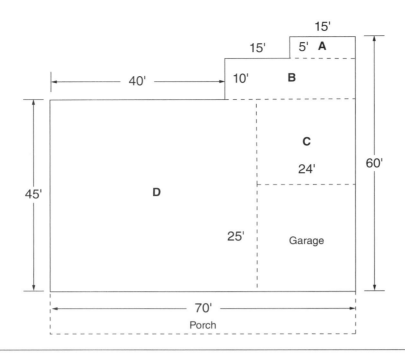

Gross Building Area (GBA)

Gross building area (GBA) includes the area enclosed by outside walls as well as attics and below-grade areas such as basements. Gross building area is typically used as an area measurement for residential properties with 1–4 units and industrial buildings. As with gross living area (GLA), gross building area does not include garages, open porches, or parking lots.

Gross Leasable Area (GLA)

Gross leasable area (GLA) is the total space that is occupied exclusively by tenants. This includes the area enclosed by outside walls as well as below grade areas such as basements and mezzanines. Not included in gross leasable area are common areas. Gross leasable area is typically used as an area measurement of shopping centers.

Net Leasable Area (NLA)

Net leasable area (NLA) is the total floor space that is rented to tenants. Not included in gross leasable area are common areas, building foyers, hallways, or space devoted to heating, cooling, elevators or other utility areas of a building.

LESSON 2 REVIEW QUESTIONS

1. 16" × 8" = _____ square feet or _____ square inches

2. 86 square yards = _____ square feet

3. 3 yards × 2' = _____ square feet or _____ square yards

4. Calculate the area of a triangle with a base of 40" and a height of 15".

5. Compute the area of the following figure:

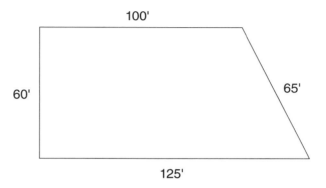

Use the figure below to answer questions 6, 7, and 8.

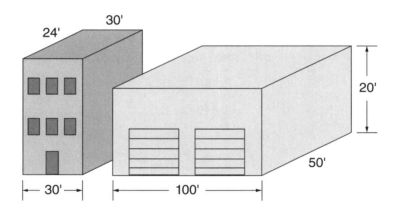

6. What is the cubic area of the garage space?

7. What is the square-foot area of the two-story office area?

8. What is the total building area in square feet?

LESSON 2 REVIEW ANSWERS

1. $16' \times 8" = $ **10.67 square feet;** $[16 \times (8 \div 12)]$ square feet or **1,536 square inches;** $(16 \times 12) \times 8$ square inches

2. 86 square yards = **774 square feet;** (86×9) square feet

3. 3 yards $\times 2' = $ **18 square feet;** $[(3 \times 3) \times 2]$ square feet or **2 square yards;** $[3 \times (2 \div 3)]$ square yards

4. A= ½(bh) = ½ $\times$ (40" $\times$ 15") = ½ $\times$ (600 sq. in) = **300 sq. in.**

5. Area of rectangle = l $\times$ w = 100' $\times$ 60' = 6,000 sq. ft.
   Area of triangle = ½(bh) = ½(125' – 100')(60') = ½(25' $\times$ 60')
   = ½(1,500 sq. ft.) = 750 sq. ft.
   Total area = 6,000 sq. ft. + 750 sq. ft. = **6,750 sq. ft.**

6. Volume of rectangular prism (garage) = lwh
   = 50' $\times$ 100' $\times$ 20'= **100,000 cubic feet**

7. Area of rectangle (office area) = l $\times$ w = 24' $\times$ 30'
   = 720 sq. ft. $\times$ 2 floors = **1,440 square feet**

8. Total area of building = office area + garage area
   = 1,440 sq. ft. + (50' $\times$ 100') = 1,440 sq. ft. + 5,000 sq. ft.
   = **6,440 sq. ft.**

LESSON 3: Statistics—Basic Concepts

WHAT IS STATISTICS?

Statistics is the mathematics of collecting, classifying, and interpreting numerical data to determine if certain values represent characteristics of a population. In statistics, a **population** is a set of measurements that describes some phenomenon. A population could be a group of individuals, objects, or items. For example, a population can be all single-family homes located within a certain town or village that are within a certain *parameter.*

A **parameter** is a characteristic of a population. For example, an appraiser might be interested in the average sales price of all *two-bedroom, 1,600-square-foot* (the parameter) single-family homes. Because most populations are too large to observe, a *sample* must be taken for statistical measurement.

A **sample** is a subset of measurements selected from a population. A **statistic** is a characteristic of a sample. A **sampling frame** is a source from which a sample is drawn. It is simply a list of all the members of a population.

> Statistics is what the analyst knows; the parameters are what he or she wants to know.

Statistics enables one to make an educated guess about a population parameter (the sales price of all two-bedroom 1,600-square-foot single-family homes), based on the statistic computed from a sample. It is important that the sample chosen is typical of the population. In other words, the sample must be representative of the population.

Sampling Techniques

Not only is it important to choose a sample that is representative of the population, but the method used in choosing that sample is also important. There are several sampling techniques.

Random Sampling   A **random sample** is one in which every member of the population is chosen by chance. Each member has a known, but *not necessarily equal,* chance (probability) of being picked. A **simple random sample** is one in which every member of the population has an *equal* chance (probability) of being picked.

By using random sampling, the likelihood of *bias* is reduced. **Bias** is a preconceived opinion. The advantage of using random sampling is that it requires minimum advance knowledge of a population. This technique best suits situations where the population is fairly homogeneous (of the same kind; not heterogeneous) and not much information is available about the population.

Systematic Sampling   **Systematic sampling** is the selection of every *n*th element from a sample frame. For a very large population, it is appropriate to choose every *n*th element from that population. For example, if your population consists of 50,000 or more people, you might choose every 10th person, every 20th person, every 30th person, and so on. Every member of that population has an *equal* chance (probability) of being chosen; therefore, this technique is similar to simple random sampling. In order to ensure that the chosen sample does not hide a pattern, which compromises the randomness, a starting point must be selected.

Stratified Sampling   **Stratified sampling** groups the population into relatively homogenous subgroups or subpopulations called **stratums.** Random or systematic sampling can then be applied within each stratum. For example, within a population of single-family homes sold within the last six months, subpopulations can be formed by grouping these homes into stratums of 0–2,000 square feet of gross living area (GLA), 2,100–3,500 square feet of GLA, 3,600–5,000 square feet of GLA, and so on. The technique requires accurate information about the population and may introduce bias. This technique should not be used when a population cannot be grouped into homogenous subgroups.

Cluster Sampling   **Cluster sampling** is a sampling technique that divides the entire population into groups, or clusters (usually counties, census tracts, or other boundaries). Random sampling is then applied to each member of that cluster. In other words, each member of the selected cluster is included in the sample. Alternately, a systematic sampling technique can be applied to a cluster. The advantage of using this sampling technique is that it may be more practical and/or economical than simple random sampling or stratified sampling.

Sample Size   It is extremely important to determine how many members of a population should be selected in order to properly represent the population. The size of the sample is simply the number of members in the sample. For example, if six single-family homes were used by an appraiser to represent the market, then the sample size is equal to six. Samples that are too large can waste time, resources, and money, but samples that are too small may lead to inaccurate results.

MEASURES OF CENTRAL TENDENCY

Measures of central tendency are numbers that cluster around the middle of a set of values. For example, the central tendency may be the typical sales price of a single-family home.

A **data set** is a set of data, which are observations, or measurements of a specific variable. Data sets must be arranged in an orderly fashion before calculating various measures of central tendency; namely, the median and the mode. Data arranged in order of size is called an **array.** In other words, the arrangement of data is in increasing or decreasing order. The following is an example of an array using the sales prices of seven single-family homes:

$450,000

$395,000

$390,000

$390,000

$389,000

$380,000

$375,000

Note that the sales prices are in descending order.

Three common measures of central tendency, the "middle" numbers, are the *mean, median,* and *mode.* All three measures of central tendency can identify the typical phenomena in a population or sample. Discussions of all three follow.

Mean

The most familiar and basic statistical measure is the arithmetic **mean,** which is an average value for a group of numerical observations. The mean is the sum of all data values divided by the total number of data values. The typical denotation for the mean of a sample is $\bar{x}$ (read as X bar).

The formula for the sample mean is usually denoted as follows:

$$\bar{x} = \frac{\sum\limits_{i=1}^{N} x_i}{N}$$

or

$$\bar{x} = \frac{x_1 + x_2 + x_3 + x_4 + \ldots + x_N}{N}$$

Where, N = number of observations

x = data value

Σ = *the summation of*

■ **In Practice**

Calculate the mean of the following data set:

{4, 9, 6, 8}

Solution:

The number of observations is 4 because there are four numbers.

$$\text{mean} = \bar{x} = \frac{4+9+6+8}{4} = 6.75$$

Median

The **median** is the middle value in an array of numbers. This middle value has an equal number of values above and below it. In other words, half of the array will have values less than or equal to the median and half of the array will have values equal to or greater than the median. To find the median of a data set, arrange all the observations from lowest value to highest value or from highest value to lowest value, creating an array, and pick the middle one. If there is an even number of observations, calculate the mean of the two middle values.

For example: The median of the previously described array is $390,000.

$450,000

$395,000

$390,000

→ **$390,000**

$389,000

$380,000

$375,000

Adding an observation of $370,000 to this array changes the median to $389,500.

$450,000

$395,000

$390,000

→ **$390,000**
$$\left.\begin{array}{c} \\ \\ \end{array}\right\} \quad \frac{\$390,000 + \$389,000}{2} = \$389,500$$
→ **$389,000**

$380,000

$375,000

$370,000

Mode

The **mode** is the most frequently occurring number in an array. There is no formula to learn; simply choose the number that appears most frequently in the data set or array. For example, the mode of the following array is $390,000.

$450,000

$395,000

→ **$390,000**

→ **$390,000**

$389,000

$380,000

$375,000

$370,000

In this array, $390,000 appears twice, while the other values only appear once.

If a data set has two modes, it is called a **bimodal** data set. Some data sets do not have modes. For example, the following data set does not have a mode because each data value only appears once.

{65, 75, 98, 101, 200}

■ **In Practice**

Calculate the mean, median, and mode of the following data set, which represents the annual rent per square foot of a sample of office building rents.

{$23, $19, $18, $24, $25, $20, $23}

Solution:

■ First, arrange the data set into an array (arranging in descending or ascending order).

1. $18
2. $19
3. $20
4. $23
5. $23
6. $24
7. $25   ·

■ Then, calculate the mean:

$$\text{mean} = \bar{x} = \frac{18 + 19 + 20 + 23 + 23 + 24 + 25}{7} = 21.71$$

The mean is, therefore, $22 annual rent per square foot, *rounded*.

■ Next, find the median:

$18

$19

$20

→ **$23**

$23

$24

$25

The median is the middle value. In this case, the median is $23 annual rent per square foot.

- Finally, find the mode:

    $18

    $19

    $20

    → **$23**

    → **$23**

    $24

    $25

The mode is $23 annual rent per square foot because it appears twice.

Notice that the mean is $22, the median is $23, and the mode is $23. When studying the distribution of all three measures of central tendency, whether or not they are all equal in value has great significance.

OUTLIERS

Within a data set, an **outlier** is a single observation that is extremely different than the rest of the other numbers in a data set. For example, consider the following data set, which represents the annual rent per square foot of a sample of retail units.

{$14, $12, $15, $13, $37, $13, $14, $11}

To include the $37 annual rent per square foot (the outlier) would bring up the sample mean to $16 annual rent per square foot (rounded); however, not a single observation in the data set is equal to $16 annual rent per square foot. Without the outlier, the mean is reduced to $13 annual rent per square foot. Outliers can be an indication of either faulty data or an error in the sampling process. It is important to note that even if the outlier is a legitimate number, since it lies so far away from most of the data, it can cause computational and inference errors. In this example, perhaps the $37 annual rent per square foot represents the rent for a very small retail unit relative to the rest of the retail units within the sample. Economy of scale dictates that if you have two units of equal utility, condition, location, etc., the smaller unit will rent for more dollars per square foot than the larger unit. Therefore, the sampling process should be reviewed and the actual size of the retail units within the sample should be more similar to each other.

One way to deal with an outlier is to delete it from the sample data set completely. This, however, should be the last resort, and only considered when the outlier is very far away from the rest of the data, as in the case of the previous data set. There is a shortcoming to just deleting the outlier. For example, perhaps the outlier is representative of a developing trend within the marketplace. In this example, after additional samples of more recent data were taken, rents closer to $37 annual rent per square foot might be uncovered, thereby indicating an upward trend in market rents.

Another option would be to keep the outlier and perform the analysis with and without it, noticing and noting the differences in the results.

It is clear that checking for any unusual data values (outliers) and investigating the probable cause should be a regular part of the data collection process. Your thorough knowledge of the appraisal assignment and the market that you are analyzing will dictate what you will do with them once you find them.

Selecting a Measure of Central Tendency

It is prudent to review the strength and weakness of each measure of central tendency before selecting a measure to represent a population. For example, while the mean is the most frequently used measure, it does have its drawbacks.

- Mean vs. Median and Mode

  The mean is sometimes preferred because it uses every observation in the data set; however, using the median or mode is more accurate when there are extreme values (outliers) in the data set. Using the mean when there are outliers distorts what should be considered a typical result. The median and the mode are insensitive to outliers. However, there is a risk when using the mode, if the mode happens to be an outlier.

- Mode vs. Mean and Median

  While the mode is the weakest measurement, it makes sense for **nominal data**, which is data that does not consist of numerical values. For example, taking a sample of American names for baby boys, the name that appears most frequently may be Michael. The mode would then be the name Michael.

  Another appropriate use of the mode is to paint a more realistic picture. For example, a sample consisting of the number of bedrooms per single-family home may have a mean of 2.5, a median of 3.5, and a mode of 3. Using the three bedrooms as representative of what is typical is more desirable than using 2.5 bedrooms or 3.5 bedrooms.

MEASURES OF VARIABILITY

The concept of comparing individual data set values to a distribution of data set values is fundamental to statistics. In addition to the measures of central tendency, which only uncover the center of distribution, other measures are used to describe data. *Variability* refers to how individual values in a data set differ from each other. **Measures of variability** measure how spread out values in a data set are, in other words, whether or not values cluster around the mean or median or are scattered. Three frequently used measures of variability are *range, variance,* and *standard deviation.*

Range

The simplest and most obvious measure of variation is the *range*. **Range** is simply the difference between the largest and the smallest values in a data set. However, range only measures the most varied values of the data set.

For example, the following is an array indicating sales prices of seven two-bedroom homes:

$250,000

$200,000

$192,000

$190,000

$188,000

$185,000

$160,000

The highest sales price is $250,000 and the lowest is $160,000; therefore, the range is **$90,000** ($250,000 – $160,000).

■ **In Practice**

Determine the range of the following data set:

{56, 44, 63, 60, 42, 52, 56, 51}

Solution:

First arrange the data set into an array.

42

44

51

52

56

56

60

63

The highest number is 63 and the lowest number is 42, so the range is 21 (63 – 42).

Variance

Variance is a measure of how spread out a distribution is, a measure of the dispersion of a data set around the mean. To calculate the variance, calculate the sum of the squares of the differences (deviations) from the mean, and then divide by the total number of observations minus 1.

$$\text{Variance} = s^2 = \frac{\sum_{i=1}^{N}(x_i - \overline{x})^2}{N-1}$$

Where N = number of observations

x = data value

Σ = *the summation of*

$\overline{x}$ = sample mean

Note that the $N - 1$ in the denominator is used when computing the *sample* variance. When computing the *population* variance, use N alone in the denominator.

Computing the variance by dividing by N, instead of $N - 1$, gives an underestimate of the population variance because the sample mean is an estimate of the population mean, which is unknown. In practice, for a large N, the distinction is often a minor one.

For example, using the array in the range example calculate the variance.

■ First calculate the mean.

$$42$$

$$44$$

$$51$$

$$52$$

$$56$$

$$56$$

$$60$$

$$\underline{63}$$

Total   424

$$\text{mean} = (424 \div 8) = 53$$

■ Next, calculate the deviations from the mean for each observation. Square them and then total them.

Deviations from the mean	Squares of deviations from the mean
$(42 - 53) = -11$	$(42 - 53)^2 = (-11)^2 = 121$
$(44 - 53) = -9$	$(44 - 53)^2 = (-9)^2 = 81$
$(51 - 53) = -2$	$(51 - 53) = (-2)^2 = 4$
$(52 - 53) = -1$	$(52 - 53)^2 = (-1)^2 = 1$
$(56 - 53) = 3$	$(56 - 53)^2 = (3)^2 = 9$
$(56 - 53) = 3$	$(56 - 53)^2 = (3)^2 = 9$
$(60 - 53) = 7$	$(60 - 53)^2 = (7)^2 = 49$
$(63 - 53) = 10$	$(63 - 53)^2 = (10)^2 = \underline{100}$

374

■ Finally, divide the total squares of deviations from the mean by the number of observations minus 1.

$$\text{Variance} = (374 \div 7) = 53.4$$

Standard Deviation

Standard deviation is another statistical measure of the dispersion or variability in a distribution. Standard deviation is the square root of the arithmetic mean of the squares of the deviations from the sample mean. Simply put, it is the square root of the variance of a data set. It measures how spread out the values in a data set are. The more spread apart the data is, the higher the deviation, hence a less reliable sample. Another way of thinking of standard deviation is as a measure of uncertainty.

The square root of the variance provides the standard deviation ($\sqrt{s^2}$).

$$s = \sqrt{\frac{\sum_{i=1}^{N}(x_i - \bar{x})^2}{N-1}}$$

For example, the standard deviation of the previous data set is the square root of the variance = $\sqrt{s^2} = \sqrt{53.4} = 7.3$.

For a single data set (i.e., a data set of only one unit of comparison), the standard deviation does not tell us much. However, comparing the standard deviation of two or more data sets (units of comparisons) can reveal the reliability of using one unit of comparison compared to the other. A *unit of comparison* is a per-unit indicator. In other words, if the standard deviation of the price per square foot is greater than the standard deviation of the price per front foot, this indicates that the price per front foot data values are clustered (less scattered) about their mean. This allows for a more accurate prediction of what is typical in the market (population). The price per front foot will also have a lower *coefficient of variance* (COV), as discussed further in this lesson.

Properties of Variance and Standard Deviation

The variance and the standard deviation are always positive numbers. If all of the data values in a data set are equal, there is no variability and the variance and the standard deviation will equal 0. Similar to the arithmetic mean, variance and standard deviation use every observation, including outliers.

A larger standard deviation indicates that the data values are far from the mean, while a smaller standard deviation indicates that they are clustered closely around the mean and are, therefore, a more reliable indicator.

Coefficient of Variance (COV)

Coefficient of variance (COV) of a sample is the ratio of the standard deviation to the mean. It is a dimensionless number (that is, it has no physical unit associated with it) that can be used to compare the amount of variance between populations or samples. The COV is the degree to which a set of data points vary. The coefficient of variance is an important measure of reliability. The *larger* this number is, the *greater* the variability in your data. When assessing precision, the *smaller* the COV, the *better* the precision, thus the more reliable predictor of the *dependent variable*. The formula of the COV follows:

$$COV = \frac{S}{\bar{x}}$$

Where   S = standard deviation

$\bar{x}$ = the sample mean

The COV can also be displayed as a percentage. Using the preceding example, divide the standard deviation of 7.9 by the sample mean of 53.

$$COV = \frac{7.9}{53} = 0.15 \text{ or } 15\%$$

The result is a coefficient of variance of 0.15 or 15 percent.

As mentioned earlier, the COV is a useful tool to determine the reliability of data collected when comparing one set of data (unit of comparison) to another. For example, suppose two different data sets are collected from a sample. By calculating the COV, we can determine which of the two units of comparison is the most reliable indicator of value. The more reliable indicator of value will be the data set with the COV closest to zero.

Once it is established which of the two units of comparison is the more reliable, the mean of that data set (the mean of the unit of comparison) is then applied to the subject, resulting in an estimate of the dependent variable. The dependent variable in this case, of course, is the value of the subject.

For example, an appraiser seeks to determine what the more reliable indicator of value is for the subject, which is a 2,800-square-foot three-unit apartment building. Data was collected from a sample of five apartment

FIGURE A.7
Sample of Five Apartment Buildings

Sale Number	Sales Price	Gross Building Area (Sq. Ft.)	Sales Price per Square Foot, Rounded	Number of Units	Sales Price per Unit
1	$300,000	2,500	$120	3	$100,000
2	$325,000	3,000	$108	4	$81,250
3	$330,000	3,000	$110	4	$82,500
4	$358,000	3,600	$99	5	$71,600
5	$360,000	3,600	$100	5	$72,000

buildings, all with various gross building areas and unit counts. Each data set represents a different unit of comparison; in this case, the sales price per square foot and the sales price per apartment unit.

- First, arrange the *price per square foot* data set into an array and calculate the mean.

99

100

108

110

$\underline{120}$

Total = 537

Mean = (537 ÷ 5) = \$107

- Next, calculate the deviations from the mean for each observation, square them, and then total them.

Deviations from the mean	Squares of deviations from the mean
(99 – 107) = -8	(99 – 107)^2 = (-8)^2 = 64
(100 – 107) = -7	(100 – 107)^2 = (-7)^2 = 49
(108 – 107) = 1	(108 – 107)^2 = (1)^2 = 1
(110 – 107) = 3	(110 – 107)^2 = (3)^2 = 9
(120 – 107) = 13	(120 – 107)^2 = (13)^2 = $\underline{169}$
	292

- Next, divide the total squares of deviations from the mean by the number of observations minus 1.

variance = s^2 = (292 ÷ 4) = 73

- Next, calculate the square root of the variance, which results in the standard deviation $(\sqrt{s^2})$ = $\sqrt{73}$ = 8.5

- Then, calculate the coefficient of variance (COV) by dividing the standard deviation by the sample mean:

COV = (8.5 ÷ 107) = 0.079439

Note: Sometimes COVs can be very small numbers; therefore, it is best to set your calculator to six decimal points.

- Arrange the *price per unit* data set into an array and calculate the mean.

71,600

72,000

81,250

82,500

100,000
_____

Total = 407,350

mean = (407,350 ÷ 5) = $81,470

- Calculate the deviations from the mean for each observation, square them, and then total them.

Deviations from the mean	Squares of deviations from the mean
(71,600 – 81,470) = -9,870	(71,600 – 81,470)² = (-9,870)² = 97,416,900
(72,000 – 81,470) = -9,470	(72,000 – 81,470)² = (-9,470)² = 89,680,900
(81,250 – 81,470) = -220	(81,250 – 81,470)² = (-220)² = 48,400
(82,500 – 81,470) = 1,030	(82,500 – 81,470)² = (1,030)² = 1,060,900
(100,000 – 81,470) = 18,530	(100,000 – 81,470)² = (18,530)² = 343,360,900
	531,568,000

- Next, divide the total squares of deviations from the mean by the number of observations minus 1.

variance = s^2 = (531,568,000 ÷ 4) = 132,892,000

- Then, calculate the square root of the variance, which results in the standard deviation.

$$(\sqrt{s^2}) = \sqrt{132,892,000} = 11,527.9$$

- Finally, calculate the coefficient of variance (COV) by dividing the standard deviation by the sample mean.

COV = (11,527.9 ÷ 81,470) = 0.141499

It is clear that the coefficient of variance for the sales price per square foot is much closer to zero than the coefficient of variance for the sales price per unit (0.079439 versus 0.141499). Therefore, price per square foot is the more reliable indicator of value. To estimate the value of the subject, simply multiply the mean of the price per square foot by the square footage of the subject.

$$\$107 \times 2{,}800 \text{ sq. ft.} = \$299{,}600$$

It should be obvious by now that calculating the COV can be a very lengthy process. Using a calculator to determine the standard deviation and mean reduces this time to a matter of seconds.

Weighted Average

The **weighted average** is a method of computing an arithmetic mean of a set of numbers in which some of the elements of the set carry more weight (importance) than others. Each element is assigned a weight factor depending upon its relative position to the others in the data set. Use the following steps to compute weighted averages:

1. Multiply the element by its weight
2. Add up the products of the element multiplied by its weight to arrive at total value
3. Add the weights themselves to get a total weight
4. Divide the total value by the total weight

For example, suppose a data set contains the final adjusted sales price of three comparable sales:

Sale 1:	$330,000
Sale 2:	$310,000
Sale 3:	$308,000

While performing the sales comparison approach, the appraiser may feel that comparable sale 1 was the *most* similar to the subject, requiring the least amount of adjustments. That appraiser would then give the greatest weight to sale 1.

Sale 1:	$330,000 × 10 = $3,300,000
Sale 2:	$310,000 × 5 = $1,550,000
Sale 3:	$308,000 × 5 = $1,540,000
Total	20 $6,390,000

Weighted average = $6,390,000 ÷ 20 = $319,500

In this example, sale 2 and sale 3 are given the same weight because they are of equal importance.

Rather than choosing an arbitrary number like 20, weight factors can be expressed as percentages as long as the aggregate of all assigned weights adds up to 100 percent. Applying percentage weights to the previous example will result in the same outcome. Note, just as in the previous example, the weight assigned to sale 1 is twice that of the weight assigned to each sale 2 and sale 3.

Sale 1:	$330,000 × 0.50 =	$165,000
Sale 2:	$310,000 × 0.25 =	$77,500
Sale 3:	$308,000 × 0.25 =	$77,000
Total		= $319,500

Rather than simply using the arithmetic mean of $316,000, the weighted average can then be used, as it may be more representative of what is typical of the population (the ultimate goal). The language used in the reconciliation of the sales comparison approach might then include words like, "Comparable sale 1 was given greatest weight, as it is most similar to the subject."

Appraisers use statistics to support assumptions made about a market that eventually lead to an estimate of value. The appraiser needs to choose the relevant information in order to draw valid inferences from the sample to the population being studied. The use of measures of central tendency in conjunction with measures of variability enables the appraiser to derive logical conclusions about a population (market) based on information that is known to be true about a sample. This lesson's discussion of statistical techniques was a brief overview. A more thorough study of statistical techniques is beyond the scope of this text; however, advanced texts, courses, and software are available.

GRAPHICAL REPRESENTATION

In statistical analysis, the data collected can be made more understandable by the use of visuals. The data can be displayed pictorially with the use of graphic displays, such as *bar charts, scatter charts,* and *frequency histograms.*

For example, Figure A.8 shows relevant data collected from a sample of six three-bedroom one-story homes that have various gross living areas and that have sold within the last six months.

FIGURE A.8
Sample of Six Homes Sold in the Last Six Months

Sale Number	Sales Price	Gross Living Area (Sq. Ft.)
1	$230,000	1,400
2	$245,000	1,555
3	$258,000	1,800
4	$263,000	1,955
5	$280,000	2,220
6	$292,000	2,400

This data can displayed using a vertical **bar chart** (see Figure A.9) or a horizontal bar chart (see Figure A.10).

This bar chart shows that the home with 2,400 square feet of gross living area sold for the highest price.

When the goal is to display the relationship between two different elements, a **scatter plot** should be used. For example, the information gathered from the sample of six single-family one-story home sales can be displayed pictorially using a scatter plot (see Figure A.11).

When an appraiser has collected information from a sample, it is necessary to construct a scatter plot in order to determine if there is a relationship

FIGURE A.9
Vertical Bar Chart

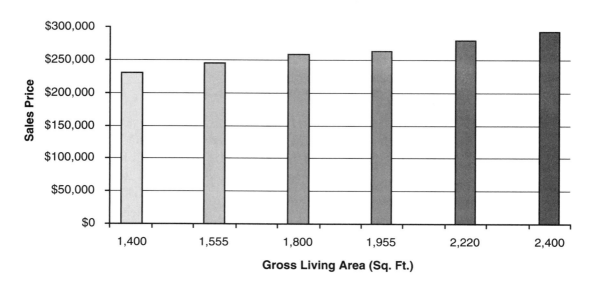

FIGURE A.10
Horizontal Bar Chart

between two elements and, if so, whether it is a positive or a negative relationship. It is obvious that the points on the scatter plot indicate a *positive* relationship between the gross living area (GLA) expressed in square feet and the sales price. In other words, as the gross living area increases, so does the sales price.

FIGURE A.11
Scatter Plot

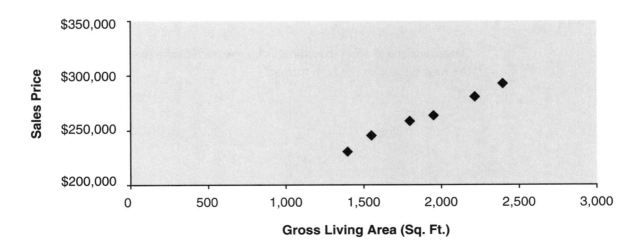

FIGURE A.12
Plot of Cartesian Coordinates (4,3)

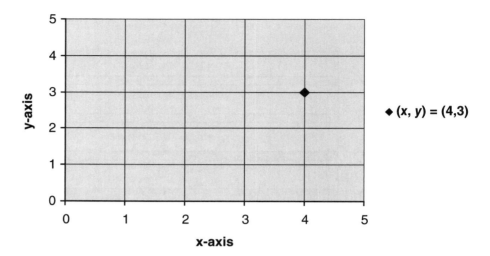

PLOTTING POINTS ON A GRAPH

To understand correlation and regression analysis, it is important first to understand the concept of graphing of data points (x- and y-coordinates). Figure A.12 shows a horizontal axis **(x-axis)** and a vertical axis **(y-axis).** The point shown in this figure has an **x-coordinate** of 4, because it is in line with the 4 on the x-axis, and a **y-coordinate** of 3, because it is in line with the 3 on the y-axis. Simply stated, $x = 4$ and $y = 3$, which can be abbreviated to (x,y) or (4,3).

These x and y coordinates are often referred to as the *Cartesian coordinates.* The French philosopher and mathematician René Descartes introduced this system of specifying a point by using two intersecting axes as measuring guides. This system is known as the **Cartesian coordinate system**.

■ **In Practice**

Determine the x- and y-coordinates for the each of the labeled six points shown on the next page. Use the (x, y) format.

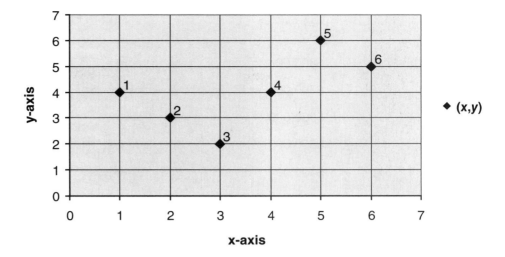

Solution:

Data point 1: (1,4)

Data point 2: (2,3)

Data point 3: (3,2)

Data point 4: (4,4)

Data point 5: (5,6)

Data point 6: (6,5)

■ **In Practice**

Plot the following x- and y-coordinates:

Square Feet (x-coordinate)	Sales Price (y-coordinate)
2,000	$230,000
3,000	$300,000
4,000	$400,000
5,000	$450,000
6,000	$500,000
7,000	$550,000

Square Feet vs. Sales Price

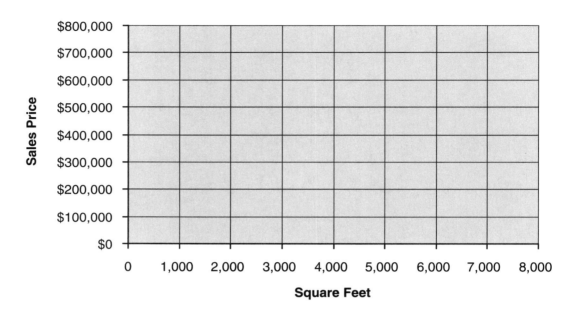

Solution:

Square Feet vs. Sales Price

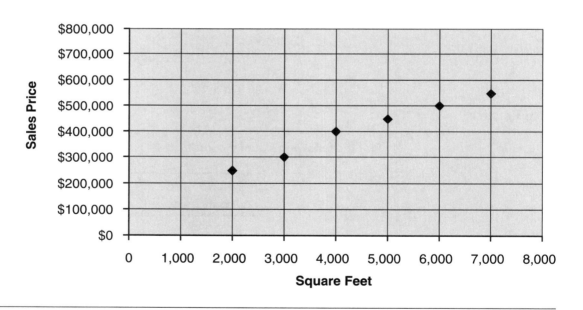

FREQUENCY HISTOGRAM

The *frequency histogram* is a commonly used graphical representation in statistics. A **frequency histogram** is essentially a bar chart that depicts how many observations are in each numerical category. The numerical categories are ordered smallest to largest and are referred to as **class intervals.** For example, after taking a sample of sales prices of three-bedroom homes within a particular market, you want to determine how many homes sold within a particular price category.

To chart a frequency histogram, first place the data set (sales prices) into an array.

$210,000

$215,000

$225,000

$239,000

$241,000

$242,000

$245,000

$248,000

$249,000

$250,000

$251,000

$258,000

$260,000

$260,000

$267,000

$277,000

$305,000

$306,000

$308,000

$320,000

$337,000

$347,000

$355,000

$368,000

$392,000

Next, categorize the sales prices into class intervals, making sure that you do not overlap data. In other words, no data value should fall into two class intervals.

Sales Price (Class Intervals)
$200,000–$250,000
$251,000–$300,000
$301,000–$350,000
$351,000–$400,000

Next, make a table showing the distribution of your data. The number of observations within each class interval is referred to as the **class frequency.**

Number of Homes (Class Frequency)	Sales Price (Class Intervals)
10	$200,000–$250,000
6	$251,000–$300,000
6	$301,000–$350,000
3	$351,000–$400,000

Finally, create a frequency histogram placing the class intervals on the horizontal axis (x-axis) and the class frequencies of occurrence on the vertical axis (y-axis). (See Figure A.13.)

The height of the individual bars of a frequency histogram represents the number of homes that sold within each sales price range (class interval). A histogram is a more interesting organizational summary of a data set than a table is. Histograms show the breakdown of numerical data and are very useful when used to compare one group or time period to another. However, histograms can be misleading if the scales for both the x-axis and y-axis are not in proportion. For example, using a smaller scale on the vertical axis (y-axis) of a histogram will exaggerate the differences. Conversely, using a larger scale on the vertical axis (y-axis) will minimize the differences. Additionally, how the data is categorized into class intervals will affect the appearance of the histogram.

FIGURE A.13
Frequency Histogram

FREQUENCY DISTRIBUTIONS

Frequency distributions use a smooth curve to connect data points on a graph. Like the frequency histogram, the class intervals are placed on the horizontal axis (x-axis) and the class frequencies of occurrence are placed on the vertical axis (y-axis). (See Figure A.14.)

Skewness of a Frequency Distribution

The mean, mode, and median not only convey useful information about the central tendencies, but also about the *skewness* of a frequency distribution. **Skewness** is a measure of symmetry or lack of symmetry. A histogram is an effective graphical representation of skewness of a data set. The distribution

FIGURE A.14
Symmetric Data in a Histogram

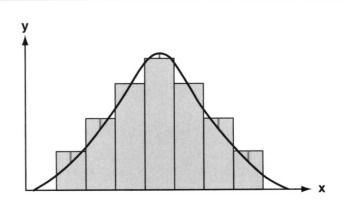

FIGURE A.15
Symmetric Distribution: Mode = Mean = Median

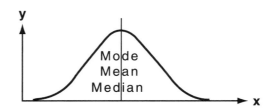

of a data set is symmetrical if it looks the same to the left and to the right of the central data point.

If a frequency distribution is symmetrical, then the smooth curve forms a bell-shaped curve. The bell-shaped curve that is formed with symmetrical distribution is also referred to as a *normal distribution*. A **normal distribution** of data means that most of the data set values are close to the mean. If the data is perfectly *symmetrical* (no skew), then the mean, median, and mode are all equal (see Figure A.15).

The more skewed a distribution is, the more different the measures of central tendencies are from each other. A *positively skewed* distribution has a longer tail to the right, meaning that the data set has outliers on the upper end. The mode is less than the median, which is less than the mean (see Figure A.16).

A *negatively skewed* distribution has a longer tail to the left, meaning that the data set has outliers toward the lower end. With a negatively skewed distribution, the mean is less than the median, which is less than the mode (see Figure A.17).

A bimodal distribution has two peaks (see Figure A.18). In other words, the data set has two modes (bimodal). A bimodal distribution may be indicative of an incorrect sampling process. The sample may not be homogenous, and the statistical inference may be for two different populations. For example,

FIGURE A.16
Positively Skewed Distribution: Mode < Median < Mean

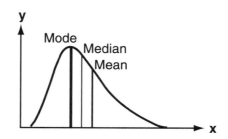

FIGURE A.17
Negatively Skewed Distribution: Mean < Median < Mode

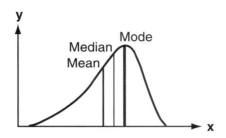

a sample of sales prices of two-bedroom homes taken from a population of home sales occurring over one year's time. The sample may be bimodal, which can indicate that the time frame should be lessened, because the most frequent sales price (mode) during such a long period of time probably changed.

Normal Distribution

Normal distribution plays a key role in the theory and practice of statistical inference. Remember that as an appraiser you take samples with the hope that you can make inferences about the population.

Properties of a Normal Curve   A normal curve tells us how far a sample is likely to be from the population. The properties of a normal curve help determine the relative standing of a particular result in the distribution. A discussion of the properties of a normal curve follows.

The shape of the curve is symmetrical with a bump in the middle and two tails off to the left and right. The curve is symmetrical because each half of the curve is the mirror image of the other half. The mean and the median are of equal value and are the center points where half of the data lie on either side.

FIGURE A.18
Bimodal Distribution

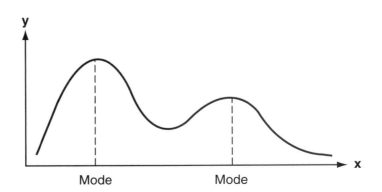

FIGURE A.19
The Empirical Rule

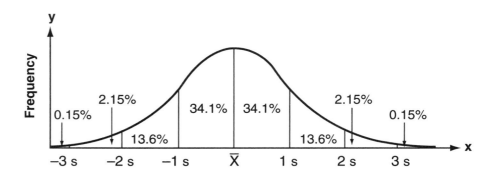

When looking at distribution, the variability of the distribution is also important. Recall from Lesson 1 of this section that the standard deviation is a statistical measure of the variability in a distribution. The standard deviation (s or $\sqrt{s^2}$) tells us how tightly all of the values in a data set are clustered around the mean. When the data values are closer to the mean, the bell will be steep and the standard deviation will be small, and when the data values are less clustered (more scattered) around the mean, the bell curve will be relatively flatter and the standard deviation will be relatively larger. With a normal distribution, the standard deviation has special significance because of the empirical rule. The **empirical rule** measures the spread of data using the mean and the standard deviation in a normal distribution using distances of 1, 2, or 3 standard deviations from the mean to mark off milestones (see Figure A.19). The empirical rule states that the area under the normal curve represents that

- 68% of the data falls within 1 standard deviation of the mean,

- 95% of the data falls within 2 standard deviations of the mean, and

- 99.7% of the data falls within 3 standard deviations of the mean.

You can use the properties of a normal curve, the symmetry of the normal distribution, and the empirical rule to formulate opinions about your sample. For example, if the sample mean and median of your sample of sales prices of two-bedroom homes within a specific market are both $230,000 and the standard deviation of the sample was calculated at $4,933, using the empirical rule, you can say the following:

- 68% of sold two-bedroom homes will sell for between $225,067 and $234,933 [$230,000 +/− (1 standard deviation × $4,933)].

- 95% of sold two-bedroom homes will sell for between $221,202 and $239,866 [$230,000 +/− (2 standard deviations × $4,933)].

- 99.7% of sold two-bedroom homes will sell for between $215,201 and $244,799 [$230,000 +/− (3 standard deviations × $4,933)].

Based on this information, you can answer the following questions:

1. What percentage of sold two-bedroom homes will have sales prices of $230,000 or more?

    Answer: 50%, since the median is $230,000 and half of the sales prices are greater than the median.

2. What percentage of sold two-bedroom homes will have sales prices of $239,866 or more?

    Answer: 2.5%, because 95% of the two-bedroom home sales are between $221,202 and $239,866, and given that the total area under the curve is equal to 100%, the area under the remaining two tails is equal to 5%. Sales prices of $239,866 represent only one side of the tail, the positive side, so dividing the 5% by 2 results in 2.5%.

Most analysts stay with the 95% range when reporting their results, since going out 3 standard deviations on either side of the mean represents only a small percentage of the data. It is important to remember that the results using the empirical rule are rounded and are approximations only.

LESSON 3 REVIEW QUESTIONS

1. A(n) _____ standard deviation indicates that the data values are far from the mean, while a(n) _____ standard deviation indicates that they are clustered closely around the mean and are, therefore, a more reliable indicator.

2. Extreme values in a data set are referred to as
   a. ranges.
   b. outliers.
   c. means.
   d. medians.

3. Standard deviation is simply the square root of the _____.

4. A(n) _____ is a data set that has been organized according to size.

5. The difference between the largest and the smallest values in a data set is the
   a. outlier.
   b. mean.
   c. median.
   d. range.

6. The range, variance, and standard deviation are measures of
   a. variance.
   b. central tendency.
   c. variability.
   d. deviations.

7. Calculate the mean, median, and mode of the following data set of a sample containing price per square foot:

   {$156, $125, $177, $124, $125, $170, $150}

8. Calculate the sample variance and sample standard deviations of the following data set:

   {11, 15, 16, 20, 23}

9. A sample is a subset of a(n) _____.

10. A parameter is a characteristic of a(n) _____.

11. _____ is a preconceived opinion.

12. Dividing an entire population into clusters is an example of
    a. random sampling.
    b. stratified sampling.
    c. systematic sampling.
    d. cluster sampling.

13. Choosing every tenth member of a population is an example of
    a. random sampling.
    b. stratified sampling.
    c. systematic sampling.
    d. cluster sampling.

14. Grouping a population into stratums is an example of
    a. random sampling.
    b. stratified sampling.
    c. systematic sampling.
    d. cluster sampling.

15. The mean, median, and mode are common measures of
    a. variance.
    b. central tendency.
    c. variability.
    d. deviations.

16. Determine the range of the following data set:

    {66, 55, 77, 66, 52, 80}

17. A statistic is a characteristic of a(n) _____.

18. A(n) _____ is often too large to measure.

19. When comparing two different units of comparison, the one with the coefficient of variance closest to zero is the _least/more_ reliable indicator of value.

20. The formula for the coefficient of variance (COV) is
    a. standard deviation ÷ sample mean.
    b. sample mean ÷ variance.
    c. sample mean squared.
    d. square root of the variance.

21. The horizontal axis is called the ___-axis.

22. The vertical axis represents the _____-axis.

23. These x- and y-coordinates are often referred to as the _____ coordinates.

24. Identify these two sets of x-coordinates and y-coordinates. Use the (x,y) format.

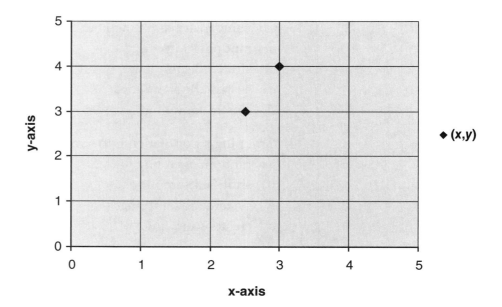

25. Graph the following four sets of x- and y-coordinates:

(2,2), (1,3), (4.5,4), (3,5)

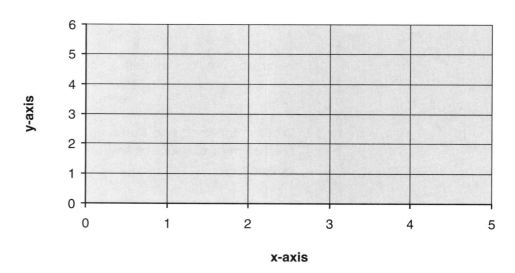

26. Similar to a bar chart, the _____ depicts how many observations are in each numerical category.

27. A numerical category is known as a(n) _____ interval.

28. The number of observations within each class interval is referred to as the class _____.

29. When a frequency distribution is negatively skewed, the mode is _____ than the median and mean.

30. When a frequency distribution is positively skewed, the mode is _____ than the median and mean.

31. The _____ (s or $\sqrt{s^2}$) tells us how tightly all of values in a data set are clustered around the mean.

32. The _____ measures the spread of data using the mean and the standard deviation in a normal distribution

33. The empirical rule states that _____% of the data falls within 1 standard deviation of the mean.

34. The empirical rule states that _____% of the data falls within 2 standard deviations of the mean.

LESSON 3 REVIEW ANSWERS

1. larger; smaller

2. b

3. variance

4. array

5. d

6. c

7. $124
   125
   125
   150
   156
   170
   <u>177</u>
   $1,027

mean = ($1,027 ÷ 7) = 147, *rounded*

median = 150

mode = 125

8. {11, 15, 16, 20, 23}, mean = (85 ÷ 5) = 17

Squares of deviations from the mean

$(11 - 17)^2 = (-6)^2 \quad = 36$

$(15 - 17)^2 = (-2)^2 \quad = 4$

$(16 - 17)^2 = (-1)^2 \quad = 1$

$(20 - 17)^2 = (3)^2 \quad = 9$

$(23 - 17)^2 = (6)^2 \quad = \underline{36}$

86

Divide the total squares of deviations from the mean by the number of observations minus 1.

Variance = (86 ÷ 4) = 21.5, standard deviation = $\sqrt{21.5}$ = 4.6

9. population

10. population

11. Bias

12. d

13. c

14. c

15. b

16. range = (80 − 52) = 28

17. sample

18. population

19. more

20. a

21. x

22. y

23. Cartesian

24. (2.5,3) and (3,4)

25.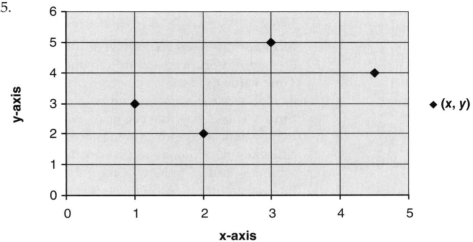

26. frequency histogram

27. class

28. frequency

29. greater

30. less

31. standard deviation

32. empirical rule

33. 68

34. 95

LESSON 4: Mathematics of Finance

TIME VALUE OF MONEY

Most appraisal assignments require the use of the income approach; therefore, appraisers need a thorough understanding of the time value of money. **Time value of money** is the core principle of finance that holds that money available at the present time is worth more than the same amount in the future. This is possible because of money's earning capacity. For example, money deposited into a savings account will earn interest. Therefore, a specific amount of money received today is more desirable than receiving that same amount of money in the future. Time value of money results from the concept of interest. *Interest* is the cost of using someone else's money. It is a charge for borrowing money, usually expressed as a percentage of the amount borrowed *(principal)*. There are two types of interest: *simple interest* and *compound interest*.

Simple Interest and Compound Interest

Simple interest is interest earned on the principal only, not including any annual accrued (accumulated) interest. For example, if you were to earn 5% annual interest on an original amount of $100, over the next five years, your interest earned would be calculated as follows:

Year 1: 5% × $100.00 = 0.05 × $100 = $5 in interest for a total of $105

Year 2: 5% × $100.00 = 0.05 × $100 = $5 in interest for a total of $110

Year 3: 5% × $100.00 = 0.05 × $100 = $5 in interest for a total of $115

Year 4: 5% × $100.00 = 0.05 × $100 = $5 in interest for a total of $120

Year 5: 5% × $100.00 = 0.05 × $100 = $5 in interest for a total of $125

Compound interest is interest computed on the original principal plus any accrued interest. For example, if you earn 5% compound interest on an original amount of $100, over the next five years, your interest earned would be calculated as follows:

Year 1: 5% × $100.00 = 0.05 × $100.00 = $5 in interest for a total of $105.00

Year 2: 5% × $105.00 = 0.05 × $105.00 = $5.25 in interest for a total of $110.25

Year 3: 5% × $110.25 = 0.05 × $110.25 = $5.51 in interest for a total of $115.76

Year 4: 5% × $115.76 = 0.05 × $115.76 = $5.79 in interest for a total of $121.55

Year 5: 5% × $121.55 = 0.05 × $121.55 = $6.08 in interest for a total of $127.63

From these two examples, it is obvious that at the end of year 5 the total accumulated amount is greater when computed using compound interest rather than simple interest.

The most important component of compound interest is the compounding period. The **compounding period** is the interval at which interest is actually paid. It is the length of time that elapses before interest compounds. The interval can be annually, quarterly, monthly, or daily. In the previous example, the compounding period is annually. At the end of the first interval, the interest is calculated and then added to the principal. With compound interest, at the end of all subsequent intervals, the interest is calculated on the principal plus interest from previous intervals. Compound interest may be calculated either at the beginning of each interval or at the end of each interval.

Compounding and Discounting

Compounding is the financial concept of converting today's money into an equivalent amount at some time in the future, a **future value.** The future value consists of the principal amount, plus any accrued interest. Compounding assumes that earned interest is reinvested and continues to earn interest over the time period. **Discounting** is the financial concept of converting an estimated future income into a **present value** using a **discount rate.** Discounting an expected future cash flow is the basis of the income approach. Simply stated, it is the present value of a future benefit. The compounding and discounting processes involve four variables:

1. The time period
2. The interest rate
3. The future value (expected future cash flow)
4. The present value

In order to calculate any one of these variables, the other three variables need to be known.

In the preceding compound interest example, three variables were known:

1. Time period: 5 years
2. Interest rate: 5%
3. Present value: $100

Hint: For greater accuracy, set your calculator to six decimal points.

SIX FUNCTIONS OF A DOLLAR

Compound Factors and Discount Factors

There are six basic time value of money factors, known as the **six functions of a dollar**. Published tables with factors of all six functions of a dollar can be used. These tables are known as **Ellwood tables**, named after the late L.W. Ellwood. Ellwood tables were based on the six functions of a dollar formulas and were widely used prior to the modern financial calculator. Table A.1 shows factors for a 10% annual interest rate, compounded annually (compound interval of one year) over time periods from 1 year to 50 years.

To use a published table, the dollar amount being considered, whether the amount is loaned, borrowed, or invested, is multiplied by the appropriate factor in order to arrive at the present value or future value.

The six columns contain factors for each function of a dollar. Each function of a dollar can also be expressed mathematically. Following is a discussion of all six functions of a dollar, their factors, and the associated mathematical formulas.

1. Column 1: **Future value of $1**—The future value of one dollar is the amount that $1 can grow to over a specific period of time. For example, at the end of 5 years, $1 compounded annually (at the end of each year) at a 10% annual interest rate will grow to $1.61; $1 × 1.610510. (See column 1 of Table A.1.)

    Formula: Future value of $1 = $(1 + i)^n$

    Where, i = interest rate

    n = number of time periods

    Using the same example:

    $(1 + 0.10)^5 = (1.10)^5 = 1.610510$; $1 × 1.610510 = $1.61

2. Column 2: **Future value annuity of $1 per year**—The future value of one dollar per period (*annuity*) is the amount that constant periodic investment of $1 can grow to over a specific period of time. An **annuity** is a level stream of cash flow for a fixed period of time. For example, at the end of 5 years $1 invested at the end of every year compounded annually at a 10% annual interest rate will grow to $6.11; $1 × 6.105100. (See column 2 of Table A.1.)

    Formula: Future value of $1 per period = $\dfrac{(1 + i)^n - 1}{i}$

    Where, i = interest rate

    n = number of time periods

TABLE A.1
Six Functions of a Dollar

10.00% Annual Interest Rate						
	1 Future Value of $1	2 Future Value Annuity of $1 per Year	3 Sinking Fund Factor	4 Present Value of $1 (Reversion)	5 Present Value Annuity of $1 per Year	6 Payment to Amortize $1	
Years							Years
1	1.100000	1.000000	1.000000	0.909091	0.909091	1.100000	1
2	1.210000	2.100000	0.476190	0.826446	1.735537	0.576190	2
3	1.331000	3.310000	0.302115	0.751315	2.486852	0.402115	3
4	1.464100	4.641000	0.215471	0.683013	3.169865	0.315471	4
5	1.610510	6.105100	0.163797	0.620921	3.790787	0.263797	5
6	1.771561	7.715610	0.129607	0.564474	4.355261	0.229607	6
7	1.948717	9.487171	0.105405	0.513158	4.868419	0.205405	7
8	2.143589	11.435888	0.087444	0.466507	5.334926	0.187444	8
9	2.357948	13.579477	0.073641	0.424098	5.759024	0.173641	9
10	2.593742	15.937425	0.062745	0.385543	6.144567	0.162745	10
11	2.853117	18.531167	0.053963	0.350494	6.495061	0.153963	11
12	3.138428	21.384284	0.046763	0.318631	6.813692	0.146763	12
13	3.452271	24.522712	0.040779	0.289664	7.103356	0.140779	13
14	3.797498	27.974983	0.035746	0.263331	7.366687	0.135746	14
15	4.177248	31.772482	0.031474	0.239392	7.606080	0.131474	15
16	4.594973	35.949730	0.027817	0.217629	7.823709	0.127817	16
17	5.054470	40.544703	0.024664	0.197845	8.021553	0.124664	17
18	5.559917	45.599173	0.021930	0.179859	8.201412	0.121930	18
19	6.115909	51.159090	0.019547	0.163508	8.364920	0.119547	19
20	6.727500	57.274999	0.017460	0.148644	8.513564	0.117460	20
21	7.400250	64.002499	0.015624	0.135131	8.648694	0.115624	21
22	8.140275	71.402749	0.014005	0.122846	8.771540	0.114005	22
23	8.954302	79.543024	0.012572	0.111678	8.883218	0.112572	23
24	9.849733	88.497327	0.011300	0.101526	8.984744	0.111300	24
25	10.834706	98.347059	0.010168	0.092296	9.077040	0.110168	25
26	11.918177	109.181765	0.009159	0.083905	9.160945	0.109159	26
27	13.109994	121.099942	0.008258	0.076278	9.237223	0.108258	27
28	14.420994	134.209936	0.007451	0.069343	9.306567	0.107451	28
29	15.863093	148.630930	0.006728	0.063039	9.369606	0.106728	29
30	17.449402	164.494023	0.006079	0.057309	9.426914	0.106079	30
31	19.194342	181.943425	0.005496	0.052099	9.479013	0.105496	31
32	21.113777	201.137767	0.004972	0.047362	9.526376	0.104972	32
33	23.225154	222.251544	0.004499	0.043057	9.569432	0.104499	33
34	25.547670	245.476699	0.004074	0.039143	9.608575	0.104074	34
35	28.102437	271.024368	0.003690	0.035584	9.644159	0.103690	35
36	30.912681	299.126805	0.003343	0.032349	9.676508	0.103343	36
37	34.003949	330.039486	0.003030	0.029408	9.705917	0.103030	37
38	37.404343	364.043434	0.002747	0.026735	9.732651	0.102747	38
39	41.144778	401.447778	0.002491	0.024304	9.756956	0.102491	39
40	45.259256	442.592556	0.002259	0.022095	9.779051	0.102259	40
41	49.785181	487.851811	0.002050	0.020086	9.799137	0.102050	41
42	54.763699	537.636992	0.001860	0.018260	9.817397	0.101860	42
43	60.240069	592.400692	0.001688	0.016600	9.833998	0.101688	43
44	66.264076	652.640761	0.001532	0.015091	9.849089	0.101532	44
45	72.890484	718.904837	0.001391	0.013719	9.862808	0.101391	45
46	80.179532	791.795321	0.001263	0.012472	9.875280	0.101263	46
47	88.197485	871.974853	0.001147	0.011338	9.886618	0.101147	47
48	97.017234	960.172338	0.001041	0.010307	9.896926	0.101041	48
49	106.718957	1057.189572	0.000946	0.009370	9.906296	0.100946	49
50	117.390853	1163.908529	0.000859	0.008519	9.914814	0.100859	50

Using the same example:

$$\frac{(1 + 0.10)^5 - 1}{0.10} = \frac{(1.6105100) - 1}{0.10} = \frac{0.610510}{0.10}$$

$$= 6.105100 = \$1 \times 6.105100$$

$$= \$6.11$$

Where, $i = 0.10$

$n = 5$

3. Column 3: **Sinking fund factor**—The sinking fund factor represents the level percentage factor that must be invested at the end of each period in order to accumulate $1. For example, if a lump sum of $1 is needed at the end of the 5-year period, $ 0.16 must be invested at a 10% annual interest rate at the end of each year for 5 years. Calculate this by multiplying $1 by the sinking fund factor of 0.163797. (See column 3 of Table A.1.)

Formula: Sinking fund factor $= \dfrac{i}{(1 + i)^n - 1}$

Where, i = interest rate

n = number of time periods

Using the same example:

$$\frac{0.10}{(1 + 0.10)^5 - 1} = \frac{0.10}{(1.610510) - 1} = \frac{0.10}{0.610510}$$

$$= 0.163797$$

$$= \$1 \times 0.163797 = \$0.16$$

Where, $i = 0.10$

$n = 5$

4. Column 4: **Present value of $1 (reversion)**—The present value of one dollar (*reversion*) is the amount that must be invested now in order to receive $1 in the future (discounting). A **reversion** is a return of rights that are due some time in the future. For example, in order to accumulate $1 at the end of 5 years, $0.62 must be invested at a 10% annual interest rate compounded annually. Calculate this by multiplying $1 by the present value of $1 factor of 0.620921. (See column 4 of Table A.1.)

Formula: Present value of $1 $= \dfrac{1}{(1 + i)^n}$

Where, i = interest rate

n = number of time periods

Using the same example:

$$\frac{1}{(1 + 0.10)^5} = \frac{1}{(1.610510)} = 0.620921$$

$$= 0.620921 \times \$1 = \$0.62$$

Where, $i = 0.10$

$n = 5$

5. Column 5: **Present value annuity of $1 per year**—The present value of one dollar per period (*annuity*) is the amount needed to be invested now, in order to receive a constant series of equal cash flows of $1 for a specified period (discounting).

An annuity is a level stream of cash flows for a fixed period of time. For example, in order to receive a series of equal cash flows of $1 for 5 years, $3.79 would need to be invested at the 10% annual interest rate compounded annually. Calculate this by multiplying $1 by the present value annuity of $1 per year factor of 3.790787. (See column 5 of Table A.1.)

Formula: Present value of $1 per period $= \dfrac{1 - \dfrac{1}{(1 + i)^n}}{i}$

Where, $i =$ interest rate

$n =$ number of time periods

Using the same example:

$$\frac{1 - \dfrac{1}{(1 + 0.10)^5}}{0.10} = \frac{0.379079}{0.10}$$

$$= 3.790787 = \$1 \times 3.790787$$

$$= \$3.79$$

Where, $i = 0.10$

$n = 5$

6. Column 6: **Payment to amortize $1**—This is the periodic payment amount needed in order to repay a $1 loan with interest paid at a specific rate over a specified time on the outstanding balance. For example, if a lump sum of $1 was borrowed for 5 years at a 10% interest rate compounded annually, the yearly payment (including principal and interest) needed to pay the loan off in full is $0.26. Calculate this by multiplying $1 by the payment to amortize $1 factor of 0.263797. (See column 6 of Table A.1.)

Formula: Payment to amortize $1: $\dfrac{i}{1 - \dfrac{1}{(1 + i)^n}}$

Where, i = interest rate

n = number of time periods

Using the same example:

$$\frac{0.10}{1 - \dfrac{1}{(1 + 0.10)^5}} = \frac{0.10}{1 - \dfrac{1}{(1.610510)}} = \frac{0.10}{1 - 0.620921}$$

$$= \frac{0.10}{0.379079} = 0.263797$$

$$= \$1 \times 0.263797 = \$0.26$$

Where, i = 0.10

n = 5

The six functions of a dollar calculations above all used $1 as the present value or the future value. Any dollar amount can be multiplied by the factors.

Calculating a Mortgage Payment

Mortgage payments, which include principal and interest, are typically paid monthly; therefore, the interest owed also compounds monthly. The number of periods and the interest rate need to be adjusted. Divide the annual interest rate (i) by the number of monthly compounding periods in one year (12). Then multiply the number of time periods (n) by the number of compounding periods.

$$\text{Monthly payment to amortize } \$1\!: \frac{i}{1 - \dfrac{1}{(1 + i)^n}}$$

Where, i = interest rate ÷ 12

n = number of time periods × 12

For example, a 30-year loan will have 12 compounding periods per year. Over 30 years there will be 360 payments (30 years × 12 compounding periods). An annual interest rate of 7% is then actually a monthly rate of 0.005833 (0.07 ÷ 12).

$$\text{Monthly payment to amortize } \$1\!: \frac{0.005833}{1 - \dfrac{1}{(1 + 0.005833)^{360}}}$$

$$\frac{0.005833}{1 - (0.123206)} = \frac{0.005833}{0.876794} = 0.006653$$

$$\text{Where, } i = 0.07 \div 12$$

$$n = 30 \times 12$$

It is very easy to calculate the monthly mortgage payment on a 30-year loan borrowed at an annual rate of 7%. Simply multiply the loan amount (present value) by the payment to amortize $1 factor.

For a $250,000 loan amount, the monthly mortgage payment for 30 years will be $1,663.25 ($250,000 × 0.006653). After the last month in the 30th year, the amount due (future value) will be 0. At that time, the loan will be fully amortized.

Financial Calculators

A table for each and every possible combination of compounding intervals (holding periods) and interest rates is needed in order to calculate the six functions of a dollar. Obviously, one would have to have access to a very large collection of tables. Rather than using tables and long mathematical calculations, financial calculators and computer programs can perform all six functions of a dollar calculations. It is important to remember that a solution that is calculated with a given factor, or one that was obtained from an Ellwood table, will differ slightly from a solution calculated using the financial function keys on a financial calculator.

There are a variety of financial calculators available on the market today. Regardless of the brand of financial calculator, the following keys would be used:

n—time period

i—interest rate*

FV—future value

PV—present value

PMT—payment (paid out or received)

Note: When entering interest rate into most financial calculators, the number is entered as is; the calculator knows that it is a percentage and therefore converts it within. For example, 10% is entered as 10, not 0.10.

■ **In Practice**

What is the monthly payment required to fully amortize a $350,000 loan over 15 years, assuming a 7% annual interest rate? The compound interest factor for 7% interest compounded monthly for 15 years is 0.008988.

Solution:

Monthly payment = $3,145.80; (0.008988 × $350,000)

Solution (Calculator):

$$n = 180 \ (15 \times 12)$$

$$i = 0.5833 \ (7 \div 12)$$

$$FV = 0 \ (\text{implied})$$

$$PV = \$350,000$$

Solve for PMT

$$\textbf{Payment} = \textbf{\$3,145.90*}$$

Note: The difference in the solutions is due to rounding.

■ In Practice

You need to borrow $40,000. You qualify for a $40,000 loan to be paid in full at the end of 10 years. The annual interest rate is 7.75% compounded monthly. The compound interest factor for 7.75% interest compounded monthly for 10 years is 0.012001. Calculate what you would need to pay each month for 10 years in order to pay off this loan.

Solution:

Multiply the amount borrowed (present value) by the payment to amortize $1 factor given.

$$\textbf{\$40,000} \times \textbf{0.012001} = \textbf{\$480.04}$$

Therefore, after the last month of the 10th year, the amount due (future value) will be 0; at that time, the loan will be fully amortized.

Solution (Calculator):

$$n = 120 \ (10 \times 12)$$

$$i = 0.645833 \ (7.75 \div 12)$$

$$FV = 0 \ (\text{implied})$$

$$PV = \$40,000$$

Solve for PMT

Payment = $480.04

■ **In Practice**

What will a $5,000 investment at a 5% annual interest rate compounded annually grow to after 6 years? The future value of $1 factor for 5% annual compounding for 6 years is 1.340096.

Solution:

Multiply $5,000 (present value) by the future value of $1 factor given.

$5,000 × 1.340096 = $6,700.48

Therefore, $5,000 will grow to $6,700.48 after 6 years of compounding at an annual interest rate of 5%.

Solution (Calculator):

$$n = 6$$

$$i = 5$$

PV = $5,000

PMT = 0 (implied)

Solve for FV

Future value = $6,700.47*

Note: The difference in the solutions is due to rounding.

This discussion, while brief, introduced the financial concepts used in the income approach. Courses and texts dedicated entirely to this topic are available to appraisers, as proficiency in advanced financial calculations is necessary for certain appraisal assignments.

Within each approach to value, the various mathematical calculations discussed in this section apply. For example, the *cost approach* utilizes area calculations for land as well as area, volume, and perimeter calculations for improvements.

Necessary calculations within the *sales comparison approach* include adjustments using a paired sales analysis (a methodized process to extract adjustments) and reconciling to a value within this approach.

The *income approach* employs income capitalization, gross rent multiplier calculations, and six functions of a dollar.

LESSON 4 REVIEW QUESTIONS

1. Time _____ of _____ states that money available today is worth more than the same amount in the future.

2. Performing compounding and discounting calculations involves the variable of
   a. future value.
   b. time period.
   c. interest rate.
   d. all of the above.

3. _____ is the process of converting an estimated future income into a present value.

4. The principal amount plus any accrued interest is the
   a. future value.
   b. present value.
   c. compound interest.
   d. simple interest.

5. _____ is interest that is computed on the original principal plus any the accrued interest.

6. What is the monthly payment required to fully amortize a $200,000 loan over 30 years, assuming a 7.25% annual interest rate? The compound interest factor for 7.25% interest compounded monthly for 30 years is 0.006822.

7. The present value of $1 factor is also referred to as the _____ factor.

LESSON 4 REVIEW ANSWERS

1. value; money

2. d

3. Discounting

4. a

5. Compound interest

6. monthly payment = $1,364.40 (0.006822 × $200,000)

    Calculator Solution:

    $n = 360$; (30 × 12)

    $i = 0.604167$ (7.25 ÷ 12)

    FV = 0 (implied)

    PV = $200,000

    Solve for PMT

    Payment = $1,364.35*

    Note: The difference in the solutions is due to rounding.

7. reversion

appendix

FORMS OF OWNERSHIP

LEARNING OBJECTIVES

By the end of this appendix, participants will be able to

- be familiar with the various forms of ownership;

- distinguish the difference between the various forms of ownership including joint tenancy, tenancy in common, and tenancy by the entirety;

- understand the concept of right of survivorship;

- describe the difference between condominium ownership and cooperative ownership;

- understand the difference between a living trust and a testamentary trust;

- describe the benefits of land trusts;

- understand the concept of time-sharing;

- identify and define the four unities of ownership;

- identify the benefits of cooperative ownership; and

- distinguish between time-share estate and time-share use.

KEY TERMS

beneficiary

community property

condominium

cooperative ownership

corporation

Declaration of
    Condominium

devisee

general partnership

grantee

grantor

joint tenancy

joint venture

land trust

limited liability
    company (LLC)

limited partnership

marital property

partition

planned unit
    development (PUD)

proprietary lease

real estate investment
    trust (REIT)

right of survivorship

separate property

settlor

severalty

special assessment

syndicate

tenancy by the entirety

tenancy in common

tenancy in partnership

tenant

time-share estate

time-share use

time-sharing

trust

trust company

trustee

trustor

unities of ownership

FORMS OF PROPERTY OWNERSHIP

The form of ownership in which a title is held is usually determined by the purchaser (**grantee**) and is communicated to the seller (**grantor**) prior to drafting the deed. The owner(s) can change a form of ownership anytime. This can be done by executing and recording a new deed that conveys the desired form of ownership.

OWNERSHIP IN SEVERALTY (SEPARATE OWNERSHIP)

When title to real estate is vested in one individual, that individual owns the property, the entire bundle of rights, in **severalty.** An "individual" can be a natural person or a legal person, such as a corporation. The term *severalty* comes from the fact that a sole owner is "severed" from other owners. The ownership rights are still subject to governmental and private restrictions discussed. The individual is the sole recipient of all benefits derived from the property, but also has sole liability for any debts and obligations associated with the property.

CO-OWNERSHIP

When title of real estate is vested in two or more individuals, these individuals are considered to be *co-owners* or *concurrent owners.* Several forms of co-ownership are recognized, such as *tenancy in common, joint tenancy, tenancy by the entirety, community property,* and *tenancy in partnership.*

Tenancy in Common

When a property is owned by two or more individuals as **tenants in common,** each co-owner (**tenant**) holds an undivided fractional interest in the property, subject to a specific agreement between them. Each tenant has the right of possession of the entire property and cannot be excluded by the other tenants. It is the ownership interest that is divided, not the physical property. For example, if an individual has 50 percent interest in a parcel containing 100 acres, that individual has 50 percent interest in the entire 100 acres, not 100 percent interest in 50 acres.

Each co-tenant can sell, convey, mortgage, or transfer his or her interest in a property. However, an individual co-tenant cannot transfer the entire property without the permission of the other co-owner(s). With tenancy in common, there is *no right of survivorship.* (See Joint Tenancy.) Upon the death of an individual co-tenant, the decedent's interest passes to his or her heirs or **devisees** (a devisee is the person whom is given property by a will) according to a will. (See Figure B.1.)

FIGURE B.1
Tenancy in Common

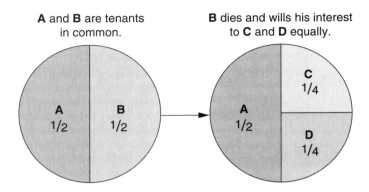

Joint Tenancy

Joint tenancy occurs when a property is owned by two or more individuals. As with tenancy in common, each co-owner (tenant) holds an undivided fractional interest in the property, subject to a specific agreement between them.

There are four legal requirements, **unities of ownership,** required in order to create a joint tenancy:

1. Unity of **P**ossession
2. Unity of **I**nterest
3. Unity of **T**itle
4. Unity of **T**ime

Use the acronym PITT to help recall the four unities of ownership.

These four unities are present when all tenants acquire the right of possession, with equal interest (equal shares), and the *title* at the same *time*.

With joint tenancy comes the *right of survivorship*. **Right of survivorship** means that upon the death of one of the joint tenants, the decedent's interest automatically passes to the surviving owner(s)/tenant(s). A joint tenant cannot transfer title of his or her share by a will. As each joint tenant of the joint tenancy dies, the surviving joint tenant(s) receive the deceased tenant's interest. The joint tenancy remains intact; only the number of tenants decreases.

The joint tenancy continues until there is only one owner, who then will hold title in *severalty*. As mentioned earlier, individual ownership or ownership in severalty allows for the right of a sole owner to pass ownership by will to his or her heirs. (See Figure B.2.)

FIGURE B.2
Joint Tenancy with Right of Survivorship

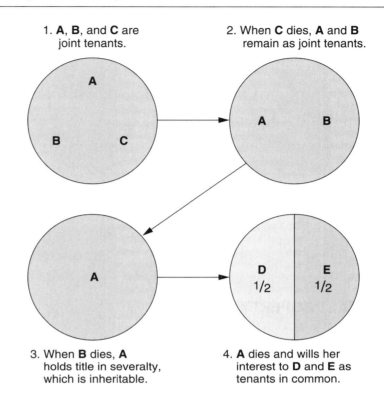

1. **A**, **B**, and **C** are joint tenants.

2. When **C** dies, **A** and **B** remain as joint tenants.

3. When **B** dies, **A** holds title in severalty, which is inheritable.

4. **A** dies and wills her interest to **D** and **E** as tenants in common.

Destroying one of the four unities of ownership can eliminate a joint tenancy. If a living joint tenant conveys his or her interest, the new owner does not become a joint tenant. The new owner becomes a *tenant in common* with the remaining joint tenants. If there were only two joint tenants, then the joint tenancy is completely terminated. With more than two joint tenants, the joint tenancy remains between only those original joint tenants; however, a tenancy in common relationship will exist between the new owner and original joint tenants. For example, A, B, and C are the original joint tenants. A conveys his or her interest to D. D now becomes a tenant in common with B and C, while B and C still have a joint tenancy. (See Figure B.3.)

It is important to note that when property is held in co-ownership or joint ownership, the unity of possession can be severed without transfer of title or creating a new interest. This is known as **partition** and is done by filing an action in court. Usually pursuant to a judicial decree, the real property can be divided into separately owned parcels based upon the owner's proportionate shares. Partition dissolves a co-ownership relationship when all of the parties do not voluntarily agree to this termination.

FIGURE B.3
Combination of Tenancies

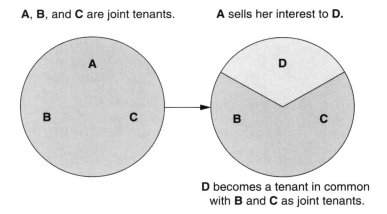

A, **B**, and **C** are joint tenants.   **A** sells her interest to **D**.

D becomes a tenant in common
with **B** and **C** as joint tenants.

MARITAL PROPERTY

Ownership rights limited to married persons are referred to as **marital property.** The issue of what constitutes a married couple is currently being debated in courts and state legislature. Two types of marital property, *tenancy by the entirety* and *community property*, are discussed below.

Tenancy by the Entirety

A form of marital property allowed by some states, limited to married couples, is known as **tenancy by the entirety.** The derivation of the term *entirety* comes from a state of being entire or complete through the marriage as if the husband and wife were one person. This form of property ownership is one in which each spouse has an equal and undivided interest in a property. Neither spouse can transfer ownership, encumber, give away, or sell their interests without permission from the other spouse. As long as the marriage exists, so does the right of survivorship. As mentioned earlier, with right of survivorship, if one spouse dies, interest automatically passes to the surviving spouse, who then becomes the sole owner. Additionally, upon the death of either spouse, the surviving spouse can benefit from sole ownership without probate proceedings. A tenancy by the entirety will be dissolved by divorce, resulting in a tenancy in common.

Community Property

Another form of marital property ownership, limited to married couples, is **community property.** Community property is all property acquired during a marriage with the exception of property acquired by gift or inheritance, and property acquired with proceeds or income from a *separate property.* **Separate property** is property owned by one spouse solely before the marriage. Any property acquired by either spouse, while married, is considered to be acquired by mutual effort. This concept of community property rights originated under Spanish law and is commonly used in some states, but not recognized in others. The laws of community property vary from state to state. Some states may even recognize unions other than traditional marriage. Unlike tenancy by the entirety or joint tenancy, community property does not automatically provide for right of survivorship. Upon the death of either spouse, the surviving spouse automatically receives *half* of the interest in the property. The other half may or may not be transferred to the decedent's heir(s) other than the surviving spouse according to a will. Depending on the state, if one spouse dies without a will (intestate), the decedent's interest may be inherited by the surviving spouse.

PARTNERSHIP PROPERTY OR TENANCY IN PARTNERSHIP

Tenancy in partnership is formed when two or more persons carry on a business for profit (*partnership*) or own property for partnership purposes. With a **general partnership,** individual partners are responsible for their portion of the distributed income as well as any partnership debts. The actions of one partner are binding on each of the other partners. With a general partnership, each partner conducting business jointly has unlimited liability, and his or her personal assets are subject to the partnership's liability regardless of individual capital contribution. A general partnership is dissolved and must be restructured if one partner dies, withdraws, or goes bankrupt. With a **limited partnership,** in addition to one or more general partners, there are one or more limited partners as well. A limited partner does not participate in the daily operations and is only liable to the extent of his or her capital contributions. In a limited partnership, the partnership agreement may provide for a continuation of the partnership upon the death, withdrawal, or bankruptcy of a partner.

All partners for purposes of the business may use the partnership property. If a partner dies, his or her interest may be passed on to the surviving partner(s). It is important to note that while the decedent's property interests may be passed on to the surviving partner(s), the decedent partner's share of business profits may or may not be transferred to his or her heir(s). With a tenancy in partnership, the partnership itself is not taxed; each partner is taxed as an individual.

A **joint venture** real estate partnership occurs when one partner is a lending institution contributing financing. The other partners can include developers and land owners contributing professional expertise and property, respectively. The partners involved carry out a single business project sharing the risk as well as the expertise. Usually, there are time limitations since the intention of joint ventures is not to form a permanent relationship.

A **syndicate** is an association of two or more people or firms authorized to undertake a duty, transact a specific business venture, or acquire real estate. A syndicate is not a legal entity; however, it can be organized into a number of ownership forms including co-ownerships of tenancy in common or joint tenancy. Syndicates can be organized into other co-ownerships such as partnerships or trusts. Syndicates are needed to spread the risk and obtain greater financial and marketing resources for large issues.

Note: In some states, a partnership is not a legal entity and therefore cannot own real estate. All partners must hold title as individuals whether in tenancy in common or joint tenancy.

CORPORATION

A **corporation** is subject to the laws of the state from which it received its charter. Since a corporation is considered a legal entity, it can own real estate in *severalty*, where the corporation is the sole owner, or as a co-owner with other corporations or individual people. A corporation is created and owned by a group of people called *shareholders*. A shareholder's ownership is represented by their holding or ownership of shares of stock. Shareholders elect a board of directors to manage and operate the corporation.

If authorized by its charter, a corporation may have the right to buy and sell real estate for any purpose. Because stock is considered personal property, shareholders do not have direct ownership interest in real estate owned by a corporation. An important aspect of a corporation is *limited liability*. Shareholders, as well as directors and officers, are not personally liable for the company's debts. Most corporations are set up with the goal of providing a return for its shareholders. The same is true for not-for-profit corporations. A disadvantage of corporate ownership is double taxation. As a legal entity, a corporation must file an income tax return and pay tax on any profits. A portion of the remaining profit is then distributed to shareholders in the form of dividends, which then become part of the individual shareowner's taxable income.

LIMITED LIABILITY COMPANY (LLC)

A **limited liability company (LLC)** is an unincorporated company formed with features of both a corporation and a partnership. The owners of an LLC are members rather than shareholders or partners. Under applicable state statute, these members cannot be held liable for the acts, debts, or obligations of the company (limited liability), and they may elect to be taxed as a partnership or a separate entity (as in a partnership).

TRUSTS

It is important to understand the concept of *trusts*. A **trust** is a fiduciary relationship in which one person or a corporation, known as a **trustee,** holds legal title to property or manages assets for the benefit of another person, known as a **beneficiary.** The **trustor** is the individual who originally owned a property and creates the trust. The trustor, trustee, and beneficiary may be individuals or legal entities, such as corporations. When a trustee is a corporation, it is referred to as a **trust company.**

A trust may be temporary, conditional, or permanent. To illustrate, suppose a generous uncle (trustor) wishes to pay for the education of his niece (beneficiary). He may convey title to one of his income-producing properties to the niece's mother (trustee). In this case, the trust instructs the trustee to use income of the property for the education of the niece.

It is important to note that a trustee's power is limited by the trust agreement set forth by the trustor either by will or deed in trust. For example, one trust agreement might allow the trustee to manage a property, while another trust agreement may allow only the collection of income from a different property. With a trust agreement, since the beneficiary's interest is considered to be personal property and not real estate, any judgment against a beneficiary is not necessarily a lien against the real estate.

Benefits of Trusts

Trusts are created for a variety of reasons, including possible tax savings for the trustor, providing funds for an anticipated future need, to provide anonymity of a property owner, and improved asset management. Tax experts as well as legal experts need to be consulted as the legal and tax implications can be complex.

There are several different types of trusts. A *living trust* is created for the trustor and administered by another party during the trustor's (property owner) lifetime. An important fact to note is that with a living trust, the trustor is usually the beneficiary. A living trust may be formed because the trustor is either incapable of managing or unwilling to manage his or her assets. The trust can continue throughout the lifetime of the beneficiary, until the beneficiary reaches a certain predetermined age, or until some other condition of the trust agreement is met. The trust can be revocable or irrevocable, depending upon the trustor's wishes. Living trusts are frequently established by married couples acting as co-trustors/beneficiaries.

A *testamentary trust* is a trust established by a person's will; hence it does not come into existence until the death of the trustor (property owner). Chiefly wealthy individuals who are concerned about their beneficiaries' ability, possibly due to being of tender age, to administer large amounts of assets use testamentary trusts.

With a **land trust,** the trustor is usually the beneficiary and upon the beneficiary's death, the title held in trust then is conveyed to the decedent's heir(s). The person establishing the land trust is also referred to as a **settlor.** A settlor can name more than one beneficiary, and if the property conveyed in trust is co-owned, multiple beneficiaries can be named. Corporations as well as individuals can be beneficiaries. A land trust typically lasts no longer than 20 years; however, there can be a time extension if all beneficiaries sign an agreement.

Benefits of Land Trusts

The major advantage of a land trust is to *avoid any kind of encumbrance* (liens). Since the beneficiary's interest is considered to be personal property and not real estate, a lien cannot be placed against the real estate. Tax liens are the exception. In addition to the aforementioned benefit, other benefits include, but are not limited to, the following:

- **Anonymity,** the principal benefit of a land trust. Usually the name of the beneficiary is not listed in public records, thereby allowing *anonymity.* This allows for a developer to acquire larger parcels of land without the general public's knowledge.

- Easier **transferability,** since transfer can be made by simply changing the beneficiary. There may be tax consequences, however.

- No **marital property rights.** A land trust is also *not subject to marital property rights;* therefore, only one spouse may convey title dependent upon the trust agreement. However, it depends on when the trust was established relative to the time of marriage and whose funds were used.

- **Collateral.** *A beneficiary's rights* can also be *pledged as collateral* (a property or asset that is offered to secure a loan or other credit).

- **Reduction in probate expenses.** There may be a *reduction in probate expenses* since a property owner can easily transfer beneficiary interest in the event of death, and a succession of beneficiaries can also be established.

Real Estate Investment Trust (REIT)

A **real estate investment trust (REIT)** is an investment trust that acquires, manages, or finances a group of income-producing properties using capital from multiple investors. Individuals can either invest in REITs by purchasing shares directly on an open exchange or by investing in a mutual fund that specializes in public real estate. There are special tax considerations with a REIT, and typically an investor may expect high yields. REITs include properties such as hotels, shopping malls, apartment buildings, and office buildings. REITs are subject to complex restrictions and regulations, requiring the counsel of a specialized attorney.

SPECIAL FORMS OF OWNERSHIP

Most forms of ownership include the land, building, and all appurtenances (rights, privileges, etc). However, with other forms of ownership, where the bundle of rights is separated, ownership may include more or less features. These forms include: *condominium, PUDs, cooperatives,* and *time-sharing.*

Condominium Ownership

Condominium is a form of ownership involving separate ownership of individual units within a multiunit building and a specified share of the remainder, such as in the common areas of an apartment building. The most common type of condominium has been residential. However, in recent years condominium ownership includes industrial buildings, office spaces, and retail units. The individual ownership includes the airspace within the interior walls, the floors, and ceiling. The undivided interest includes the common elements within the development. Common elements typically include parking lots, hallways, stairs, lobby area, roof, and the exterior structure itself. The individual owners usually form a condominium association. The main purpose of the association is to maintain and manage all of the commonly held interests. The association, which is nonprofit, charges unit owners a monthly association fee that is based on the percentage each unit owner has in the project itself. For example, if a project has five residential condominium units, with a mixture of 2,000-square-foot units and 1,000-square-foot units, the owners of the 2,000-square-foot units will pay higher monthly association fees than the other smaller units. A special assessment may be charged in addition to the regular fees. **Special assessment** charges pay for any expenses not provided for in a standard reserve fund. This may include the unscheduled repaving of a parking lot, an unscheduled new roof, or unforeseen damage to the exterior structure. (See Figure B.4.)

FIGURE B.4
Condominium Ownership

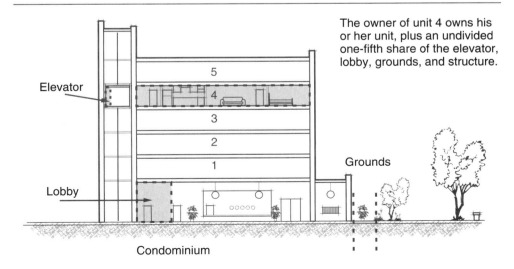

The owner of unit 4 owns his or her unit, plus an undivided one-fifth share of the elevator, lobby, grounds, and structure.

In some states, an owner of an existing building or a developer of a new project establishes a condominium by recording a **Declaration of Condominium.** The *declaration* includes the legal description of all units and the common elements, bylaws that will govern the actions of the owners' association, illustrations indicating all unit boundaries vertical and horizontal, and any restrictive covenants controlling the use of the ownership rights. For example, some associations may not allow for pets.

Once a property is declared as a condominium, each unit becomes a separate unit that can be owned by one or more individuals. A unit can be separately leased, mortgaged, or sold. Real estate taxes are assessed for each unit separately. All real estate taxes are collected for each unit separately, and any default in the payment of real estate taxes may result in a tax lien causing a foreclosure sale of the individual unit. The ownership of other units within the project would not be affected. Additionally, the condominium association can impose a lien on the title of an individual unit, if there is a default in the association fees. As with the tax lien, this would not affect the other owners in the project.

Planned Unit Developments (PUDs)

A **planned unit development (PUD)** is a planned mixed- or multizoning-use development; for example, housing, recreation, and commercial land uses are all located within a development or subdivision. The developer of a PUD may set aside land for open space or other public amenity. The individual units, which can be town homes, detached single-family homes, and condominiums, are owned in fee simple. As with condominium ownership, individual units can be sold, mortgaged, or leased. There are common elements similar to a condominium project. Often, there are charges levied for the maintenance of common elements. Common elements include green-belts maintenance, entrance security guards, and subdivision entrance signs.

Cooperative Ownership

A **cooperative ownership** is established when a corporation holds title to real estate (land and building) and offers stock to prospective tenants/shareholders. The price of the stock is essentially the purchase price of the individual unit. A purchaser becomes a shareholder in the cooperation and receives *a proprietary lease (owner's lease)* to the unit, usually an apartment, during the life of the corporation. A **proprietary lease** is a contract where an owner of a property conveys exclusive possession, control, or enjoyment for a specified term. The tenant/shareholder is obliged to pay his or her share of the costs to operate and manage the property in the form of *monthly maintenance fees.* These fees are based on the percentage of the shareholders' holdings. Shareholders elect officers and directors to operate and control the corporation. The use of property management companies is very common. The management company assists in the operation and maintenance of the entire parcel. The costs to operate and manage the parcel include real estate taxes, replacement reserves, janitorial services, utilities, repairs and maintenance, and insurance. Bylaws are also established, and individual shareholders must abide by them. Shares in the cooperation may be transferred; however, some cooperatives require the tenant/shareholder to sell stock back to cooperation for the original purchase price. This allows the corporation to realize any profits upon the resale of the stock.

An advantage of cooperative ownership is that the tenants/shareholders can vote to allow or deny prospective shareholders into the *corporation*. A stringent investigation into the financial ability of all prospective shareholders is important. This not only allows the tenants/shareholders to pick their neighbors, but it also protects the corporation from foreclosure. Unlike condominium ownership, any default on maintenance payments by a shareholder becomes the responsibility of the remaining shareholders. If the corporation defaults on mortgage or real estate taxes, the result can be a foreclosure. This will then eradicate interests held by *all* tenants/shareholders.

Other advantages of cooperative ownership include the freedom from maintenance and income tax advantages. Since tenants/shareholders do pay a portion of the real estate taxes, there may be income tax benefits. Cooperative owners do not own real estate since shares in stock are considered to be personal property. While the entire property may be financed, lending institutions may consider the shares of stock as acceptable collateral for financing.

Time-Sharing

With **time-sharing,** there is a limited ownership interest in, or rights to use and occupy, a unit for a specified time or period. Units are usually within a recreational property. There are two types of time-sharing. With a **time-share estate,** a purchaser receives a deed that conveys title to a unit for a specified time of the year. A time-share estate allows the purchaser the right to sell, lease, or bequeath the time-share. This interest can also be mortgaged. Within time-sharing, there are two categories: *time-share ownership* and *interval ownership.* With a *time-share ownership plan,* time-share owners are all tenants in common who have possessory rights to use or occupy a unit, such as a hotel room in a resort or residential apartment, for a specified amount of time, during a specific time of year stipulated by the deed. With *interval ownership,* the ownership term only lasts for a specified time period. At the end of the ownership term, the ownership reverts back to the interval owners as tenants in common, or the time owners may enter into a new agreement. This reversion can occur if provided for.

Time-share owners and interval owners are assessed for operating and maintenance expenses based on the amount of ownership periods purchased. These expenses include prorated real estate taxes, insurance, common area maintenance, and management. A time-share located in warmer climate areas is likely to be more expensive during winter months than in summer months. Usually, 50 out of 52 weeks in a year are sold, leaving 2 weeks for maintenance.

With **time-share use,** a purchaser does not receive a deed that conveys title to a unit, but receives only the right to *use* a time-share unit and all accommodations for a fixed or variable time period.

APPENDIX B REVIEW QUESTIONS

1. The right of survivorship is most closely associated with what form of ownership?
   a. Joint tenancy
   b. Tenancy in common
   c. Beneficiary
   d. Trustor

2. Which is *NOT* a common element in a condominium project?
   a. Living room carpet
   b. Parking lot
   c. Project swimming pool
   d. Exterior structural walls

3. The unity of _____ requires co-owners to receive their titles at the same time.
   a. time
   b. possession
   c. title
   d. interest

4. Which are the four unities of ownership?
   a. Time, title, interest, possession
   b. Tenancy in common, joint tenancy, servility, possession
   c. Time, title, survivorship, heir
   d. Trustee, trustor, beneficiary, trust

5. Which of the following reveals a cooperative ownership?
   a. Shareholder stock certificate
   b. A real estate tax bill for the individual unit
   c. Monthly maintenance fees
   d. Both a and c

6. Fee simple interest is involved in all of the following *EXCEPT*
   a. time-sharing.
   b. condominium.
   c. planned unit development (PUD).
   d. tenancy in common.

7. Which is *NOT* a benefit of land trusts?
   a. Anonymity
   b. Easier transferability
   c. Exemption from real estate taxes
   d. Possible reduction in probate costs

8. What form of co-ownership exists when real estate is owned by two or more individuals who each hold an undivided fractional interest in the property?
   a. Joint tenancy
   b. Tenancy in common
   c. Severalty
   d. Both a and b

9. A tenancy by the entirety may be held by
   a. a brother and a sister.
   b. a corporation and an individual.
   c. a husband and wife.
   d. any of the above.

10. Condominium ownership includes which type of properties?
    a. Industrial
    b. Residential
    c. Retail
    d. All of the above

11. A trust established by a person's will and not effective until the death of the trustor is a
    a. testamentary trust.
    b. living trust.
    c. trustor.
    d. settlor trust.

12. A _____ ownership is established when a corporation holds title to real estate and offers stock to prospective tenants/shareholders.
    a. condominium
    b. cooperative
    c. planned unit development (PUD)
    d. joint venture

13. _____ pay for any unforeseen expenses not provided in a reserve fund.

    a. Trusts
    b. Liens
    c. Special assessment charges
    d. Bylaws

14. Which is considered to be a special form of ownership?

    a. Cooperative
    b. Time-sharing
    c. Condominium
    d. All of the above

15. With cooperative ownership, a purchaser becomes a shareholder in the cooperation and receives a _____ lease, or owner's lease, to a unit during the life of the corporation.

    a. tenant's
    b. proprietary
    c. corporation
    d. None of the above

APPENDIX B REVIEW ANSWERS

1. a

2. a

3. a

4. a

5. d

6. a

7. c

8. d

9. c

10. d

11. a

12. b

13. c

14. d

15. b

ANSWER KEY

SECTION 1 REVIEW ANSWERS

1. **b** The principle of substitution related to the cost approach states that no person is justified in paying more for a property than he or she can build new without any undue delay.

2. **c** Functional obsolescence is a form of depreciation. Functional depreciation, economic or external depreciation, and physical obsolescence are fictitious terms.

3. **b** Functional obsolescence refers to the market's response to a superadequacy or a deficiency. Physical depreciation is the result of general wear and tear.

4. **d** External obsolescence is a value loss that is realized as a result of the market's negative response to something that is outside of the property lines. Functional obsolescence is a value loss as a result of the market's negative response to some functionality of the property. Physical depreciation is the loss in value as a result of general wear and tear.

5. **d** In the cost approach method, the replacement cost, or the reproduction cost of a building, is first determined, then accrued depreciation is subtracted, and finally the value of the land or site as though vacant is added.

6. **c** A loss in value as a result of an overimprovement is known as a superadequacy.

7. **b** The straight-line depreciation method is the simplest method and is calculated by dividing the cost new by the useful life (expected life) to find an equal annual percentage of depreciation over the life of the asset.

8. **c** The straight-line depreciation method is the simplest method and is calculated by dividing the cost new by the useful life (expected life) to find an equal annual percentage of depreciation over the life of the asset ($200,000 ÷ 50 = $4,000).

9. **d** Because total economic life equals effective age plus remaining economic life, both b and c are correct formulas.

10. **b** Chronological age is defined as the age that the property has actually been in existence from the time of its original construction. Therefore, 36 years is the chronological, or actual, age of this home.

11. **c** Total economic life equals effective age plus remaining economic life (TEL = EA + REL).

12. **b** The breakdown method is the most detailed and comprehensive method of calculating depreciation. The age-life method does not consider curable and incurable items. The unit-in-place method determines replacement/reproduction costs new, not depreciation. The straight-line depreciation method is the simplest method.

13. **c** Quantity survey method is the most comprehensive method of costing. The costs are estimated by accounting for every item that goes into a project, including the cost of individual units of materials, labor, fees, and so on. The economic age-life method determines depreciation, not cost new. The unit-in-place method costs the major components of a structure, such as the flooring, roof, wall structure, foundation, plumbing, heating and air-conditioning, electrical, and so on. The square-foot method is similar to the unit-in-place method of costing except the property is broken down into a square-foot unit of comparison.

14. **d** *Accrued depreciation* refers to the loss of value from all causes, including physical depreciation, functional obsolescence, and external obsolescence.

15. **c** Chronological age is defined as the age that the property has actually been in existence from the time of its original construction. Therefore, the chronological, or actual, age of this building is eight years.

16. **b** Sales price of the comparable properties. Adjustments are always made to the comparables, not to the subject.

17. **a** Sales price ÷ element of comparison

18. **b** A negative $3,500 adjustment to the comparable sale. If the comparable is superior to the subject, the adjustment must be a negative adjustment to the comparable to make the comparable similar to the subject.

19. **c** Lot size is an element of comparison.

20. **d** Price per unit is a unit of comparison.

21. **c** Sales comparison approach. The sales comparison approach is most useful when there is an ample number of similar sales to the subject property (an active market). The quantity survey method is not an approach to value; it is used within the cost approach to value.

22. **b** Property rights conveyed, financing, conditions of sale, market conditions (time)

23. **c** If an element of a comparable is superior to the subject, then a negative adjustment is made to the comparable. Adjustments are always made to the comparables, not to the subject.

24. **d** If an element of a comparable is inferior to the subject, then a positive adjustment is made to the comparable. Adjustments are always made to the comparables, not to the subject.

25. **b** Net adjustments are the result of adding all negative and positive adjustments.

26. **a** Gross adjustments are the result of adding all adjustments and ignoring the signage.

27. **d** All of the above. With a relative comparison analysis, the qualitative adjustment is a rating system where the comparable is rated similar, superior, or inferior to the subject.

28. **b** The gross rent multiplier (GRM) and the gross monthly rent multiplier (GMRM) are used exclusively for residential properties.

29.

Sale Number	Value (sales price)	Gross Rent	GRM
1	$700,000	$48,947	14.3
2	$695,000	$49,000	14.2
3	$690,000	$47,000	14.7
4	$689,000	$48,000	14.4
5	$690,000	$47,500	14.5

30. $681,600 ($4,000 × 12 months × 14.2)

31. 12.9 ($645,000 ÷ $50,000)

32. $593,400 ($46,000 × 12.9)

33.   EGIM = 6.05 ($456,000 ÷ $75,330)

    EGI = $76,000

            + $5,000

            $81,000

    –7% $5,670

            $75,330

34.   direct capitalization

35. **a** 0

36.   negative

37.   Extrapolation

38.   Interpolation

39.   dependent

40.   independent

41. **c** is horizontal

42. **d** all of the above.

43. **c** both a and b.

44. **c** no correlation between the variables.

45. **a** slopes downhill.

46. **b** y-intercept.

47.

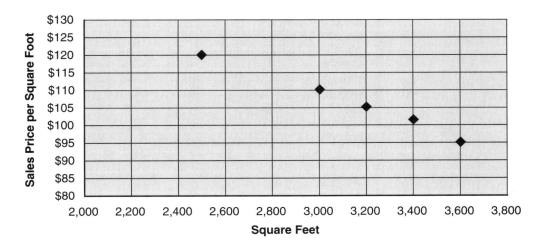

Sales Price per Square Foot vs. Size of Building

48. **b** $110 and $120.

49.

Sale Number	Sales Price	Gross Building Area (Sq. Ft.)	Sales Price per Square Foot, Rounded	Number of Units	Sales Price per Unit	Number of Bedrooms	Sales Price per Bedroom
1	$1,200,000	11000	$109	18	$66,667	48	$25,000
2	$1,500,000	12000	$125	14	$107,143	22	$68,182
3	$1,000,000	11500	$87	20	$50,000	40	$25,000
4	$1,600,000	14000	$114	21	$76,190	30	$53,333
5	$1,650,000	14500	$114	28	$58,929	20	$82,500

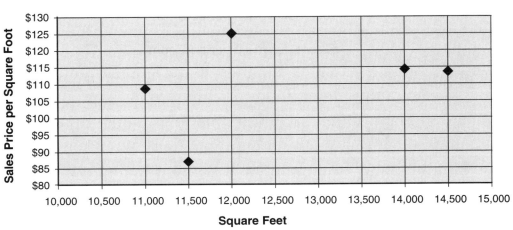

Sales Price per Square Foot vs. Building Size

Sales Price per Unit vs. Number of Units

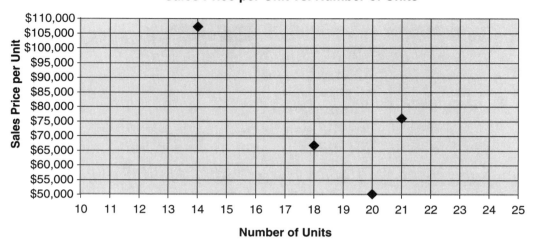

Sales Price per Bedroom vs. Number of Bedrooms

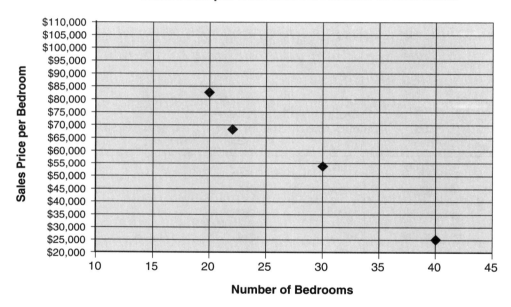

50. **c** sales price per bedroom

51. **c** sales price per bedroom

Index